England from a Side-Saddle

Derek J. Taylor

England from a Side-Saddle

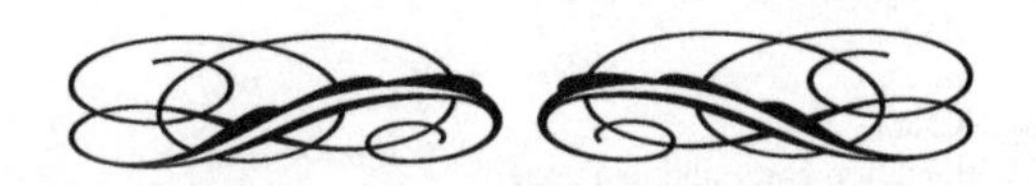

The Great Journeys of Celia Fiennes

To Lindsay Stanberry-Flynn.

Cover illustration painted by Jane Dunn

First published 2021
This paperback edition first published 2023

The History Press
97 St George's Place, Cheltenham,
Gloucestershire, GL50 3QB
www.thehistorypress.co.uk

British Library Cataloguing in Publication Data.
A catalogue record for this book is available from the British Library.

ISBN 978 1 80399 359 1

Typesetting and origination by The History Press
Printed and bound in Great Britain by TJ Books Limited, Padstow, Cornwall.

Trees for Life

Author's Note

In the many quotes I have used from Celia Fiennes' diary, I have taken the liberty of making the style of her prose a little more accessible to the twenty-first-century reader. At the end of the seventeenth century, there wasn't the standardisation of spelling, capital letters and abbreviations that we take for granted today, and some of the words she uses have now dropped out of use or changed their meaning. I have felt it important not to let these unfamiliar peculiarities act as a barrier to our appreciation of the value of what this remarkable traveller has to tell us about life in late seventeenth-century England and about her own character and motives in making her journeys. At the same time though, my aim has been to preserve the precise meaning, archaic feel and sometimes delight or distaste expressed in her original manuscript.

There's an example of her writing, unedited, in the Appendix.

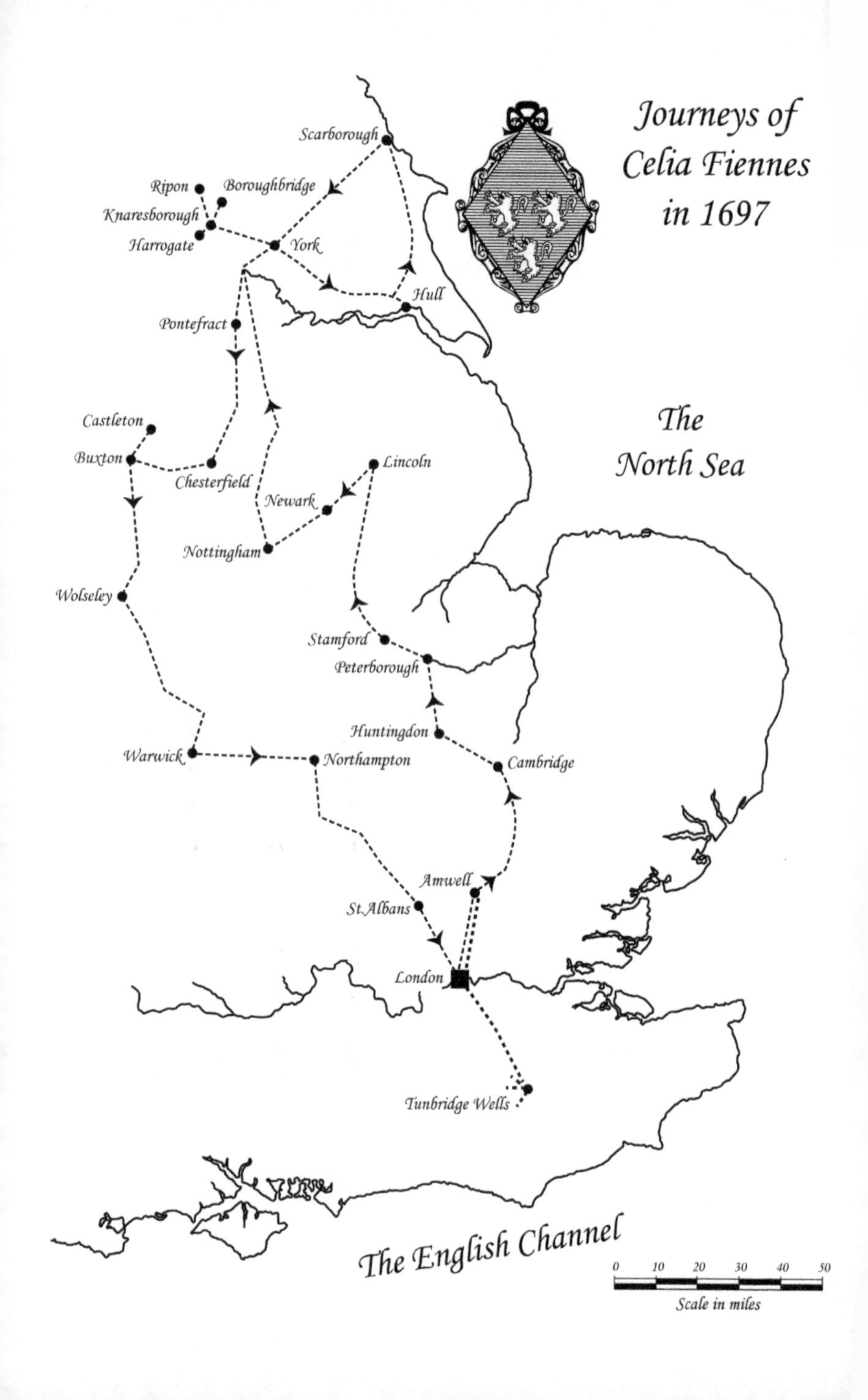
Journeys of
Celia Fiennes
in 1697
Scarborough
Ripon
Boroughbridge
Knaresborough
Harrogate
York
Hull
Pontefract
Castleton
Buxton
Chesterfield
Lincoln
Newark
Nottingham
The
North Sea
Wolseley
Stamford
Peterborough
Huntingdon
Cambridge
Warwick
Northampton
Amwell
St.Albans
London
Tunbridge Wells
The English Channel
0
10
20
30
40
50
Scale in miles

The 'Great Journey'
of Celia Fiennes
in 1698
Scotland
The Irish Sea
The North Sea
Aitchison Bank
Newcastle
Carlisle
Haltwhistle
Penrith
Durham
Richmond
Kendal
Lancaster
Harrogate
Leeds
Liverpool
Manchester
Flint
Chester
Wolseley
Derby
Shrewsbury
Peterborough
Norwich
Leicester
Ely
Huntingdon
Worcester
Colchester
Gloucester
Amwed
Windsor
London
The Bristol Channel
Bristol
Bath
Newton Toney
Salisbury
Winchester
Hartland Pt.
Taunton
Exeter
Launceston
Dorchester
Plymouth
Penzance
The English Channel
0 10 20 30 40 50 100
Scale in miles

Contents

Prologue

Broughton Castle

THE EXCITEMENT OF INK BLOTS

If all persons, both ladies and much more gentlemen,
would spend some of their time in journeys to visit their native land,
it would be a sovereign remedy to cure laziness.

'If she were alive today,' says Martin, 'she could have been a war correspondent. She was brave. She was determined. She was curious about the world out there – beyond where the rest of us normally go. And, of course, she felt compelled to write about what she saw.'

Celia Fiennes was Martin Fiennes' great-great-great-great-great-great-great-great-great-great aunt. He's invited me to Broughton Castle, the Fiennes family's ancestral home, to see the original diary where she wrote about her journeys, thousands of miles on horseback around England at the end of the seventeenth century. It was a time when women didn't do such things. It was too dangerous for a start. As she herself discovered, once you got away from towns, highwaymen lay in wait for the unwary, many roads were unsigned marshy tracks, and lodgings could be filthy and vermin ridden. And it certainly wasn't an aristocratic lady's role in life to get on a horse and wander off – Lord knows where! – out of touch for months on end.

Broughton Castle stands within a 40ft-wide moat in open countryside near Banbury in Oxfordshire. It's been the official residence of the Fiennes family – their aristocratic title is the Lords Saye and Sele (pronounced 'say and seal') – since the fourteenth century. The family's roots go back even further. Its members have helped mould English history since the first of them came over

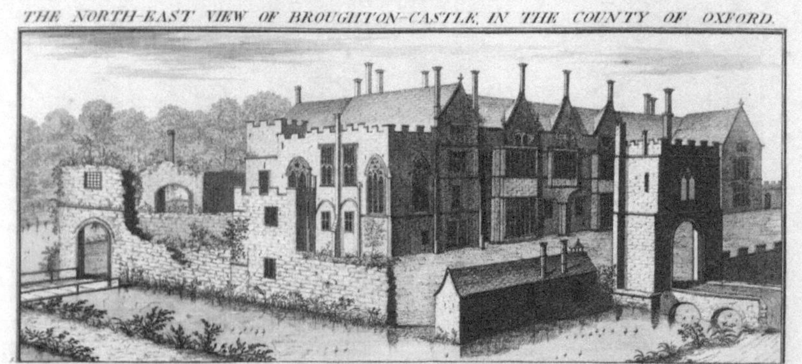

Broughton Castle near Banbury, ancestral home of the Lords Saye and Sele. She remarks that it was 'much left to decay and ruin when my brother came to it'. It had been damaged when besieged by Royalists during the Civil War. This drawing from 1729 shows that it was largely repaired by then. (From Broughton Castle, by permission of Martin Fiennes)

with William the Conqueror in 1066; one was among the barons who forced King John to agree Magna Carta; another fought with Henry V at Agincourt; and William Fiennes, 8th Lord Saye and Sele, was a leading Parliamentarian during the English Civil War in the mid-seventeenth century. William had fifteen grandchildren, one of whom was Celia.

We're in the castle's Great Hall, its grey stone walls rising 30ft or so to a ceiling studded at regular intervals with what look like over-sized, upside-down chess bishops. It's Sunday afternoon, and a dozen paying visitors are wandering around, squinting at the pictures of elegant ladies and military gentlemen and pointing up to where four glinting suits of armour keep an eyeless watch over the whole scene. As we pause by a wall-rack of rapier-like swords alongside a small sign saying 'Please do not touch', I explain my plan to Martin. The idea is to retrace her horse's hoof-steps around England.

'By side-saddle?' he asks with a wink.

''Fraid not,' I reply. 'My riding days – if I ever had any – are long gone. And anyway, if you tried to go on horseback along the same routes she took, you could find yourself in the outside lane of the M5, or on some other equally inhospitable stretch of tarmac.' I explain that it'll be strictly by car for me, or on foot where any of the old roads she took have survived. And I'll be stopping at the places she did – which she wrote about in her diaries. By seeing what she had to say about England three centuries ago, I want to try to understand how people lived, worked, relaxed and suffered back then.

Martin nods his approval. 'And of course,' he adds, 'we have so few details about her life other than from her travel diaries. The words she wrote are our only real clue to the woman herself, what she was like, what made her tick, why she did what she did.'

What we *do* know about Celia Fiennes' life is this. She was born on 7 June 1662. She first got a taste for travel when she was 20, and during the next fourteen years, her writings show she made nine excursions, some probably by coach and some on horseback, mostly within 40 miles of where she lived, first from the family home at Newton Toney in Wiltshire and then from London, where she moved in 1691 on the death of her mother.

It was in May 1697, a month before her 35th birthday, that she struck out on the first of two great journeys. She followed a winding route up to Scarborough on the Yorkshire coast and back, a distance of around 1,100 miles. The second of her trips – the one she herself calls 'My Great Journey' – was during the summer of the following year. It was some 1,900 miles long and took her north to Carlisle, briefly across the Scottish border, then south all the way to Land's End in Cornwall. Over the two summers, she visited every county in England. In her journals she not only tells us about the roads she rides (often muddy and treacherous), the towns she stops at and the people she meets (some she admires, some she criticises for their laziness or pities for what she regards as their misguided religious beliefs) – she's also fascinated by industry and commerce: the workshops, the markets, shipping, and especially the coal pits and tin mines. What she tells us is significant. The wheels of the Industrial Revolution would soon begin to judder and turn. Celia Fiennes was describing an England that was about to change forever.

Martin bends down to a dark oak settle, one of those that doubles as a chest, and, raising the lid, pulls out two small, slightly scuffed leather-bound books. 'Here they are,' he says, 'the hand-written journals of the great lady herself', and he takes them over to a table in front of the main fireplace. I'd expected to see a pile of dog-eared old papers, but he explains that they were bound together like this in the nineteenth century.

The larger of the two books measures around 6in by 4in with a dark green leather cover. When he opens it, we see tightly written pages of neat, sloping lettering. Martin tells me this version is probably one copied out by a secretary as it also has a brief introduction in a more ragged and squashed style, which ends with Celia Fiennes' own signature in carefully rounded, large characters.

He then opens the smaller book. 'We know this one is in her own handwriting,' he explains, seeing straightaway that this again is in the more straggly style of the Introduction. Whoever bound her manuscripts into this smaller of the two books, however, made a savage job of it. The pages have been cropped so the writing looks as though it's almost falling off the edge of the pages.

But it's not only the style of her penmanship which is so immediately identifiable. There's something else about her original diaries that occurs to me now as Martin and I leaf through the smaller book of her diaries. When I look at the words that she herself scratched onto these pieces of thin paper 300 years ago, with all their grammatical eccentricities and in her own distinctive handwriting – a little faded and browned now, and mingled with the occasional splodge of spilt ink – it's as though we're time-travelling. I could imagine we're looking over her shoulder as she blows on the paper to dry the ink before putting it away in a drawer. And I share this thought with Martin. 'It's so personal,' I say. 'Not like a dress she might have worn, or a plate she might have eaten from. Nobody wrote like her, nobody thought like her, nobody else saw the world as she did. And here, right in front of us, as if we can touch them, we have her thoughts and impressions recorded for us as though she's just dashed them off.'

Celia Fiennes was a pioneer. She undertook her great journeys around England a quarter of a century before Daniel Defoe, author of *Robinson Crusoe*, rode around the country and published *A Tour thru' the Whole Island of Great Britain*. And it would be a further 100 years before William Cobbett would do the same and tell the world about it in his *Rural Rides*. Unlike their books, her journals were unknown until, in 1888, one of her descendants paid to have them published and they reached a very limited public. Since then, they've been valued by academics studying late seventeenth-century social history, but beyond that there's only been the odd chapter about her in a couple of general histories or the occasional brief quotes in local guidebooks. Why then has she been so neglected? Is it because she was a woman, her writing and observations thought unworthy of the attention given to Defoe and Cobbett?

I ask Martin what he thinks. And in reply he opens, with careful fingers, the larger of the two books at the first page. 'Even she,' he says, 'apparently felt her writings were of limited interest.' And together, we decipher her opening words beneath the heading 'To the reader':

> *As this was never designed for, nor likely to fall into the hands of, any but my near relations, there needs not much to be said to excuse or recommend it.*

This sounds like modesty – suggesting the wider world won't be interested in what she has to say. Modesty maybe, or more likely she's reflecting the limited ambitions that were expected of women at the end of the seventeenth century. Women's diaries didn't get published – it was as simple as that.

But Celia Fiennes was both a child of her time and much more – as the next lines she wrote in her introduction tell us. She addresses head-on the other question that comes to our minds. Why did she decide to do what no other women of her time dared to do? Why did she travel unaccompanied by a husband or a father? She writes:

> *My journeys were begun to regain my health by variety and change of air and exercise. So, whatever promoted that was pursued.*

By 'regain', does she mean that she'd been ill and needed to recover? We don't know. But apart from very occasionally feeling a little sick (once or twice from eating rye bread), she always seems to be energetic and fit on her journeys.

She then adds something more revealing of her character. She wants to make sure 'my mind should not appear totally unoccupied'. And once we've got these polite, formulaic opening remarks out of the way, the real Celia Fiennes suddenly springs from the page, a person of strong opinions, proud of her achievements, and not timid about telling the rest of the world – men, women and even political leaders – to stop being such hypochondriacs, get out there and follow her example. She gives them a severe lesson:

> *... if all persons, both ladies and much more gentlemen, would spend some of their time in journeys to visit their native land, and be curious to inform themselves and make observations of the pleasant prospects,*

good buildings, different produces and manufactures of each place, … it would be a sovereign remedy to cure, or preserve from, these epidemic diseases of vapours – should I add laziness?

What's more, she goes on, it might put a put a stop to all this fashionable yearning for foreign tourism.

It would also form such an idea of England, add much to its glory and esteem in our minds, and cure the evil itch of overvaluing foreign parts.

Her large, well-formed signature at the end of the introduction leaves no doubt whose advice this is. Only intended for her family? I don't think so. She may not have thought it possible that the words of a woman could be published. But unlikely or not, she must have

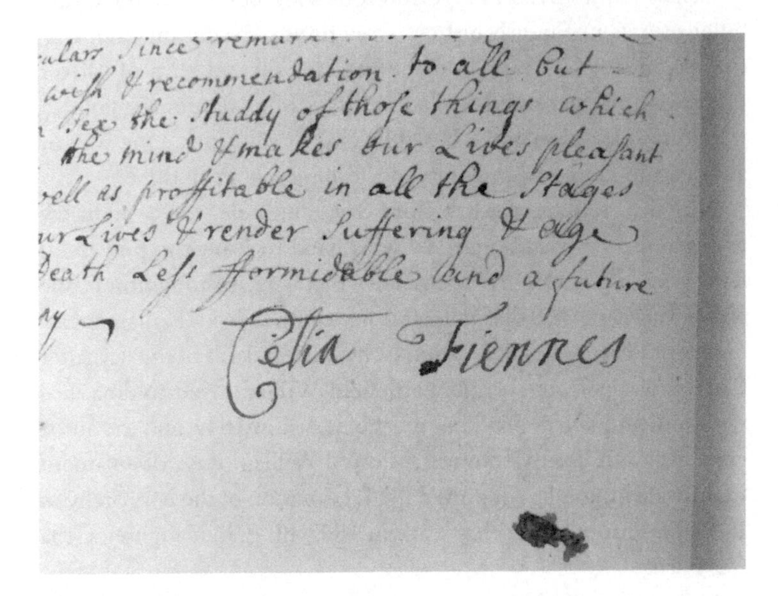
ular since remar
wish & recommendation to all but
Sex the studdy of those things which
the mind & makes our Lives pleasant
well as proffitable in all the Stages
ur Lives & render Suffering & age
Death Less fformidable and a future
ay
Celia Fiennes

Her signature at the end of the Introduction to the diaries. (From Broughton Castle, by permission of Martin Fiennes)

hoped that could happen. And she seems to understand that the opinion of a woman about the state of the world could be just as valuable as that of any man – a very rare, if not unique, attitude in the late seventeenth century.

Before I leave, Martin takes me on a tour of the castle. First we go over to the far side of the Great Hall to a painting of a middle-aged man wearing a lace neck-ruff and a tight-fitting leather jacket, his hair thinning on top but curling over his ears, his moustache and beard ending in three sharp points like the angles of a stretched triangle. He's fixing us with a no-nonsense stare. No smile. 'This is Celia's grandfather, William Fiennes,' explains Martin. 'The king nicknamed him "Old Subtlety" because of the cunning way he dealt with politics at court.'

Celia Fiennes lived in a period following one of the most turbulent times in English history – religious persecution, civil war, the execution of a king and the military dictatorship of Oliver Cromwell, all the products of a lethal mix of revolutionary politics, religious extremism and a belief in violent solutions. One way or another the Fiennes family played a leading role in all three.

William Fiennes, the 8th Lord Saye and Sele, was a mainstay of a group of Parliamentarians who tried to limit the powers of King Charles I during the 1630s. They met here at Broughton Castle and in the Civil War that followed, he commanded a Parliamentary regiment but he wasn't an extremist by the standards of the day. After Charles was defeated on the battlefield, William tried to do a deal with him and failed. The king was beheaded in 1649, and the autocratic rule of Oliver Cromwell followed. William was not an ardent Cromwellian, and he supported the Restoration of the Monarchy in 1660. Two months after his death in 1662, his granddaughter, Celia was born.

Next, Martin leads us up a winding stone staircase to a long gallery where rows of Fiennes' ancestors look down at us from each side. We stop before the portrait of a young man, clean-shaven, handsome, his dark hair brushed back and falling in curls behind his shoulders. 'This is Celia's father,' he explains, 'Nathaniel, a younger son of William. Notice the heading on the picture calls him "Colonel", so this was at the early stage of his career.'

Nathaniel fought for the Parliamentarians at the Battle of Edgehill in 1642 and was commended for his bravery. He was promoted to commander of the Parliamentarian troops at Bristol but found his forces outnumbered and surrendered the city to the Royalists. For this, he was court-martialled, and found himself – briefly – under sentence of death, before being pardoned.

He was already the MP for Banbury. Though a fervent supporter of the Parliamentary cause, he tried, like his father, to soften the policies of the extremists. He supported Cromwell but tried to talk him out of declaring himself Lord Protector of England and instead to take the more traditional course and crown himself king, again without success.

Religion in this age was more than a matter of how you prayed, it often had political ramifications too. And Nathaniel – whose speeches in parliament were described as 'spiritual' – lined up with Cromwell in arguing that preachers should stay out of politics and the law, and he supported the abolition of the rank of bishop. After Cromwell's death and the brief rule of his ineffectual son, England had a king again, and these policies were reversed: the Anglican Church with its hierarchy came back to the fore and Nathaniel found himself elbowed aside. He was now in that religious minority – Protestants who disagreed with the rituals of the Church of England – known as Dissenters.

And so, Nathanial retired from public life, his elder brother inherited the Saye and Sele title along with the estate at Broughton Castle and Nathaniel and his family settled in the village of Newton Toney near Salisbury. He married Frances Whitehead, from another family devoted to the rebellion against the king – her father was a colonel in the Civil War. It was Newton Toney where Celia, the fourth of Nathaniel and Frances' five daughters, spent her childhood. Unfortunately, we can't visit the family house; it was demolished in 1710 and a new one built in its place.

Celia's mother, Frances, was a fierce proponent of the beliefs and practices of Protestant Dissent. She appointed a disgraced Nonconformist as her private chaplain, and in 1671 she was fined for holding an illegal service at her house in Newton Toney. She turned their village into something of a Nonconformist centre. By 1676, there were twenty-six Dissenters living there, which was a triumph at a time when the civil rights of such believers were restricted by law. Frances' assertive character must have been an example to her daughter and showed her what a woman could achieve with independence and determination.

Celia's father, Nathaniel, died in 1669 when she was 7 years old. He never got to witness the fulfilment of what he'd fought and argued for – one of the most momentous events in English history. In the year 1688, the Dutch prince, William of Orange landed on the shore of Devon with his wife, Mary. They were Protestants. Parliament offered William the throne, to replace the Catholic, James II. A deal was done with the new king. It was an abiding and revolutionary agreement that would define the way England – and later the United Kingdom – is governed to this day. It was all contained in two powerful, interlocking principles:

> Monarchs would no longer have absolute power.
> Parliament was now supreme.

It had all been achieved without a shot being fired and became known as the Glorious – or sometimes the Bloodless – Revolution.

Celia Fiennes was 27 years old when this happened. As we follow her journeys through her diaries, we'll be asking just how much her attitude to what she saw around England was influenced by the family tradition that her grandfather and father had established; a tradition of public service, and compromise over extremism, while

For a long time, this was thought to be the only portrait of Celia Fiennes. However, artists used the dove to symbolise that the person in the painting had died, and this portrait dates from the 1670s – Fiennes lived till 1741. In addition, the plunging neckline would not have been to her Puritan liking. It's probably of one of her cousins. (From Broughton Castle, by permission of Martin Fiennes)

remaining true to the principles of Protestant Dissent. And how much was she a product of that Glorious Revolution of 1689 and all that it gave to the country?

As we head back to the staircase, Martin pauses in front of a painting of a young woman in a voluminous blue dress, falling off her shoulders. With implausible ease, she's gripping a dove in her right hand while her left stretches out one of its wings as though she's giving a lesson in ornithological anatomy.

'Now this one,' he says, 'was thought to be of Celia Fiennes herself.'

'Really!' I exclaim, as a moment of hope converts 'thought to be' in my head to 'could be'. 'But …' I bend for a closer look at the young woman's sad and slightly swollen eyes. 'But … I thought there weren't any portraits of her.'

'Don't get too excited,' says Martin. 'We're pretty sure it's not her, I'm afraid. There was a long-held theory it was but there are a number of things that point against it. For a start, Celia was not the sort of woman who would have allowed herself to be portrayed with a plunging neckline – she was a little too straight-laced for that. And then there's the dove she's holding, that was a symbol that the person in the painting had died. Her style of dress,' he points to the young woman's flowing blue robe, 'dates it around the 1670s. But, of course, Celia lived till 1741.'

'So, who is it?' I ask.

'We think she's one of her cousins, who died in childbirth about this time. I'm afraid we'll never know what Celia looked like.' Then with a reassuring smile, he adds, 'But, you know, what you're planning to do, getting deep into her diaries and seeing the world as she saw it, could tell us far more about the woman than any flattering painting could ever do.'

With that, I thank and shake the hand of Celia Fiennes' great-great-great-great-great-great-great-great-great-great nephew, and, as I make my way back to the car park, I start to plan how we'll follow her on the first of her great journeys around England in the year 1697.

Her First Great Journey 1697

1

North from London

A RISKY RIDE

The road lay under water,
which is very unsafe for strangers to pass.

Within an hour or so of riding away from the safety of her London home, Celia Fiennes was facing the first hazards on her journey. Once you left behind the houses, inns and markets of the city – whichever direction you travelled – you were on some of the most dangerous grounds in the country. Blackheath, for example, to the south-east, she described as 'a noted robbing place'. And it was the same in Hounslow, Hampstead and Primrose Hill. The heaths and commons all around London were the favourite haunts of highwaymen. Celia Fiennes' first day out on her summer-long journey of 1697 – a 25-mile ride north – took her along some of the riskiest routes. On Finchley Common in 1687, the notorious William Cady had robbed a gentlewoman at gunpoint and killed her manservant, before two men happened to arrive and shot his horse from under him. In 1691, near Barnet, there was a shoot-out between a gang of highwaymen and several locals, leaving three men dead and several horses killed. Then in 1694, at Stoke Newington, a man named John Smith was arrested having 'committed divers robberies on the road near that town'. He was hanged for murder.

That day, however, Celia Fiennes reaches her destination without incident. As we'll discover later, she won't always be so lucky.

She opens her diary with words that reflect little of the sights, delights and dangers she'll face over the months to come:

HERE BEGINS MY NORTHERN JOURNEY IN MAY 1697. From London to Amwellbury in Hertfordshire 19 miles. Thence to Bishops Stortford in Essex 13 miles, which is a very pretty, neat market town, a good church and a delicate spring of water which has a wall built round it, very sweet and clear water for drinking. There is a little river runs by the town that feeds several mills.

Her first night's stay is in the village of Great Amwell near Ware in Hertfordshire. This is where her cousin, Susannah Filmer, lived, at Amwellbury House. It's almost certainly the only residence she visits that's not open to the public today, and there's only the odd doorway that she would recognise in the place now – it's been rebuilt over the centuries.

She then does some country-house visiting. First at Audley End in Suffolk:

A house of the Earl of Sussex which makes a noble appearance like a town, so many towers and buildings of stone within a park,

Then to Littlebury in north-west Essex. Everything seems perfect for the next 12 miles:

All the country is pleasant between this and Cambridge. You go in sight of so many neat villages, with rows of trees about them and very neatly built churches.

So to Cambridge. Though she admires the colleges and describes them in detail, she's not so keen on the town itself.

The buildings are old and indifferent, the streets mostly narrow.

'Old' to her is often a term of disdain.

A day or two later she visits Burghley House near Stamford – and in general she praises it:

> *The house looks very nobly, the gardens very fine within one another, with lower and higher walls, statues and fine grass walks.*

But she condemns its chapel as 'old and not to abide' – in other words, she couldn't stand it.

Undramatic as these descriptions may be, her tastes are beginning to emerge. She likes things – houses, churches, streets, gardens – to be modern and especially to be 'neat'. It's a word she uses countless times in her diaries. It implies that she doesn't like the world to be disorganised and wants it to be controlled. In this, she's in line with the mainstream philosophy of her time. This was the Age of Enlightenment, when it was believed that the brain and ingenuity of humans could now triumph over the wildness of nature. It was a time when even horticultural vistas which stretched beyond a statue, a fountain or a row of trees should be trained on some reassuring works of humans, such as church steeples or the right-angled walls of a great house.

At Burghley House, we also learn something about her attitude to her own sex. Although she admires the quality of the artwork in the paintings of female figures, she goes on to say:

> *But they were all without garments or very little. That was the only fault, the immodesty of the pictures especially in My Lord's apartment.*

She makes a similar comment at Lord Sandwich's house, Hinchingbrooke at Huntingdon:

> *Over one of the chimneys is a fine picture of Venus, were it not too much unclothed.*

'The Sleeping Venus' by Daniel Seiter is almost certainly one of the paintings Fiennes saw on her visit to Burghley House. She remarked that 'they were all without garments or very little. That was the only fault.' A mild criticism of an image that more extreme Puritans would have regarded as wicked. (From the Burghley House Collection)

She'd been brought up according to Puritan beliefs and strictures, and that could explain her distaste for any hint of female nudity. But there's more to it than that. Look at the painting opposite, 'The Sleeping Venus' by Daniel Seiter. It had been brought from Rome in 1684 by the then-master of Burghley, the 5th Earl of Exeter, so was almost certainly one of the paintings she saw. A strict Puritan would have regarded it as shameless and wicked, without any saving features. Celia Fiennes is less extreme. Nudity is the 'only fault' in Burghley House's art collection, not an overriding one. So she appears to be on the more liberal wing of late seventeenth-century Puritanism.

And she has other objections to an exposed female thigh or breast that appear to be more to do with her personal dislikes rather than her religious beliefs. As we'll discover later on her journey when she briefly crosses into Scotland, she's scathing about 'the women and great girls bare-legged', who she condemns because they 'sat hovering between their bed and the chimney corner all idle doing nothing'.

She equates flaunting flesh with laziness. Her disdain of idleness is clear in her Introduction to her journal. She has some specific advice for her sister women. They should quit their boring lives, and:

> *... study how to be serviceable to their neighbours, especially the poor ... This would spare them the uneasy thoughts how to pass away tedious days, and time would not be a burden, when not at a card or dice table.*

It's a reminder that it would have been all too easy for her to waste her days in pointless games with similarly bored women friends. But that was not Celia Fiennes.

The flirtatious, disreputable off-the-shoulder dress seems to be more than immorality, it goes with slothfulness and a failure by women to improve themselves. She believes women should make themselves useful members of society.

My own journey, following her north from London, takes me through an hour and a quarter's worth of traffic lights, junctions, roundabouts, lane-changing, and queues behind smelly lorries before I join the A10, swoop under the M25 and then start to catch a glimpse of the odd fields and woodland amid the many housing estates as the car now glides smoothly over a newly tarmacked road surface. There's nothing unusual of course about this experience of twenty-first-century travelling. We all take it for granted. But its very familiarity can be a barrier to understanding what the same journey would have been like in 1697. Of course, it's obvious that everything I've listed – from traffic lights to tarmac – were absent back then. But that's not the same as being able to see in our mind's eye – or for that matter, feel in aching and bruised arms, legs and spine – what roads were like back then. We might think all we have to do is picture ourselves on some narrow country lane we know well, and that's it. Yes, that'll start to get us time-travelling. But it won't do much more than lift us off the launch-pad. The biggest difference for today's traveller compared with 320 years ago was the state of repair of the roads themselves. You might say, 'Oh, I can understand that. You should see the potholes round our way.' Forget it. The almost constant challenge that Celia Fiennes has to face on her 3,000 miles or more of travels, criss-crossing the country from end to end, is the unreliable and at times dangerous ground – or lack of anything resembling a firm surface – beneath her horse's hooves.

Flooded roads are a particular problem for her. This, for instance, is not far from her cousin's house at Amwellbury.

It's a low flat ground all here about, so that with the least rain it is overflowed by the river, as it was when I was there, so that the road lay under water, which is very unsafe for strangers to pass, by reason of the holes and quick-sands and loose bottom.

The road around Dunmow in Essex is 'mostly clay' and for '8 long miles, it's a very deep way especially after rain'. This phrase 'long miles' is a favourite of hers. She seems to mean each mile took a long time to negotiate, in this case because the road was 'deep', which is her way of saying the surface isn't firm, so her horse's hooves dig deep into it and slow her progress. It's also worth noting that, although the statute mile had been defined a century earlier in 1593, in many parts of England it often still wasn't recognised.

And so it goes on. In Huntingdonshire, she remarks that the land 'after rains, is in some places deep'. Near Stilton, it's the same.

> *This is in part of the fenny country. In a mile or two the ground is all wet and marshy.*

Muddy or even flooded roads, however, are not the only hazard she has to face. Far from it. Every part of the country seems to offer its own challenges.

While we're talking about roads in the late seventeenth century, we'll take a moment to review the kind of challenges she faces – in one form or another – on almost every day of her travels. Thus, in the north Cotswolds, she tells us:

> *Thence up a vast stony, high, hazardous hill of near two miles long ascending all the way from Weston-sub-Edge – this is in sight of Chipping Campden. So to Morton-in-Marsh, 6 miles down as steep a stony hill for 2 miles.*

Uneven, stony tracks on steep slopes present their own difficulties. For instance, in Dorset:

> *From Lyme Regis, the ways are also difficult by reason of the very steep hills up and down, full of large smooth pebbles that make the strange horses* [i.e. ones not used to it] *slip and uneasy to go.*

We can judge how serious this is for her by the effect on the horses' hooves. In Cumberland, she writes:

These stony hills and ways pull off a horse's shoe, and wear them so thin that it was a constant charge to shoe my horses every 2 or 3 days.

A third problem – after the mud and the rock-strewn, steep slopes – is the width of the roads. Today even the narrowest of single-track roads can take a tractor and will usually have passing places. Here's what she encounters just outside Plymouth.

The ways now become so difficult that one could scarcely pass by each other, even single horses, and so dirty in many places, and just a track for one horse's feet, the banks on either side so near. And the quicksets [hedges] *and trees that grow on these banks loosen them and so make them moulder down* [crumble] *sometimes, which would be in danger of quite swallowing up the way.*

And sometimes, she meets all hazards at the same time – floods, rocky slopes and no room to pass. At Leigh near Axminster, she reports,

I went through narrow, stony lanes up hills and down, which steeps cause the water from rains to trill [surge, cascade] *down on the low ground so that for a few hours or a day there will be no passing at the bottom, which happened while I was at Leigh. One night's rain put the cattle in the meadows swimming, and hindered us from going to church – the water would have come over the windows of the coach.*

She'd been staying over the Saturday night with a relative, a Mr Hendley who lived nearby, and presumably they'd all planned to go to church the next morning in his coach.

If travellers on horseback found the roads hazardous, coach passengers weren't always much more comfortable. She recalls one trip only a few miles from her mother's home in Wiltshire.

Our coach was once wedged by the wheel in the stones, so that several men were forced to lift us out.

Privately owned carriages might have springs, but public transport coaches did not. They were often slow and uncomfortable. The stagecoach, which had first appeared in England in 1640, was heavy and cumbersome. There were three classes of passenger. Those who paid most were packed inside, while second-class passengers balanced in a large open basket attached to the back. Third class sat on the roof with the luggage, with only a handrail to grasp to stop slithering off as the vehicle pitched into the frequent craters – to call them 'potholes' would flatter them. Up front were either four or six horses, lurching you forward at an average speed of 4mph.

So, were any of England's roads safe and comfortable to travel in 1697? The answer is – yes, sometimes. There were occasions, for instance, when she finds nothing worth telling us about the state of the road. She writes, for example, without further comment:

> *Thence to Saxmundham 8 miles more.*

We can assume there was no problem in that part of Suffolk. At other times – near Colchester for example – she tells us the way was pretty good … only to then point out a contrast:

> *except 4 or 5 miles they call the 'Severals', a sort of deep moor ground and woody.*

There was one notable and fairly consistent exception to the bad-roads routine. The streets in towns and cities give her least to complain about. After her reference to the 'deep moor' approaching Colchester for instance, she discovers much to commend in the town itself, which has:

> *well-pitched streets, which are broad enough for two coaches to go abreast, besides a pitched walk on either side by the houses.*

'Pitched' is a favourite word of hers. It means 'paved', probably with flat stones, and has nothing to do with tar or the camber of the surface. Her compliments are a tribute to the effective government of many towns. By the end of the seventeenth century, those that were flourishing centres of trade and industry had elected mayors who oversaw taxation and expenditure on projects – such as providing clean, safe streets – vital to help grow their economy.

Outside the towns, however, in rural parishes, where the only occupation was often farming the bit of land you rented from the local lord, there was no such motive for fixing up the roads.

At the end of the seventeenth century, most of England's main roads outside towns were in a worse state than when the Romans had left 1,300 years earlier. Throughout the medieval era, long-distance traders – their merchandise of wool or salt, for instance, carried on packhorses – had made use of the stone-paved roads the Romans had built. But as the centuries passed, constant use had eroded and crumbled them. The alternative was to follow the ancient trackways that predated the Romans, unpaved, unfenced paths, marked out only by the footsteps and hoofprints of 2,000 years. Whichever way you chose – as Celia Fiennes shows us – it was likely to be dusty in dry weather, muddy and treacherous after rain, sometimes boulder-strewn and frighteningly steep, impassable in winter, and with craters big enough to trap a yard-high carriage wheel.

So, was anyone responsible for maintaining England's roads in Celia Fiennes' day? There was a medieval tradition that it was the job of the local landlord. On her approach to Ely in Cambridgeshire, she reports:

> *You pass on a gravel causeway, which the Bishop is charged to repair. Else there would be no passing in the summer. In the winter, this causeway is overflowed and they have no way but by boats to pass in.*

The Bishop was Ely's chief landowner and, according to an ancient feudal custom, could require his tenants to 'make and maintain two furlongs of the causeway'. Fiennes' remark seems to indicate that this was a help here, in the summer anyway, though not in the wetter months. But at least the Bishop of Ely did something to help the traveller. However, in most parts of the countryside, it was rare that the local lord took much interest in such matters.

The first co-ordinated attempt to improve the lamentable highway system came during Henry VIII's reign. Heavy wagons and springless carts were becoming more common, and they churned up the roads and made them even more muddy and cratered. At the same time, a wagon needed a wider track than a packhorse. The official response came with an Act of Parliament in 1555 which placed an obligation on each parish to maintain the roads within its boundaries. Anyone who held a certain amount of land had to supply two men, with horse or ox, as well as a cart and tools, to work for four consecutive days a year – later extended to six – on mending and maintaining nearby roads. At the same time, in each parish, 'two honest persons' should be chosen to serve as Surveyors of the Highways, who would oversee the work and could fine anyone who failed to supply the requisite labour.

However, in summary, it was all pretty much a waste of time. First, there was no local expertise in road building or maintenance, so chucking the odd shovelful of loose stones on a constantly waterlogged track or shifting the soil around to fill the holes achieved next to nothing. And anyway, who'd want to be a Surveyor of Highways? You'd be unskilled, probably unpaid, and certainly unpopular. And finally, most people felt it was one thing to make sure the little roads which locals needed to move around the parish were made safe, but it was quite another to have to work – without reward – on the long-distance routes used by traders and other travellers who were merely passing through and made no contribution, either in labour or cash, to the work. So, roads in much of the country continued to be neglected and, what's more, fell into an even worse state during the later seventeenth century as increasing numbers of passenger coach services and freight carts were gouging, grinding and eroding what was left of England's highways. That was the state of the roads, then, that Celia Fiennes describes in all their stony, narrow and flooded shame.

Change, however, was on the way. Not a rapid revolution, but a few solid grains of hope had appeared in the otherwise chaotic mess.

Half a century before Celia Fiennes rode north from London, in the tiny village of Standon in Hertfordshire, the local people had come up with a novel idea. The old Roman road known as Ermine Street passed through their parish and was a popular route for merchants plying their trade between the north-east of England and London. Instead of the poor folk of Standon having to work unpaid on the upkeep of the road, they proposed that the traders themselves fund the repairs. The suggestion was put to a justice of the peace at the county's quarter sessions. There doesn't seem to have been much reaction at first – in fact, not for another seventeen years. Then in 1663, Parliament passed a law allowing ('allowing' note, not 'requiring') justices in the counties of Hertfordshire, Cambridgeshire and Huntingdonshire, through which Ermine Street passed, to levy a toll on those who travelled the road, the cash to be used to pay for its maintenance.

The first tolls to be collected were at the tiny hamlet of Wadesmill in Hertfordshire, where the surface of the old Roman road was being wrecked by the regular traffic of wagons carrying barley to the maltings at the town of Ware to the south. All did not, however, go to plan. The barley traders resented the new tax, and so steered their wagons away from Wadesmill and its toll-collector, along an alternative route (which, incidentally, became so popular it's still in use today – it's the A1(M) motorway). And that was it. The idea of tolls funding road repairs progressed little for another thirty years.

In 1695, Parliament decided to give it another try, and, at the very moment that Celia Fiennes was journeying through England, began to pass a series of acts extending the old law to other parts of the land where 'the lanes are in a ruinous and dangerous state and the several parishes are unable of themselves to repair the same'. And it allowed the collection of tolls 'to be paid for all such horses, coaches, carts, wagons, droves and gangs of cattle as shall pass, be led or droven in or through the said way'.

What may be the first account by a toll-payer of the new law in action comes from Celia Fiennes herself. She's travelling west from Norwich.

> *Thence I went to Wymondham, a little market town 5 miles, mostly on a causeway, the country being low and moorish. And the road on the causeway was in many places full of holes, though it's secured by a bar at which passengers pay a penny a horse for mending the way, for all about is not to be rode on unless it's a very dry summer.*

It sounds as though the money collected from the tolls hadn't done much to improve the quality of Wymondham's road. But it was early days, and perhaps not enough cash had yet been amassed to begin to pay the workers' wages.

Over the next century and a half, 'turnpikes' – as the toll bars were known – began to appear all across the land. The word has an uncertain origin. A pike was – in military parlance – a long pole with a spike on the end, so by association the pole which barred the way to travellers until they paid the toll was also called a pike. Then once the cash was handed over, the pike was turned either upwards or sideways to let the traveller through. Another, more exciting, version stems from the practice of young bloods, who – reluctant to fork out the required penny for their horse – would gallop up to the bar and jump over it. To stop this abuse, spikes – like those on the end of a military pike – were sometimes fitted on top of the bar, which, once the toll was paid, could be turned so the sharp points faced safely down. The term 'turnpike' may have stuck because it described both these systems.

In the decade following Celia Fiennes' great journeys, management of turnpikes passed from justices of the peace to committees of independent trustees, who could borrow money to carry out

An early turnpike. 'Passengers pay a penny a horse for mending the way.' (Public Domain)

road building and repair against the promise of future income from tolls. But turnpikes were far from a success. A Royal Society report of 1737 claimed that if all 'turnpikes were taken down and the roads not touched for seven years, they would be a great deal better than they are now'. They were not popular – there were even riots against them. Nevertheless, by the 1750s, what became known as 'turnpike mania' took hold, as thousands of trusts were made responsible for over 15,000 miles of roads. They continued to be the system for repairing most roads into the nineteenth century. Their death knell was sounded, not by a bell, but a whistle – from a steam-powered locomotive. At Wymondham, for instance –where Celia Fiennes witnesses the birth of the turnpike – the old horse-drawn coach service ceased to operate within a year of the opening of the Norwich to London railway in 1844. Travellers preferred the speed and comfort of the train to the old horse-drawn coach service, and a year later the turnpike at Wymondham was shut.

Turnpikes have left their legacy across Britain. Anyone visiting Wymondham today who turns off the bypass on to the 'London Road', will find themselves alongside an unprepossessing twentieth-century building, once a house and now an office. The place itself may not have much of a history, but its name does. It's called

'Turnpike Farm' and marks where the very first toll-collector lived on the job. More historic buildings – with names like 'Pike Cottage' or 'Turnpike House' – can be seen all over the country. They often have a small tower at one end with a window near the top, so the collector could see travellers approaching well before they arrived. And the turnpike has left its mark in the present-day United States. A 'turnpike' there is a major highway where vehicles are charged a toll, one of the most famous being the 'Mass Pike', the Massachusetts Turnpike.

But all this was well into the future. As we follow Celia Fiennes' journeys in the days ahead along those flooded, steep, rocky, narrow tracks, we should remember that all the problems were made much worse for her simply because she was a woman. She had to contend with a basic, physical disadvantage that no male counterparts who might venture out from towns and cities had to worry about.

Long before the days of women in trousers, at a time when ladies of the higher social station wore flared skirts reaching below the ankle, they had no choice but to ride side-saddle. This involved a strain on the spine and hips with one leg hoisted in a contorted position across the horse's back for hours on end. And there were other challenges. Men could mount the animal by themselves, but it often took two helpers to hoist up a side-saddler. And there were more dangerous implications. The side-saddler didn't have the security of one leg on either flank of the horse. If your mount bolted and fell, a male rider – legs astride – was often thrown clear. The woman was more likely to slide off her side-saddle and end up beneath the toppling animal with a risk of breaking her back or even being killed.

Thus, the simple problem of how to travel from A to B was not so simple. At the end of the seventeenth century, it meant the prospect of discomfort and even danger for Celia Fiennes every day that she set off up the road.

2

To Nottingham and Harrogate

BEER, BATHING AND PRAYING

Some of the Papists I saw there had so much zeal
as to continue a quarter of an hour
on their knees at their prayers in the well.

One of the delights of delving into Celia Fiennes' diaries is discovering what she thought about places we love, especially those we have a soft spot for because we grew up there. A friend of mine was keen to know her opinion of Harrogate, the genteel Yorkshire spa town where he came from.

'Aha,' I said with a superior grin, 'she says the water there smelled so dreadful, she couldn't even force her horse to get near it.' I resisted boasting of the contrast with what she writes about the town where I spent my youth and went to school.

Nottingham is the neatest town I have seen, built of stone and delicate, with large and long streets much like London, and the houses lofty and well-built.

To reach Nottingham, Celia Fiennes follows a zig-zag route north via Lincoln. There, she makes for the cathedral. However, it's not the glory-to-God splendour of its architecture that she tells us about. Instead, she recounts how she climbed the 250 steps up the tower to 'Great Tom's Nest', Great Tom being the minster's giant bell. It's so big that:

> *Eight persons may very well stand up in the hollow of the bell together. It's as much as a man can reach to the top of the bell with his hand when he is inside. It's rarely ever rung and only then by* [pushing] *the clapper to each side. Which we did, and it sounds all over the town.*

This is typical Celia Fiennes, having a go herself. And when she reaches Nottingham, she combines her observations on the industry of the town with again setting her hand to it herself.

> *They make brick and tile in the town. But the manufacture mostly consists in weaving of stockings, which is a very ingenious art. There was a man that spun glass and made several things – birds and beasts. I spun some of the glass myself, and I saw him make a swan presently with different coloured glass.*

She's particularly struck by Nottingham's central square.

> *The Market Place is very broad, out of which runs a very large street much like Holborn. The buildings are fine, and there is a piazza all along one side of one of the streets, with stone pillars for walking beneath. It runs the length of the street which is a mile long.*

Anyone who knows Nottingham today will recognise its fine Old Market Square. That's where we're bound now. I pull off the M1 west of the city, and at the Park-and-Ride take advantage of the city's clean, frequent and swift tram service to propel me through streets I once knew well and into the city centre. The Square is dominated by the Council House, a banal name for one of the grandest tributes to civic pride in England. Its neoclassical splendour, eight pillars across the front rising 100ft and topped by a dome 100ft more, might tempt us to wonder whether its baroque style dates back to Celia Fiennes' time here, or at least to soon after. But it's not so. It was built in the 1920s. It's neo-neoclassical, but no less imposing for that.

The Square this morning is as peaceful as in Celia Fiennes' time. It's a huge area – the size of two football fields – paved with white stones. There are several hundred people here today, some sitting on the stone walls around the edge, others – like me – scuttling across to reach the opposite street, ahead of me its garish signs of the very twenty-first-century Ladbrokes, Mod Pizza and Five Guys restaurant. But there is just a trace of something that Celia Fiennes might have recognised: brown marble pillars prop up the front of each building with a hint at the piazza arcade she reported seeing.

It's not just the glassblowing, the wide streets and the Market Place that she admires in this city. It's how it serves more basic bodily needs too.

> *Nottingham is famous for good ale. So for cellars, they are all dug out of the rocks and so are very cool. At the Crown Inn is a cellar of 60 steps down, all in the rock with archways over your head. In the cellar I drank good ale. We were very well entertained and very reasonably so at the Blackmoors Head.*

In the late seventeenth century, unpolluted drinking water was hard to find. Beer was the usual - safe – thirst-quencher of all classes. But Celia Fiennes' interest appears to go beyond that practicality, she writes as though she enjoys a tasty pint of her favourite alcoholic tipple. Not what we might expect from a lady of minor aristocratic, Puritan upbringing. So, have we discovered a surprising new side to her character? Or is it more to do with her constant curiosity about the way people make things? However much she likes drinking ale, she's also investigating the peculiar and beneficial way that Nottinghamites have traditionally brewed it – in caves.

The Crown Inn and the Blackmoors Head that she mentions have long disappeared. But another pub with a similar story is still thriving. Leave the Square, along Friar Lane, turning left onto Castle Road, with the rockface rising on the right around a corner tower of Nottingham Castle, and there, a few yards down a leafy pathway, stand the white walls of what I'm looking for. One of England's historic gems, in the pub category anyway, and also as it happens where, as a 16-year-old, I'd come to defy the law with my mates after a game of rugby on a Saturday and knock back a half of that Nottingham ale that Celia Fiennes so extolled. From 100yds away, I can see the name high on its walls: Ye Olde Trip to Jerusalem.

What makes 'The Trip', as it's known hereabouts, so different starts to emerge from outside. And I'm not just talking about its name – allegedly derived from the Crusaders who gathered here before setting off to try to drive the Saracens out of the Holy Land. The Trip looks as though it's the front half of a house tacked onto a towering rock-face – Nottingham Castle sits above it. Walk through the door and we straightaway see that 'tacked onto' is not what it is at all. The interior of the pub stretches in front of me, away to the side and up above. Its walls and ceiling are a rough, pock-marked, pinkish grey stone. Most of the pub is inside one vast cave. I say 'one', but I know from visits here years ago that it also has cellars stretching down and under the rock supporting the castle for scores of yards in several directions.

Caves are found all over or – I should say – under Nottingham. They're not natural. The rock here is a soft sandstone, and the many cellars and caverns have been hacked out by hand, the first of them, probably here where I'm sitting now, around 900 years ago. At the end of the seventeenth century when Celia Fiennes visited Nottingham, most of its inns made use of underground passageways, as did the Crown Inn that she mentions. In an age well before ale began to be delivered to the pub door from a central brewery, each inn made its own and allowed it to ferment down in the cellars.

The management of The Trip are sensitive to the place's history, and if they're not too busy – like today – the landlady will give you a tour. So, once the lunchtime crush has slackened off, she takes me to see a giant chimney round the corner from the bar. It's been chipped out of the rock. It's like an empty inglenook fireplace about 8ft by 10ft wide, which I step inside and peer upwards. It's not like any chimney you'll have seen before: it's the same wide shaft all the way up for what looks like 60ft or 70ft, to where daylight streams in. This is where they did the malting. There would have been a fire down here at the bottom, and the particularly wide chimney was because there were wooden trays a few feet up the shaft where the barley was laid out on the heat. My guide explains that the next step in the brewing process ideally needs a constant temperature summer and winter for the fermentation, which was provided by Nottingham's caves. The result was the high-quality beer which Celia Fiennes so enjoys.

I thank my guide, get a cheery 'You're welcome, duck', finish my coffee, and it's back by tram to the Park-and-Ride.

Then it's on up into Yorkshire. Celia Fiennes always makes a bee-line for any spas within a few days' ride. She's a steadfast believer in their health-giving benefits – hardly surprising since medical practice in the late seventeenth century was limited to invasive surgery unsupported by any logic, anaesthetic or sterilisation of equipment, plus the administration of a few crushed herbs, backed up by blood-letting, which was carried out by a barber between haircuts.

The word 'spa' today conjures images of elegant promenading and aristocratic balls in Georgian England. And indeed, spas as holiday retreats for the wealthy were just starting to catch on in Celia Fiennes' time, as we'll discover later when she journeys to Tunbridge Wells. In the nineteenth century, Harrogate would become Yorkshire's Tunbridge, attracting many an idle noble not only from across Britain but from a wider Europe too. Today, it's no longer where people flock to taste its waters or stroll up and down looking fashionable. But its four-star hotels, flower-filled parks and Betty's Tea Rooms ensure that the name Harrogate has remained synonymous with gentility, if a little more Hyacinth Bouquet than Duchess of Devonshire these days.

Back in 1697, Harrogate and its spas were not yet the posh holiday resort it would later become. As well as being the haunt of those seeking cures for their ailments, the town and the surrounding area also drew in religious pilgrims. Fiennes explains:

> *We went over a marshy common to the spa at Knaresborough* [3 miles from Harrogate]. *There is a little chapel cut out of the rock and arched and carved with figures of saints, I suppose. It's called Saint Robert's chapel. He is esteemed a very devout man. His effigy is carved at the entrance, and there is an altar that was decked with flowers and the ground with rushes for the devout that did frequent it. Several Papists were there about and many came to the spa and did say their prayers there.*

The belief that springs or natural wells were holy places went back way before Christian times. Holy wells had been so popular with pagan worshippers that the early Christian Church tried to ban such devotions. It failed, and so priests adopted the ever-effective strategy of if-you-can't-beat-'em-join-'em and started to preach that these wells were really sites special to Christian saints. It's been estimated that at one time or another the average British county each had around forty of these watery shrines. The idea that they had healing powers seems to have begun early too, and throughout their history, there were claims that if you recited the right prayers or made the expected offerings to your deity, their water could cure eye problems, infertility, lameness, insanity, skin complaints, leprosy, assorted palsies and agues as well as children's disabilities such as rickets and polio.

Protestants in the seventeenth century rejected the idea that wells and springs had some sort of miraculous powers and that was the view that Celia Fiennes, along with most of her compatriots, subscribed to by 1697 when she visited Harrogate.

The term 'Papists' is significant. We would regard it as an insult and in some ways it was. It was the term deliberately chosen by England's non-Catholics to demean their religious opponents. Catholics were now in a minority and, technically at least, were outcasts. But they were no longer outcasts in the sense that they had to be persecuted.

Change had come with the Bloodless Revolution of 1688–89, when the Protestant monarchs William and Mary had replaced the last Roman Catholic ruler of England. One of the first Acts of Parliament in the new regime embedded a degree of religious tolerance in the constitution. Over the previous 150 years, the mere sight of citizens praying in a different way from their neighbours had opened deep divisions in English society, had brought torture and burning at the stake for heretics, and was in part responsible for the slaughter in the Civil War and the oppressive regime of Oliver Cromwell. In the post-1689 era, while the new law made the Church of England the keeper of the country's predominant religion, most other Protestants were also free to practise their beliefs. However, tolerance did not extend to Catholics. Their system of worship was still illegal. Nevertheless, in practice, it soon emerged that little or no action was usually taken against them. Opposition to those dubbed by Celia Fiennes 'Papists' was now expressed in words, rather than in physical violence or judicial punishment. And by the end of the seventeenth century, it had become the standard way for Puritans to refer to Catholics, and to an extent that stripped out some of its sense of abuse.

Even more telling is the way that Fiennes, a devout Protestant herself of course, chooses to describe the actions of those she calls 'Papists'. She never ridicules them. Sometimes she pities them for what she sees as their misguided beliefs. But at Knaresborough, she reports on their deeds more, it seems, in a spirit of objective journalistic observation, as though she's writing about some exotic primitive tribe.

There was a Papist lady lodged where we did. And our landlady at the inn – where we were treated civilly – told us she went with this lady among these ruins where the lady would say her prayers. And one day someone had been digging and brought up the bone of a man's arm and hand and the ligature of the elbow, and in the hollow part of the joint was a jelly-like blood that was moist. This lady dipped the end of her handkerchief in it, and cut it off and put it up as a relic.

It's clear then that the ancient belief that the sacred quality of spa water could cure ill health did not, however, die with the birth of the Age of Enlightenment. And what's more, in the new Protestant world, which Celia Fiennes inhabited, the power of the waters lived on. Now though, the spa was no longer seen as a giver of miracle cures. Its springs were now the source of something believed to be more rational and scientific, a medical treatment for specific stomach upsets.

On her arrival at Harrogate itself, she lists 'four different springs of water'. Taking advantage of the first one isn't so easy.

There is the sulphur or stinking spa, not improperly termed, for the smell being so very strong and offensive that I could not force my horse near the well.

The next ones are even worse.

There are two wells together with basins in them that the spring rises up in, which is furred with a white scum which rises out of the water … It comes from brimstone mines, for the taste and smell is much of sulphur, though it has an additional offensiveness – like carrion.

But it takes more than the stink of rotting flesh to put her off.

It's a quick purger and very good for all scorbutic humours. Some persons drink a quart or two. I drank a quart in a morning for two days and hold them to be a good sort of purge if you can hold your breath so as to drink them down.

'A quick purger.' This was often seen as the great benefit of drinking certain spa waters. It seems that constipation was the common curse of this and many eras in our history. 'Scorbutic humours' is a slight puzzle. 'Scorbutic' usually means to do with scurvy, a disease of the skin and the gums, which we now know is caused by vitamin C deficiency. Celia Fiennes is using the word 'humour' in the way the ancient Greeks defined it, as one of the liquids that controlled the health of the body, a theory that persisted in medical circles way after her time. So, presumably, she means that the foul drink she's forcing down will restore the balance in her body necessary to prevent her getting scurvy.

The last Harrogate spring is different again.

> *Within a quarter of a mile is the sweet spa, a spring which rises off iron and steel of a petrifying quality which turns all things into stone.*

It was a common misbelief that a petrifying well transformed the objects which were exposed to their water – turned them to stone – by some magical process. People thought that things soaked in these springs for a few months – be they ragdolls or cartwheels – were changed into rocks that were replicas of themselves. What many people didn't realise was that the objects in fact became coated with stone because the water was so loaded with minerals.

But this spring gives Fiennes undiluted pleasure. She becomes quite poetical.

> *This clear spring runs with a swift current to the brow of the hill and then it spreads itself all around the hill, which is a rock, and so runs down like a hasty shower of small and great rain ... And this is called the Dropping Well. There is an arbour and the company used to come and eat supper there in an evening to have the pleasing prospect and the murmuring shower to divert their ear.*

We could wish that she'd told us in whose 'company' she enjoyed these pastoral evening picnics, but she doesn't.

The Dropping Well at Knaresborough, which 'runs down like a hasty shower of small and great rain'. (From the Wellcome Collection)

Six miles on from Harrogate she reaches Copgrove and a 'spring of exceeding cold water called St Mongo's Well'. Here we learn that it's not just *drinking* spa water that improves your health. You've got to dip yourself right under it too. She can't get enough of St Mungo's and she has a favourite spot.

> *I always choose to be just where the springs rise, where it's much the coldest. Setting aside the Papists' fancies of it, I cannot but think it is a very good spring being remarkably cold. And just at the head of the spring, it's so fresh, which must needs be very strengthening. It shuts up the pores of the body immediately. You cannot bear the coldness of it above 2 or 3 minutes, and then you come out and walk around the pavement, and then in again, and so 3 or 4 or 6 or 7 as many times as you please.*

The well here had been so popular at one time that the owner of the land got fed up with the crowds on his property, so fenced it off to keep the spa-fans out. But there were so many complaints that the proprietor had to give in and open it up again. By the time Celia Fiennes comes here, it sounds like St Mungo's covers an extensive area to accommodate so many devotees of its benefits.

I'm curious to see what it looks like today. This turns out not to be so easy – partly because 'St Mungo's' doesn't appear on Google maps or any others I consult. There is however a St Mongahs Lane in Copgrove village which I guess is a variation of the spelling. After making a few enquiries, I'm directed across a field (no signpost), and eventually stumble on a square of broken wooden fencing around a small, round gulley in the grass with a few bits of plastic piping scattered around. The sound of bubbling water down below is all that's left of St Mungo's today.

One question that might occur to us is how a devout Protestant aristocratic lady in the late seventeenth century coped with bathing? What did she wear? How did she preserve her modesty? Here's her answer.

> *You go in and out in linen garments. Some go in flannel.* [But] *I used my bath garments …*

Her bath garments would have been a full-length dress, covering the whole body like any other garments she wore, though of a simpler design.

> *… and I pulled them off and put on flannel when I came out to go to bed, which is best. Some will keep on their wet garments and let them dry on them and say it's more beneficial, but I did not venture it. I dipped my head quite over* [she means the water came over her] *every time I went in, and found it eased a great pain which I used to have in my head. And I was not so apt to catch cold so much as before, which I imputed to the exceeding coldness of the spring.*

> *Some of the Papists I saw there had so much zeal as to continue a quarter of an hour on their knees at their prayers in the well, but no one else could endure it so long at a time. I went in on seven different sessions and seven times every session, and would have gone in oftener, could we have staid longer.*

It's been suggested that this was the age of the hypochondriac, at least among the upper classes. For the first time in many decades, the uncertainties and threats posed by civil war, religious oppression and political upheaval had diminished, and those who didn't need to do paid work turned from fretting about their safety to fretting about their health. Such worries were understandable in an era when there was no effective medical treatment, no one understood what caused any ailment from the common cold to cancer, and at a time when you might get up feeling fine and be dead before bedtime. So, if the theory was that bathing forty-nine times in freezing Yorkshire water or downing some vile tasting drink might help, you'd go for it.

And the theory may well have been correct in one case – the 'quick purger' that Celia Fiennes was so keen on. This of course was long before anyone knew about the benefits of five helpings of fruit or vegetables a day. So what did people eat back then? As she continues her tour of Yorkshire, she's about to tell us.

3

Boroughbridge to Beverley

MEAT, FISH AND NO VEG

We had crabs bigger than my two hands,
a penny apiece.

I can't help wondering whether these purging laxatives that she'd been knocking back, not to mention all the freezing cold water she'd dunked herself in, had worked up Celia's appetite. With hardly a break for breath after the account of her dipping seven times in seven days at Harrogate spa, her diary continues:

> *Then we went to Boroughbridge, eight miles, a famous place for salmon, but then we could not find any. But we had a very large codfish there, above a yard long and more than half a yard around, very fresh and good, and cost but 8 pence.*

It's too good a deal to miss.

> *I saw as big a one, which I bought then for 6 pence, and six crabs as big as my two hands, the smallest was bigger than one of my fists. All cost but 3 pence.*

Celia Fiennes' love of fish puts her in tune with a relatively new fashion. In Tudor times, people had viewed salmon, cod, crabs and the rest as less nourishing. And there was a common prejudice among Protestants against fish because of its associations with the Catholic practice of not eating meat on Fridays. So it's a reflection of how much religious tolerance had moved on by the late seventeenth century that Celia Fiennes – a devout Protestant Dissenter – loves to eat fish and is no longer put off by any links with Catholicism.

Over the next few weeks, she rides back and forth around Ripon, Harrogate, Knaresborough and Boroughbridge before travelling across the West Riding of Yorkshire through York towards the coast ('Riding' by the way – as in 'West Riding', 'North Riding' and 'East Riding' - has nothing to do with mounting a horse, it's the old version of 'thirding', Yorkshire being divided into these three areas).

I've timed my own arrival in Ripon for a Thursday, market day. I park in a pleasant tree-bordered little car park at St Marygate (when was the last time you heard anyone describe a car park as 'pleasant tree-bordered'? It tells you a lot about Ripon), then weave my way through narrow lanes to the Market Place. Well ahead of reaching it, a cross on top of a tower flashes up over the rooftops. It turns out to be in the middle of the square, between lines of covered market stalls. Looking in on this scene are two and three-storey buildings, some mock-Tudor, some Georgian square-windowed, some – like the bank on the corner – twentieth century pretending to be neoclassical. Even the Greggs is trying to blend in, and the Sainsbury's seems to feel the need to compete – in its restraint – with the Unicorn Hotel and its rectangular façade.

When Celia Fiennes visited here, she too headed straight for the market, pausing only to remark that it's a 'pretty little town' and noting, as I had, the 'high cross on several steps'. The produce on sale however, was rather different from today.

We were there market day where provisions are very plentiful and cheap. In the market were sold then 2 good shoulders of veal. They were not very fat nor so large as our meat in London, but good meat, one for 5 pence the other for 6 pence, and a good quarter of lamb for 9 pence or 10 pence. And there were crayfish 2 pence a dozen – so we bought them.

Which raises the question how she got them cooked, given that she – and her servants – were on the road. She doesn't tell us. But we might guess that she would have handed them over to her landlady with a request to prepare them for her supper. And given her next remark, perhaps innkeepers weren't always too helpful.

> *Notwithstanding this plenty, some of the inns are very dear to strangers that they can impose on.*

There's a sound practical reason why she gives so much attention to the freshness and price of meat and fish in the markets of Yorkshire and other places far from London. To reach the capital, produce had to be transported often long distances in carts over those steep, flooded and rutted roads we've seen. That added to the market price and supplies to the capital could even be cut off entirely in the depths of winter. And it also meant that the quality of the food suffered by the time it reached Londoners' tables many days after it had been slaughtered or caught. Just after Celia Fiennes' time, a city-based doctor wrote a warning that the odour of meat was such that one should keep it away from the nose while eating it! What a joy it must have been for Fiennes, the Londoner, to feast on the freshest of local Yorkshire meat and fish.

As I stroll around among today's crowds in Ripon marketplace, I start to notice something that would have struck Celia Fiennes as odd, and I'm not talking about the obvious differences of dress style, mobile phones, or white vans parked – rear doors open – behind the stalls. It's what's on sale here. The favourite buys seem to be fruit and veg – sprouts, leeks, carrots, bananas, apples. And a close second are the fresh fish – salmon, cod, crabs and more. There are no butchers.

It's striking that throughout Celia Fiennes' food notes there's never a mention of vegetables. In fact, the word itself didn't appear in the English language in its modern sense of 'plants cultivated for food' until seventy years after she made this trip. But what about the individual greens themselves? The tally tells its own tale – and these are mentions across the *whole* of her diaries, not just Ripon or Yorkshire.

> Cabbage – nil.
> Cauliflower (or any alternative name) – nil
> Potato – nil. It had been introduced from North America a century earlier but hadn't yet caught on.
> Turnip (or its old forms *turnepe* or *neep*) – nil
> Parsnip (or *passenep* as it often was then, or again anything similar) – nil
> Artichoke – one reference, though to its shape not its taste. In the 'Physick' garden (i.e. where medicinal plants and herbs were grown) at Corpus Christi College, Oxford, she notes 'the aloe plant, which is like a great flag in shape, leaves and colour, and grows in the form of an open Hartichoake'.
> Peas and beans – one reference, though strangely she lumps them in with corn: 'In these northern counties, they have only the summer grain, as barley, oats, peas, beans, and lentils.'
> Carrots – yes! One mention, but hardly a recommendation. When she visits Castleton in Derbyshire, she sees, part-built into a cave 'several poor little houses, built of stone and thatched like little styes. One seemed a little bigger, in which a gentleman lived and his wife … Mr Middleton, who was with us, said he had dined with them there on carrots and herbs, and that the gentleman and his wife were dead a year or two since.'

And that's it for veg. A few carrots fit only for folk who lived in pig-styes then died – by Celia Fiennes' account anyway.

The explanation tells us a great deal about both seventeenth-century understanding of what food is good for you and about snobbery then. Vegetables were considered of little dietary value, so were usually absent from the daily menu of the upper classes. And ones like turnips, parsnips and carrots – with their muddy origins – were best left to those who couldn't afford meat every day.

A detail from William Hogarth's 'Industry and Idleness', 1747. Not a vegetable in sight. (The Metropolitan Museum of Art)

And what about fruit? She has mixed feelings about it, and that's probably typical of her era. Sometimes, as when she visits her aunt's house in Wolseley, she sees fruit more as a decorative item in a neat garden than as food.

> *There are very good gardens, abundance of fruit of all sorts and the finest dwarf trees I ever saw, so thick like a hedge and a huge width every single tree, and very full of fruit, of apples, pears and cherries. There are fine flowers.*

But then on another visit there, she says:

> *I ate a sort of flat strawberry, like a button.*

And again at the Duke of Bedford's house:

> *I ate a great quantity of the red coralina gooseberry, which is a large, thin-skinned, sweet gooseberry.*

By 'coralina', she meant 'coralline', a word which had entered the English language around 1630, meaning coral-coloured, i.e. a reddish-yellow. That would describe several old varieties of gooseberry that are sweet enough – like the ones she enjoyed – to be eaten straight from the bush, rather than needing to be cooked with loads of sugar.

This is quite adventurous of her, because there was a persistent belief that certain uncooked fruits could make you ill. And back in the late seventeenth century, the idea was not as silly as it sounds. People were particularly wary of the tomato, technically a fruit of course, though we often think of it as a vegetable for salads or sauces. By 1697, the tomato had been around for 150 years, but the disdain in which it was held is reflected in a – racially stereotyped – encyclopaedia entry of 1753, describing it as 'a fruit eaten either stewed or raw by the Spaniards and Italians and by the Jew families of England'. The reason why the English couldn't get to grips with the poor old tomato had more to do with their table manners than the fruit itself. Pewter plates had become the vogue for those who could afford them but pewter back then contained lead, which the acid from the tomato – unbeknown to the diner – caused to leech out with potentially poisonous results.

Other acidic fruits would have had the same effect – such as citruses. Oranges – despite the fame thirty years earlier of Nell Gwynne, orange-seller before she became actress and then mistress to the king – were still a rarity. Celia Fiennes mentions seeing them at a house near Southampton.

> *Here were fine flowers and greens, dwarf trees and orange and lemon trees in rows with fruit and flowers at the same time and some ripe. They are the first orange trees I ever saw.*

Cooked fruit, however, was generally enjoyed. And when she stays at St Austell in Cornwall, her mouth-watering delight at one dessert oozes from the page.

> *My landlady brought me one of the West Country tarts. This was the first I met with, though I had asked for them in many places in Somerset and Devonshire. It's an apple pie with a custard all on the top. It's the most acceptable entertainment that could be made for me. They scald their cream and milk in most parts of those counties, and so it's a sort of clotted cream, as we call it, with a little sugar put on the top.*

But – typical! – just when you're having a good time, this happens.

> *I was much pleased with my supper, though not with the custom of the county, which is universal smoking. Men, women and children all have their pipes of tobacco in their mouths, and so sit round the fire smoking, which was not delightful to me when I went down to talk with my landlady.*

Which brings us on to tobacco. It was now imported from the plantations of Virginia and other southern states of America. Many thousands of African slaves were forced to plant and harvest it. It had arrived in England by the late sixteenth century. To hear of children smoking shocks us of course. But in Celia Fiennes' day, opinion was divided. Some thought it was bad for you, others that it could even be a treatment for certain diseases. It had been suggested for instance that smoking tobacco could cure the pox. To which, in 1604, King James I answered that this applied only to Indian slaves, and 'here in England it is refined, and will not deign to cure here any other than cleanly and gentlemanly diseases'. Quite what a 'gentlemanly disease' might be, wouldn't we like to know? Celia Fiennes' objection seems to coincide with that of many non-smokers today. She found it unpleasant to have to breathe the stuff in from someone else puffing away, and she probably couldn't see any benefit from the habit.

Sugar, too, which her landlady had sprinkled on her pie, was the product of slave labour. It had been around in England for the past fifty years and was shipped in from the Caribbean. The plantation owners made such big profits from it that they called it 'white gold'.

Food fads had varied during the seventeenth century – at the royal court anyway. Fancy French recipes had become popular with aristocrats during the reigns of the Catholic monarchs, Charles I and II. These exotic dishes were called 'kickshaws', a poor attempt by the English gentry to pronounce *quelques chose*, the French for 'something'. The new idea was that uncooked fruit and vegetables wouldn't necessarily poison you. And the lordly classes had even begun to eat salads!

Celia Fiennes of course, as we read in her Introduction to the diaries, deplored foreign travel and urged her fellow English folk to glory in their English homeland. Food, then, which was both French and Catholic was hardly likely to find favour with her. And there were many others of the better-off classes under the Protestant rule of William and Mary who felt the same way when they organised their kitchens: plenty of meat, good fish if you could get it, cooked fruit with sugar for afters, and forget the greens.

As Celia travels on through Yorkshire, at the village of Brandesburton near Beverley she discovers delicious food can still be had in the midst of poverty. Incidentally, note the cryptic reference to 'us' without revealing who is travelling with her.

> *Here we could get no accommodation at a public house, it being a sad poor thatched place and only 2 or 3 sorry alehouses. No lodgings but at the Hall House, as it was called, where lived Quakers. The rooms were good, being the Lord of the Manor's house. These Quakers were but tenants who did entertain us kindly, made two good beds for us and also for our servants, and good bread and cheese, bacon and eggs.*

'Good bread' is something she's always on the look-out for. Top of her list is what she calls 'clap bread'. It's a kind of oatmeal cake and is so called because it's clapped or beaten until it's thin. She watches it being made, and her account is almost as good as a recipe. Here it is, divided it up into stages to make it easier to follow as you dodge between this book and the kitchen counter. Exact proportions of ingredients, timings and the type of flour you'll have to work out yourself.

> *They mix their flour with water, so soft as to roll it in their hands into a ball.*
>
> *Then they have a board, made round and something hollow in the middle, rising by degrees all round to the edge a little higher, but so little as one would take it just to be warped. This is to cast out the cake thin.*
>
> *And so they clap it round and drive it to the edge in a due proportion till driven as thin as a paper.*
>
> *Then they have a plate of iron, same size as their clap board, and so shove off the cake on it, and so set it on coals and bake it.*
>
> *When baked enough on one side, they slide it off and put the other side; their iron plate is smooth, and they take care their coals or embers are not too hot, but just enough to make it look yellow.*

The result?

> *It will bake and be as crisp and pleasant to eat as anything you can imagine.*

But, as with all good bread, you must 'eat it presently, for it's not so good if 2 or 3 days old'. Not all bread gets a five-star rating however.

> *They have much rye in Lancashire, Yorkshire and Stafford and Shropshire and so Hereford and Worcestershire, which I found very troublesome in my journeys, for they would not own they had any such thing in their bread. But it so disagrees with me as always to make me sick.*

I pull off the B6265 to follow her to one of my own favourites in York-shire, Newby Hall, a short way from Ripon. She's of the same opinion.

> *This was the finest house I saw in Yorkshire.*

Its core was the brainchild of the man who owned it when she visited the place that summer, Sir Edward Blackett. He was the local MP in the Parliament which had endorsed the 1689 Bloodless or Glorious Revolution and had invited the Protestants William and Mary to take the throne of England. Blackett employed Sir Christopher Wren to design Newby, which he did while over-seeing the construction of St Paul's Cathedral. Celia Fiennes notes:

> *His house is built of brick and quoined* [cornered] *with stone, a flat roof, leaded, with rails and balustrades and a large cupola in the middle. The front entrance is three gates of iron bars and spikes painted blue with gold tops. The brickwork between the gates and pillars with stone tops carved like flowerpots.*

For her, the place has other attractions apart from its fine – and at that time – very modern architecture.

> *There are good stables and coach house, and all the offices* [i.e. the nec-essary parts of any fine house, from stables to kitchens] *are very convenient – very good cellars, all arched, and there I drank small beer four years old not too stale, very clear good beer, well brewed.*

This, then, is how she washed down all that delicious salmon, cod and beef, how she and her contemporaries usually quenched their thirst. We've already seen in Nottingham that she was an aficionada of fine ale. Her mention of 'small beer' at Newby has nothing to do with the amount she drank, she means its strength. It contained just

1 or 2 per cent alcohol. And in an age when inadequate or non-existent sanitation often left water supplies disease-ridden, everyone – including children – quenched their thirst with weak ale. The fermentation process cleansed the liquid. Sailors were known to drink up to ten pints of it a day when working in hot weather, and large schools, such as Eton, brewed their own small beer for their pupils. There are references to small beer in Shakespeare. In *Henry IV Part 2*, Prince Hal makes fun of Falstaff who brags of quaffing pints of small beer and never getting drunk.

And what about wine? She makes very few references to drinking it. Once when she's in the town of Rye in Sussex, she makes a point of telling us:

> *Here I drank right* [not clear what she means by this, perhaps real or genuine] *French white wine, and it was exceeding good.*

By the seventeenth century, England, which had produced wine in an earlier age, was no longer a grape-growing country, not on a commercial scale anyway. This may have been in part because of changing weather patterns, and because most English wine had been produced in the monasteries, which Henry VIII had shut down. Wine in Celia Fiennes' day was usually imported – often from France. But that now posed a problem. In 1697, England was still at war with its neighbour. So the likelihood is that when she drank French wine at Rye on the south coast, it had been smuggled in.

She mentions wine too – in passing – while she's in Yorkshire. The reference tells us less about the drink and more about the woman herself, ever delighting in a freebie for her taste buds.

> *There is still this custom on a market day at Leeds. At the sign of the bush just by the bridge, anybody that will go and call for one tankard of ale and a pint of wine and pay for these only, shall be set to a table to eat with 2 or 3 dishes of good meat and a dish of sweetmeats after. Had I known this and the day which was their market, I would have come*

> *then. But I happened to come a day after. However, I did only pay for 3 tankards of ale, and I and my servants ate 'gratis'.*

And what about plain old water itself? Was it never drinkable – other than the sometimes-revolting liquid available at England's many spas? While still at Newby Hall, she remarks:

> *The house is served with water by pipes into a cistern and into the garden cellars and all offices* [again, the kitchens, laundry, etc].

Was it OK to drink? It's an open question. And when she moves on from Newby to Beverley, she reports:

> *The town is served with water by wells, walled around or rather in a square, above half one's length. And by a pulley and weight lets down or draws up the bucket which is chained to a beam. There are many of these wells in all the streets. It seems it's in imitation of Holland, they being supplied with water so.*

Again, not certain it's drinkable. Or was it just for washing clothes, and your face and body – should you wish to indulge in that luxury? For most English people, at the end of the seventeenth century, fresh – or fresh-ish – water would have been a rare luxury. Beer – small or strong – was the safer choice.

Celia Fiennes, it seems, usually stuck to that. Outside of the health-giving, though foul-smelling, sulphurous waters of a spa, there would have been little point in taking a risk with water that might be carrying dysentery or some other equally disastrous disease.

It's not that she was risk averse. She would never have undertaken her travels if she were. But there had to be a reward. She was ever prepared to take a chance, even put her life on the line, in the cause of investigation and discovery, as we're about to see when she arrives at the Yorkshire coast.

4

Hull and Scarborough

OUT ON THE WAVES

It seems to be a pretty turbulent sea.
I was on it in a little boat, but found it very rough.

Before she leaves Beverley, a grisly discovery awaits her, one that I can find no reference to in any other writers. She visits the town's massive parish church, known as the Minster, as grand as many a cathedral. Inside, she goes to see the monuments to the 4th Earl of Northumberland and his Lady.

His is very plain, only a marble stone raised up about 2 yards high.

Make your way today beneath the arches stretching high above the nave, beyond the altar and along the north aisle and you'll find the tomb. It's not quite as plain as she suggests. Its sides are decorated with carvings of intricate, miniature, pointed archways, topped with delicate stone leaves in the shapes of crosses. Buried beneath it is the body of Henry Percy, 4th Earl. He met a violent end in 1489. Yorkshire was in rebellion against the king, Henry VII. The earl, who was attempting to enforce the collection of an unpopular new tax, was killed during a skirmish with the rebels.

When Celia Fiennes came here 200 years later, the top of his monument was damaged.

His tomb was a little fallen in with a hole so big that many put their hands in and touched the body which was much of it entire. Of the

> *bones, the skull was whole and the teeth firm, though of so many years' standing.*

She doesn't tell us how this had happened, nor if she disapproves of people messing with an ancient corpse. She gives no hint whether those who touched the body did so in some sort of religious ritual, or whether she blames the church authorities for not keeping the tomb in good repair. One explanation for her own lack of squeamishness could be that a dead body – and one that you could touch – wasn't as uncommon in the late seventeenth century as it is now.

She also notes inside the church:

> *Just by the communion table is the sanctuary or place of refuge where criminals flee for safety.*

We're most of us familiar with the tradition according to which villains on the run could evade justice by rushing into a church and prostrating themselves on the altar. But is it true? The answer is: up to a point. Certainly, her use of the present tense, 'where criminals flee [not 'fled' or 'used to flee'] for safety' was inaccurate by 1697.

It is correct that in medieval times, law-breakers – even murderers – could seek protective sanctuary in a church. It was a tradition that went back to ancient Greece and Rome, and the practice was known in Anglo-Saxon England, from the seventh to the eleventh centuries. Religious sanctuary wasn't confined to these shores either, it was common throughout Christian Europe. How it began no one is entirely sure. On the face of it, the practice seems bizarre, that the institution which represents peace and order would shield the most violent in society. But for much of its history, seeking sanctuary in a church wasn't as simple as that. There were rules, notably that sanctuary-seekers must confess their crimes, and swear to leave the country within forty days, never to return. In an age when law courts and legal processes could not be relied on to bring criminals to justice, a way of getting them to plead guilty and of ridding the country of them forever, was to be applauded. It may not have been foolproof, but sanctuary was seen as a useful weapon in the fight against crime.

However, as the official legal system began to improve in later centuries, the idea that the Church would give sanctuary to criminals was seen more and more as a hindrance, rather than an aid, to justice. It was open to abuse. Criminals could for example break their word, not bother to go into exile, and instead return to a life of violence and misdeeds. And so, in the sixteenth century, Henry VIII drastically restricted when it could be used, and in 1623, the practice was officially abolished. Celia Fiennes, then, is not correct to imply that sanctuary was still open to anyone on the run from the law in 1697. It may be that she was influenced by her Puritan upbringing. Those like her, opposed to the Catholic Church, often saw sanctuary as typical of the defects of the old religion.

Outside the Minster, she spots the results of a seventeenth-century attack on the church façade, damage which is still a common sight for us today right across the country.

> *Carved on the outside with figures and images, and more than 100 pedestals that remain where statues once stood of angels and the like.*

The fate of the stone figures that had once sat on the now-empty pedestals can usually be traced back to the Civil War years when many had been torn down by Parliamentarian soldiers. Religious rivalry was then in such a frenzy that images on church façades were regarded by Puritans as the essence of the Catholic, Royalist enemy, and their destruction had even been made mandatory by law in 1643.

Next stop, Hull. To get there, I avoid the A1079, the modern road leading from the Beverley bypass, and instead drive down Long Lane, more likely to have been the route she took. For much of its length, it's little wider than a small family car, and there are ditches on either side draining the water off the flat fields all around. At one point, near a bend in the road, I stop to look at the lines of straight, narrow water-filled channels between marshy stretches of land on either side. Though not as obvious to today's speeding car driver as it would have been to a slow-paced seventeenth-century horse rider, the landscape now is still reminiscent of three centuries ago. Fiennes writes:

> *From thence we went to Hull, 6 mile all upon a causeway, secured with two little rivers running on each side, which are used to flow over their grounds, it being a great flat for several miles, and the meadows are clothed with good grass.*

Today on the drier fields, it's mainly the yellow flowers of oilseed rape that clothe the fields.

Soon, we're driving along a tree-lined boulevard. A sign tells us that the three-storey buildings visible through the leafy branches to the right are part of the University of Hull. Then minutes later, there's a housing estate and corner shops before we pass beneath a graffiti-daubed railway bridge. The suburbs are left behind. A Travelodge towers over the junction. Then it's left into Carr Lane, and we're in an open square with Queen Victoria – mini-crown balanced on head – not deigning to look down on us from her plinth in the middle.

All cities of course look very different from how they did 320 years ago. Often, though, we can find a district where old buildings crowd in on a narrow alleyway, perhaps overlooked by a castle or church that the Victorians didn't mess up, all giving us some impression of what the visitor would have seen three centuries ago. Hull is not like that. There are a couple of churches, but otherwise nothing to give a hint of what Celia Fiennes saw here in 1697. Back then, Hull looked more like a military base than a hospitable town. It was a citadel surrounded by defensive walls. Nothing survives of those fortifications today. On page 70 is a plan from around 1640 – it had changed little sixty years later.

She writes:

> *We enter the town of Hull from the southward over two drawbridges and gates.*

The map shows us that – strictly speaking – there is no gate as such to the south. That's where the Humber Estuary is on the right-hand side – north is towards the left. She must mean the entry point (on the corner of the wall at the bottom of the image) named as Beverley Gate, which lies to the south of what was commonly called North Gate (the left-hand corner). And it would be logical that, travelling from the town of Beverley, she would arrive here. She describes the configuration of the defences.

> *Ditches are around the town to the landward, and they can flood the ground for 3 miles, which is a good fortification. The garrison and platform* [the barracks and the walkway along the wall] *which is the fortification to the sea is in a very uniform figure – it's walled with a palisade. I walked around it and viewed it. And when I was on the water, it seems to run a great length, and would require many soldiers to defend the 'half-moons' and 'works'.*

'Half-moon' – also known as a semi-circular bastion – was a technical term for a curved outward bulge in the defensive wall, which enabled gunners stationed on it to shoot down at enemy soldiers along the base of the wall. By 'works' she means all the walls, towers and other structures that made up the fortifications. Her reference to being 'on the water' we'll return to shortly.

The city's defences date back to the fourteenth century and had been strengthened in the build-up to the Civil War, sixty years before she arrives here. It was during this period that those 'half-moons' and 'works' came into their own. The city was besieged twice.

At first it was a Royalist stronghold, and in 1639 before the fighting began, King Charles I was welcomed here when he came to

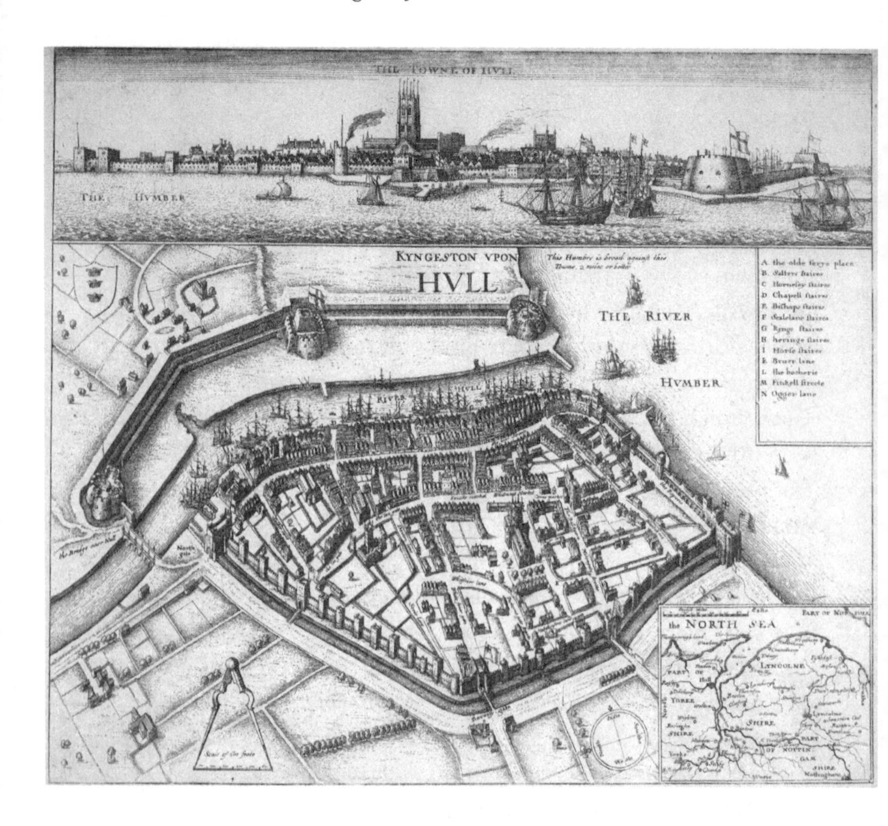

Map of Hull by Wenceslas Hollar, *c.* 1670. 'Ditches are around the town to the landward, and they can flood the ground for 3 miles, which is a good fortification.' (Wikimedia Commons)

inspect the defences and the artillery. Then three years later, as both sides prepared for war, he returned to make sure Hull was still on side. However, the town's governor, Sir John Hotham refused to let him in. The royal army surrounded its walls and the king demanded Hotham surrender. He was about to do so when, just in time, the Parliamentarians brought in reinforcements by water from the Humber Estuary. The king's forces were now on the back foot; they botched an attempt to blow up the town's gates, and then were defeated during a brief battle outside the walls.

The Royalists retreated, organised reinforcements, and in 1643 returned to besiege the city for a second time. At first, it looked like they'd bring it off – they stormed and captured two key points in the defences. But three weeks later, the Parliamentarians hit back, routed the Royalists during a seven-hour battle outside the walls, and that was it. Hull was now a Parliamentary bulwark, and it stayed so for the rest of the war.

With the end of the fighting, Hull's days as a military base were over. Its future lay in a different direction. A direction that Fiennes recognises when she arrives here fifty years later. She notes that the city:

> *... is a good trading town by means of this great river Humber that ebbs and flows like the sea, and is 3 or 4 mile across at least. It runs 20 mile hence into the sea and takes in all the great rivers – the Trent, Ouse, Aire, Don, the Derwent and the Hull.*

The city of Hull itself had gone through great changes over the previous few decades. Its economy and its people, which had suffered during the Civil War, were now thriving. As she states, it was by now 'a good trading town'. In fact, it had become England's main commercial link with Norway and – via the Baltic Sea – Sweden. On Hull's quaysides, cloth, especially baize produced in Yorkshire, was the main cargo loaded onto outgoing ships. Those arriving from Scandinavia brought in timber, iron and grain for the markets of northern England. As a trading port, Hull was second only to London. And when the Industrial Revolution took hold in the decades ahead, Liverpool was the only town to grow faster than Hull.

Those mighty, fortified city walls that Celia Fiennes describes were no longer needed. In fact, more and more, they were in the way. And eighty years after her visit to the city, their death knell was sounded. In 1774, Parliament at Westminster passed the Hull Dock Act to establish a commercial company with the right to demolish the fortified walls and clear the way for trading ships to berth. By

1829, three great docks had been built, and all sign of Hull's fighting history had been wiped out.

But, not quite.

Go to the point where she entered the old city walls – Beverley Gate – and you can discover what I mean. There's a pleasant open square amid neat (she would have liked that) rows of pruned hedges and trees that look almost artificial in their uniformity. In the middle, stone stairs lead down to what are the foundations of an old wall, polished and presented for anyone curious about the history of Hull. They're the only remains of those fortifications – with all their barracks, platforms, towers and half-moons – that for 400 years surrounded the town for a length of a mile and a half or more. A round plaque here now states:

SITE OF THE
PRINCIPAL ENTRANCE
OF THE ANCIENT WALLED
AND FORTIFIED TOWN
c. 1371 – *c.*1780
BEVERLEY GATE
HERE SIR JOHN HOTHAM
THE GOVERNOR DENIED
ENTRY IN 1642 TO KING
CHARLES I – THE FIRST
OVERT ACT OF THE
CIVIL WAR.

Trade hadn't entirely taken over Hull when Celia Fiennes visited the place in 1697. Its military connections lived on, in one limited sense. Naval vessels were built here. She observes that the Humber Estuary, into which the River Hull flows, 'carries so much water that a man-of-war of all sorts can ride it', and she manages to hitch a ride on one of these naval vessels.

> *I was on board a new man-of-war that belonged to the town and was called the 'Kingston'* [by 'belonged to' she must mean 'named after' the town whose full name is Kingston-upon-Hull]. *It was but small, well compact for provisions, and was built fit for swift sailing.*

The *Kingston* had just been launched from Hull's shipyards in March that year. It was designed – as she notes – to make speedy attacks during a sea battle, was armed with sixty canons, and was classed as 'fourth rate', a term which referred to its size – nothing to do with its quality as a fighting ship. The *Kingston* was 145ft long. It was to have a distinguished career. During the early decades of the next century, it saw action in four battles during the War of Spanish Succession, a conflict which drew in almost every nation in Europe to battle on one side or another. The *Kingston* was rebuilt twice, and sixty years after Celia Fiennes rode her decks was still going strong during encounters with the French. Then, in 1762, it was sold to a band of privateers – mercenaries – who sold their services to the Portuguese. A year later, during a sea battle off Chile, the ship was set on fire, and when the flames reached the ammunition store, it exploded. Two hundred and seventy-two men were killed, and the ship sank.

How, then, did Celia Fiennes talk her way on board a battleship of the Royal Navy for a day trip? It seems strange to us today when, apart from the occasional Open Day, worries about health and safety and the security of military intelligence mean naval decks are normally out of bounds to us civilians. But it wasn't like that during the seventeenth, eighteenth and early nineteenth centuries. This was a time when women – of all classes – were to be seen on all decks of a fighting ship when it was in port. Many of the lower ranks of sailors didn't want to be on board at all – they'd been press-ganged – and so were not allowed ashore for fear they'd never be seen again. So, to keep them entertained, local prostitutes were brought in, known – with thinly veiled decency – as 'wives'. For the officers it was a different story, though keeping them happy may still have been part of it. Allowing them to invite their (real) wives, girlfriends or sisters onto the upper decks gave them a chance to show off their manly, heroic way of life, and might have eased a lengthy separation from the family.

So how did that work in Celia Fiennes' case? She was unmarried, didn't have a beau as far as we know, and her family's connections – through her father and grandfather – had been with the army, not the navy. We can only assume that she'd met some well-placed relative or acquaintance in Hull who had a naval officer in the family. As ever, keen to try a new experience, she must have asked them to wangle an invitation onto the *Kingston* for her.

Once on board, she has a rough ride.

> *The Humber is very salty, always it rolls and tosses just like the sea, only the soil being clay turns the water and waves yellow and so it differs from the sea in colour, not else. It's a hazardous water by reason of many shores the tides meet. I was on it a pretty long way and it seems more turbulent than the Thames at Gravesend.*

There is at least one sight that remains just as it was for Celia Fiennes in 1697, and that's hidden away inside one of Hull's best-known old buildings. A couple of hundred yards east of the Princes Quay Shopping Centre (a historic name for a very twenty-first-century 'experience') stands Trinity House. The structure we see today isn't the one that she visited. The colonnaded entrance topped with a gilded coat of arms was built in 1753. The Trinity House she writes about was its predecessor dating back to the fourteenth century. The institution itself, however, has served a similar function throughout its history. Today, it's described as a charity that supports 'needy seafarers and their families'. In 1697, it's 'a home for seamen's widows, thirty of them, their allowance

16 pence per week and their fuel'. What she finds inside the old Trinity House is still here. It's a bizarre relic of a sad story. Here's her description.

> *In the middle of this room there hangs a canoe from the roof, just big enough for one man to sit in. And inside is the effigy of a man that was taken with it, all his clothes, cap and a large bag behind him wherein his fish and provisions were. These were all made of the skin of fishes and were the same which he wore when taken. The form of his face was added to resemble 'The Wild Man', as the inscription calls him, or 'The Bonny Boatman'. He was taken by a Captain Barker, and there are the man's oars and spear with him – this is all written on the boat to perpetuate the memory of it. He would not speak any language or word to them that took him, nor would he eat, so in a few days he died.*

Captain Andrew Barker, who lived in Hull, had brought the kayak and the man's clothes and possessions back with him after a trip to Greenland in 1613. It seems the people of Hull back in the seventeenth century saw the poor Inuit as more than just a wild, primitive animal. They had a soft spot for him. He was to be admired too, as 'a bonny boatman'.

Before we leave the north Yorkshire seashore, we get a hint of what lies ahead next on her great journey. She travels north by the coast road to Scarborough.

> *A very pretty seaport town built on the side of a high hill. The church stands in the most eminent place above all the town. The ruins of a large castle remain.*

Again she takes to the waves.

> *It seems to be a pretty turbulent sea. I was on it in a little boat but found it very rough even in the harbour. I suppose the cause may be from standing so open to the main.*

And in case you might think she's overplaying the danger – although she never mentions it – there's 99 per cent certainty that she could not swim. Almost no one could at this time, even most sailors. She observes:

> *... all the ships that pass go to Newcastle or that way. I see 70 sailing ships pass the point and so come onward at some distance off from the castle. I assumed them to be colliers and their convoys.*

These 'colliers' were carrying coal from Newcastle along the coast south to London. They faced dangers on their trips south. The Nine Years' War was not yet finished, and coal boats were known to be the targets of French attack. From this word 'convoys', it seems they travelled together in large numbers to make it more difficult for individual vessels to be picked off.

By 1695, these Newcastle colliers were so important to England's economy that their tonnage made up one-third of all the country's shipping. Coalmining is the subject of our next investigation, as we follow our diarist back across Yorkshire and into Derbyshire.

5

Through Yorkshire to Derbyshire

COALMINES AND THE DEVIL'S A*SE

They are forced to use gunpowder to break the stones, and it is sometimes hazardous to the people and destroys them.

The age 'when coal was king' would soon be upon these islands. Between the reign of Queen Elizabeth I and Celia Fiennes' time, coal production had increased fourteenfold. Much of it was destined for London where the amount unloaded at the docks from the 'colliers' that Fiennes witnessed in Hull had risen from a mere 11,000 tons each year to half a million. Though not quite yet deserving of the title of 'king' in the nation's economy, coal nevertheless was already showing it had power over monarchs. By 1689, the air in London had become so choked up with smoke from coal fires that King William and Queen Mary were forced to move out (William was asthmatic) and take up residence in what was then rural Kensington.

Judge how many coal-pits there must have been in north-eastern England from what Celia Fiennes tells us as she now heads south through Yorkshire.

All the country is full of coal, and the pits are so thick in the road that it is hazardous to travel for strangers.

It seems that the coal-pits and the rubble, earth and slag dug from them had spilled onto the road. When she reaches Sheffield, the result is pollution.

> *Water came down a great bank at the end of the town like a precipice with such violence that it makes a great noise, and looks extremely clear in the stream that gushes out and runs along. But it runs off a deep yellow colour, they say of a poisonous mine or soil from coal pits. I sent for a cup of it and the people in the street called out to forbid the tasting of it. And it will bear no soap so it's useless.*

What then did these coal-pits look like? Put simply, they were holes dug just deep enough to bring out coal which was close to the surface. The huge deep mines, which we think of today when we hear the word 'coalmine', began to appear only with the Industrial Revolution decades later. In Celia Fiennes' time, these shallow pits were the only means of mining. The area she talks about between Sheffield and Chesterfield in Derbyshire – as well as the district around Newcastle and Durham which she'll be visiting the following year – were ones where coal seams came close enough to the surface to be accessible from such pits.

There were hundreds of them, and their remains can still be seen near Chesterfield today, especially around the villages of Brimington, Inkersall and Duckmanton.

To investigate, I head east on the Chesterfield Road, then right into Inkersall and cut through an estate of newish brick houses to where a footpath leads into the woods. Plenty of room to park, and minutes later along the track I start to see them. You have to look carefully. They're small craters in the ground around 5 metres across and just a few feet deep. Around and outside the rim, the ground on some of them is slightly raised. These remains bear little relation to what they would have looked like when they were in operation. The miners filled them in when they couldn't be worked anymore.

The technical name for them was 'bell pits', because of their shape underground. They weren't simply cylindrical holes. When the miners reached the coal seam perhaps 10ft or 20ft down, they then dug passageways out sideways along the seam in order to get the most coal they could from every pit. The result was a shaft which was narrower at the top close to the surface and wider at the bottom – similar to the shape of a bell. The miners couldn't dig sideways very far because of the danger of the roof collapsing, so then they'd abandon that pit, and start a new one nearby – using the soil and rubble to fill in the old one. Fiennes describes the mining process.

Here we entered Derbyshire and went to Chesterfield 6 miles, and came by the coal mines where they were digging. They make their mines at the entrance like a well till they come to the coal. Then they dig all the ground about where there is coal and set pillars to support it, and so bring it to the well where, by a basket like a hand-barrow, they pull it up by cords. In the same way they let down and up the miners with a cord. Chesterfield looks low when you approach it. The coal pits and quarries of stone are all about, even just at the end of the town.

Humans have been digging out minerals like this since prehistoric times. In Norfolk, for example, at 'Grimes Graves' there are the remains of over 400 bell pits which date back 4,500 years. These ancient Norfolk pits were not for mining coal, but flint, which was needed for tools and arrowheads. One of these pits has been restored to its original state – and, of course, made safe – so that visitors can go down and see for themselves. The only difference in mining technique between those ancient pits and the ones Celia Fiennes saw is that hers used pulleys to bring up the coal. The Grimes Graves pits, however, date back to before the invention of the wheel, so miners there had to heave their flint up a ladder in baskets carried on their shoulders.

The remains of the old bell pits – filled in – can still be seen. (Public Domain, Bill Rowley)

Bell-pit mining in Derbyshire was also used for minerals other than coal, as she observes:

> *Thence to Buxton, 9 miles over those craggy hills, whose bowels are full of mines of all kinds, of black and white and veined marble. And some have mines of copper, others are tin and lead mines, in which is a great deal of silver. I have some which looks full of silver. It's so bright, just brought up out of one of the mines.*

And she tells us about the plight of those whose job is to dig out these minerals.

> *Those that work underground generally look very pale and yellow, they are forced to keep lights with them.*

It's not hard to understand how unhealthy the work must have been. Her observation that the miners are 'pale' and even 'yellow' looking would indicate that they weren't exposed to much, if any, sunlight, so presumably were working underground twelve hours or more a day.

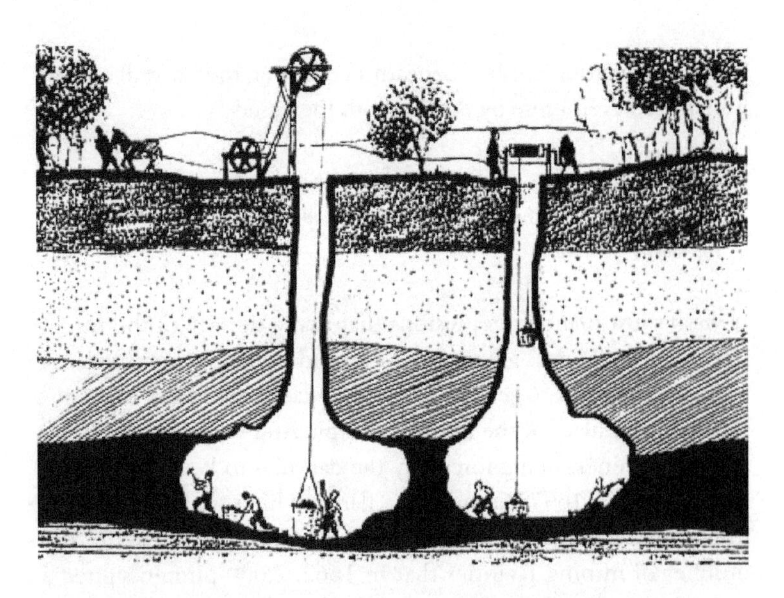

Bell pits. 'They make their mines at the entrance like a well till they come to the coal. Then they dig all the ground about.' (Public Domain)

And she gives us more details about the mining methods. Precautions against the pits falling in on the workers sound to be rudimentary.

> *They dig down their mines like a well for one man to be let down with a rope and pulley. When they find ore, they keep digging underground. In the mine that I saw, there were 3 or 4 miners at work. They dig sometimes a great way before they come to ore. They wall round the wells to secure them from mouldering* [collapsing] *in upon them.*

And a little further on at Ashbourne, she adds:

> *I saw some of their copper mines where they dig them like a well, securing the side with wood and turf bound like laths or frames across and lengthways to secure it.*

The risk of getting crushed beneath a collapsing roof or wall of rock is increased even more by the methods they used

> *And sometimes they are forced to use gunpowder to break the stones, and it is sometimes hazardous to the people and destroys them at the work,*

It wasn't just planned explosions that made the life of the miner so dangerous. There's always been a hazard in mines from firedamp – the name given to several flammable gases, especially methane, which accumulate in the bottom of a pit. And when Fiennes talks about the miners being forced by the darkness to keep 'lights with them', back in 1697 that meant a flame, which without warning might ignite any pocket of gas. Such was the concern about the number of mining fatalities that in 1662, 2,000 pitmen signed a petition to Parliament calling for measures to protect them from the dreadful consequences of accidental explosions. As far as we know, it had no effect on safety procedures. I say, 'as far as we know', because until 1852 no one kept an official tally of how many were killed in mining accidents. Occasionally parish records reveal the terrors that miners faced every day in the period when Celia Fiennes witnessed coal mining. For example, the local register for the village of Fatfield near Sunderland shows that in a single year, 1708, sixty-nine miners met their deaths hewing coal down bell pits in that one parish.

Part of the problem was that bell pits were temporary. There was a severe limit on how deep they could go and how wide they could be dug at the bottom before they started to become unsafe, which – never mind the danger to the life of the miners – meant it was impractical to keep on working them. The life of the average pit was not much more than a year. Because they were so short-lived, it wasn't thought worth the time or labour – both of which meant cost – needed to shore them up safely.

And there was another problem: water. In most places, when you dig a hole anything more than a score or so feet deep, the bottom starts to get wet. Go deeper and you find yourself in a puddle. Try to go further down still and your hole becomes so flooded that you have to stop. To construct a deep mine therefore, you need some way of pumping up to the surface what can be a flood. However, as we'll discover when Celia Fiennes reaches Cornwall, a solution to the problem would soon be found during the early years of the following century, when the first coal-powered steam engine would be used to pump out the water.

As well as flooding, there were many other challenges to be tackled – ones that plagued the new deep mines as much as the old bell pits. How to fortify walls and roofs so they wouldn't collapse and how to guard against exploding gases. But the way forward was now clear. More and more millions of tons of coal would be needed every year. Over the next century, the shift from the bell pits Celia Fiennes saw to deep mines would see coal output multiply a further five times over.

The Industrial Revolution brought fundamental change to every aspect of life for the people of England, with more and more engines powering everything from cotton mills to locomotive trains. When we consider that, we can often forget that coal – the driving force of that revolution – was itself nothing new. Celia Fiennes reminds us of this and of the challenges that lay ahead for the engineers of that Revolution.

While she's in the Derbyshire Peak District, she does some underground exploration herself. She goes caving.

First, it's to 'Pool's Hole', what today is known as Pool's Cavern on the outskirts of Buxton. It got its name, she tells us, from a man:

> *who was a robber and used to secure himself in that place. It's a large cavity underground of a great length.*

So what would the experience have been like for her back then? To find out, I leave the car in the nearby Buxton Country Park and pay my £11, which entitles me to a 20-minute tour. There are six of us in our group, and the guide, a middle-aged chap in woolly hat and gloves (I wish I'd worn the same because it's unexpectedly cold once you get more than a few yards inside), tells us the cave was formed out of the limestone 2 million years ago.

'I hope you feel you're getting your money's worth for the entry fee,' he tells us, 'Just thank your lucky stars you weren't on a tour here in the nineteenth century. The guides back then used to try to extort money out of visitors by threatening to put out the lights and run off, leaving you in the dark unless you forked out more money!' How we laugh. Nervously. 'Don't worry,' he adds, 'I'm nowhere near the light switch inside here.' We laugh again.

The lighting today has been cleverly concealed, so it casts artistic shapes of shadows across the jagged lines of the walls and roof. It gives a mysterious, slightly spooky, feel to the rock formations and side-caves as the path twists and turns the further we go inside.

Celia Fiennes' visit was rather different. For a start there was no Health and Safety requirement for the level concrete path that's beneath my feet for the length of the cave, she had none of the fences that stop me falling into the pits and holes at the side, and the only illumination would have been either an occasional candle or perhaps an oil lamp.

Just at the entrance you must creep, but presently you stand upright, its roof being very lofty, all arched in the rocks, and sounds with a great echo. The rocks are continually dropping water all about. You walk over loose stones and craggy rocks.

Remember she's wearing a flared skirt down to the ground, and her shoes are almost certainly the ones she rides in, probably not ideal.

I clambered over the top of all the stones and as I came back I passed under several of the arches like bridges; they are both ways full of loose stones and the water dropping makes them slippery, it being also very uneven by reason of the crags.

Back at the surface, she goes to see a very different cavern 2 miles away on a hillside, Eldon Hole, a wide pit that slants downwards deep into the rocks. It's not one you can explore. It's got its own dangers.

It must be of a great depth by reason of the time you can hear a stone strike the sides and ring in its descending. It's a very hazardous place, for if a man or beast be too near the edge and trip, they fall in without retrieve. It's reported that several attempts have been made to fence the whole around with a stone wall, but yet it has been all in vain. What they built up in the day would be pulled down in the night. The country here about is so full of moors or quagmires and such precipices that a stranger cannot travel without a guide, and some of them are at a loss sometimes.

When she says the walls are 'pulled down in the night', we can assume she means that the muddy, soft land and precipices that she then goes on to mention, make it impossible to construct secure foundations for any protective structures.

Four miles further on is the town of Castleton.

It's a town lies at the foot of an exceeding steep hill which could not be descended by foot or horse, but only by the roads returning to and fro on the side of the hill at least 4 times before we could gain the bottom or top of the hill.

The locals have a special name for it.

This is what they call the Devil's Arse. The hill on one end jutting out in two parts and joined at the top. In the cleft in between, you enter a great cave.

Now, here's a surprising use of language by a Puritan gentlewoman. When Daniel Defoe came this way twenty-five years later, he too reported on the name, but with rather more restraint than she did. He wrote of 'the so famed wonder called, saving our good manners, The Devil's A**e'. Why did she – unlike her male successor – spell it out in full, and without even saying anything about the coarseness of the word? Could it be that even Celia Fiennes, hardened traveller, had led a life so sheltered from gentlemanly banter that she didn't recognise its impoliteness? Hardly. Surely the sniggers of her servants or others she was with would at least have made her enquire further about the word. Perhaps this is a vivid example of an ever-attractive trait in her character – it says, 'Celia Fiennes tells it like it is.'

Her detailed observation of coalmining, her eagerness to go underground herself, and her use of blunt language all raise the question – how exceptional was her behaviour in the late seventeenth century? What was expected of upper-class women at this time?

In the latter part of the seventeenth century, instructions to 'gentlewomen' on how to behave in polite society began to appear, usually in the form of books of etiquette. One of the most popular of these volumes came out in its fifth edition in 1696. It was written by a man, incidentally, John Shirley, and was called *The accomplished ladies' rich closet of rarities*. If that's confusing, the subtitle explains all (and I pretty much mean 'all' – as subtitles go, it could be in the *Guinness Book of Records*).

The accomplished ladies' rich closet of rarities, or,
The ingenious gentlewoman and servant maids
delightful companion:
containing many excellent things for the accomplishment of the
female sex,

after the exactest manner and method,
to which is added a second part,
containing directions for the guidance of a young gentlewoman
as to her behaviour and seemly deportment, &c,
together with a new accession of many curious things and matters,
profitable to the female sex, not published in the former editions.

It deals with everything from how to make quince cakes ('clarify your sugar with the whites of eggs'), how to behave at the table ('gnaw no bones, but cut your meat decently with the help of your fork'), and how to handle servants ('be courteous and affable but not over-familiar'), and even how to run your love-life ('keep, as it were, a guard upon your hearts, to prevent the entrance either of a lawless or disadvantageous passion').

It also gives general instructions on how the gentlewoman should interact with her equals: 'You must be very modest and moderate, your words few yet to the purpose.' And taking care of your feminine beauty is apparently more important than observing the world around you: 'Keep your eyes within compass; that is let them not be too much fixed upon idle and vain objects, nor drawn away by unseemly sights. Open not your eyes too wide, thereby to distort your countenance; look not too much downward; nor with a more than ordinary elevation.'

It would be hard to define rules of behaviour more at odds with the way Celia Fiennes led her life, constantly curious, risky and defiant. How many of Celia Fiennes' upper-class female contemporaries followed such rules of etiquette is impossible to say. Nevertheless, the popularity of the book does seem to indicate that at the very least they represented the ideal of gentlewomanly behaviour in 1697.

And we today are the beneficiaries of her refusal to toe the social line. How much poorer we would now be if she'd bothered with the instructions in *The accomplished ladies' rich closet of rarities*. The last thing she was going to do was keep her eyes in line and not look at anything but what appeared in front of her. If she'd done so, for instance, on the stage of her journey across Yorkshire into Derbyshire, her diary would have been dull, uneventful, and told us nothing about coalmining and the other pre-Industrial Revolution ways of working in this part of England. Not only is Celia Fiennes a pioneering woman, she's an invaluable observer of life at the end of the seventeenth century, unmatched by her contemporaries, be they women or men.

On the next stage of her journey, we're going to examine something which would have been much closer to the hearts of her fellow aristocrats. That's the great dwelling places of the mightiest in the land. But as ever, Celia Fiennes' observations on the subject are much more than guidebook extracts. They're detailed and meticulous and will tell us a great deal about the newfangled architecture of the late seventeenth century and how it reflected a fresh way of thinking about the world around us.

6

Chatsworth

CLASSICAL, THE NEW NEAT

While you are thus amused,
suddenly there runs down a torrent of water
out of 2 pitchers in the hands of two large nymphs.

During her two great journeys over the summers of 1697 and 1698, Celia Fiennes tells us about visiting some 350 different places. It's difficult to be precise. Even if you count every inn, marketplace, dockside, glass-blowing workshop, coalmine, college or whatever that she mentions, it's still not always clear whether she's returning to somewhere she's been before or how many coalmines or markets she inspected. Three-hundred-and-fifty, then, may not be exact, but it does give an idea of the energy she put into her travels.

There's one kind of place that she rarely rides past without knocking on the door to find out more. And that's grand houses, 'stately homes' if you like. I've counted fifty-nine of them in her diaries. She doesn't always mention making contact with the duke and duchess, earl and his lady, knight of the shire or whoever it is owns the place, though sometimes she does remark, 'Thence to my relations' house'. The layout of gardens and parks, the diversity of architecture and the ornate decoration of lofty halls and even private apartments all fascinate her.

As it happens, one of the very few ways that Celia Fiennes has been remembered these days, other than in the occasional academic treatise, is in guidebooks to some of the stately homes. Those of us who love what the National Trust today calls 'exploring historic houses' may sometimes stumble on a couple of sentences attributed to Celia Fiennes to illustrate how a house or its gardens have changed since the end of the seventeenth century, or to show what she thought of some curiosity that can still be enjoyed by today's visitors.

On our journey round the country, I've chosen not to stop at all the great houses she mentions. To do so would fill a book in itself. But we can get a flavour of what it is she enjoys about such places at one house she visited before she leaves Derbyshire's Peak District, and at the same time we'll learn about her contemporaries' extraordinary loathing for something we today admire for its beauty.

Chatsworth House is one of the nation's favourite stately homes. In the 1950s, when I was taken there for the first time as a child – we lived only 30 miles away – it attracted 10,500 visitors a year. By 2018, that figure had risen to over 600,000, second only to Blenheim Palace.

As ever, the car park today is packed. I want to get a panoramic view of the vast west front of the house, so walk against the flow of the crowds – who're heading towards the side entrance – and make for a little bridge that spans the river here. Then the path to the left along the waterside by open parkland takes me to a point opposite the house – it's a couple of hundred yards away. This is how she first saw it too.

The Duke's house stands on a little rising ground above the River Derwent which runs all along the front of the house, and by a little waterfall which makes a pretty murmuring noise.

There's no waterfall here anymore, but the river level's quite high today, and away from the crowds now, I fancy I can hear a bit of 'pretty murmuring'. The 'Duke' she speaks of was William Cavendish, 1st Duke of Devonshire, and it was he who built the

Chatsworth we love. The house he inherited in 1684 looked nothing like the structure we see across the river today. The original building had been the brainchild of his great-great-grandmother, Elizabeth Cavendish, better known as Bess of Hardwick. She was one of the most remarkable figures in Tudor England and oversaw the construction of four great houses. Chatsworth, begun in 1552, was one of them. From the drawings of it that have survived, we can see it was very much of its age. It was admired for its castellated roofline and protruding towers, giving it the feel of an old fortress converted into a family home. A hundred and thirty years later however, the duke decided that was old hat. He wanted something in the latest architectural fashion, and so he commissioned one of the leading architects of the day – William Talman, considered a rival of Sir Christopher Wren – to come up with a new design. Then he set about demolishing much of Bess's work and began constructing the edifice before me now.

By the time Celia Fiennes arrived in 1697, it was eleven years since the work had begun, and it would be another ten before it would be anything like complete. She tells us:

> *The front entrance is not finished. It is formed with several large stone pillars carved. From the entrance into another court, which the house is built around, are piazzas supported with more stone pillars, under which you pass from one place* [courtyard] *to another.*

She was witnessing the birth of neoclassicism. Chatsworth captures the very essence of that movement and was one of the first great houses in Europe to do so. Its towering pillars, topped by a huge triangular pediment, every stone on its façade, every window, every doorway, from the steps at the bottom to the balustrades at the top are all symmetrical, straight-lined and rectangular in their grandeur. If, on the morning of our own visit, we could magic the appearance of the Parthenon, from its home overlooking Athens 2,400 years ago, to a spot on this Derbyshire hillside alongside Chatsworth, the similarity would be immediate. Of course, the Duke of Devonshire's creation is far from identical to the Parthenon – there are all the windows for a start. But even their symmetry and regularity across the west façade, as recorded by Fiennes, are part of a grander design.

> *It has a flat roof with barristers* [balustrades] *and flowerpots. In the front are 7 large windows, the glass diamond-cut and the panes big, 4 in a breadth 7 in height. Towards the garden are 12 windows of the same glass, 4 panes broad, 8 long. The lowest windows are made with grates before them and an aviary. There are 20 steps out of the garden on either side, and iron bars painted blue and tipped with gold.*

So why did it catch on and become so fashionable to copy the ancient Greeks?

By 1697, when Celia Fiennes came here, the educated classes across Europe now believed that the civilisation of ancient Greece, from 2,000 years earlier, best represented their own new values based on rational thought. The superstition of the medieval period and the dominance of religion in politics and philosophy during the sixteenth and earlier decades of the seventeenth centuries were now in the past. Rational thinking, underpinned by close observation, was now taking over. The Age of the Enlightenment, also known as the Age of Reason, was beginning. The ancient Greeks were admired because of the logical fact-based thinking of Pythagoras, Plato, Socrates and Aristotle, and buildings like Chatsworth reflected this. Its West Front – with its dependable, balanced, controlled beauty – was a visual image of neat, provable argument built up step by step. Chatsworth and other neoclassical buildings of the late seventeenth and the eighteenth centuries were the embodiment of the Age of Reason.

Given the philosophical foundations of Chatsworth, we might have expected that the mastermind behind it – the 1st Duke of Devonshire – would himself have been one of the great thinkers of the age. Not a bit of it. Horace Walpole wrote later that he was 'prone to take offence, ready with his sword, as with his tongue'. In a notorious squabble with a Royalist supporter named Colonel Culpepper over the ownership of some land, he grabbed Culpepper by the nose and dragged him off before beating him over the head with a cane. The noble lord was arrested and fined £30,000, then jailed for non-payment. He somehow managed to walk out of the prison gates and headed for Derbyshire, later resolving the matter with an I.O.U. – which he had no intention of paying. He then saw his chance and backed the claim by William of Orange to the throne of England – it was said he did it to win support in his row with Culpepper. The move worked, and come the Glorious Revolution of 1689, William rewarded him with the title of Duke of Devonshire.

But not only was he a brawler, but a gambler too, a fan of the races. His agent wrote, 'My Lord is now at Newmarket where most of our cash is gone.' And two weeks later, he added, 'Our noble lord is not yet returned from Newmarket and I am much afraid hath lost a great deal of money.' Back on the building site, things were getting desperate. A foreman carpenter sent him a letter: 'My men will not strike a stroke more before they be paid in full for what they have done.' But the financial resources of the nobility could seem boundless. The duke somehow raised the cash to cover the back-pay, and the huge building project was back on track.

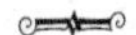

Celia Fiennes has less to say about the lofty halls and treasure-packed rooms inside the house than you'll find in any of today's guidebooks. In fact, she seems less impressed by them than she was by the external façades.

The reason is soon pretty clear. Five minutes after leaving the garden, the red carpet in the North Entrance Hall is inviting me up the dozen wide stairs into the heart of the house. I pause to look up above the mid-room pillars and the bust of a Roman emperor, to where the goddess Aurora is leading Apollo in his horse-drawn chariot, surrounded by female supporters, across a vast ceiling fresco.

One of the many ways that Chatsworth excels today is in the friendliness and knowledge of its guides. They don't steer you at an unnatural pace from room to room as though trying to get rid of you. There are one or two based in each area of the house happy to chat and tell you about whatever catches your eye. In the Hall, it's Freddie (name badge), sixties, tweed suit, tartan tie, trimmed beard.

He tells me, 'I always think the amazing thing about this grand hall is that up to the 1760s, it was actually the kitchen. And see the fireplace there,' – he points to a marble chimney breast, busts on either side, naked nymphs or similar in wood over the mantlepiece, red leather sofas waiting for someone to sit and warm their knees on a winter's day - 'buried behind it are all the old cooking ranges.'

'Wow,' is my unimaginative response. 'And the ceiling fresco?' I nod up at Aurora.

'Lovely, isn't it? It was installed in 1848.'

I thank him and move on. But that's it in a, delicately sculptured, nutshell. Behind the Parthenon look-alike exterior which we today can share with Celia Fiennes, Chatsworth's interior has changed. Most of what delights me over the next hour's wandering through its halls and up its staircases – gilded bannisters, frescoes in muted colours, statues of gods wearily reclining or pointing languidly, marble floors, intricately carved French furniture, rows of Chinese ceramic pots, drawings by Holbein and Raphael, portraits by Rembrandt and Gainsborough, Landseer's of slaughtered deer, mahogany dining chairs and much more – were not here when Celia Fiennes walked where I'm walking.

That's not to say it was all a bare, stone building site. She found much to admire.

The hall is very lofty, painted top and sides with armoury. The floors of the rooms are all finely inlaid, there is very curious carving over and round the chimney pieces, and round the looking-glasses that are

> *on the piers* [in this context, pillars of stone] *between the windows, and fine carved shelves or stands on each side of the glass. The Duchess's Closet is wainscoted with hollow burned japan, and at each corner are piers of looking glass; over the chimney is a looking glass, an oval and at the 4 corners are hollow carvings all around the glass.*

Glass mirrors were still a rarity, hence why she makes so much of them. The production of the mirrored glass itself was a problem because it tended to crack when hot, molten metal was applied to its rear surface in order to produce the reflection. Those that survived the manufacturing process tended to be fragile, small and gave only distorted images. Polished metal was the normal way to see yourself when rouging or shaving. Mirrors as we know them weren't common till 150 years after Celia Fiennes was writing. So the ones she saw at Chatsworth were ahead of their time.

The most unusual apartment she describes is the 'bathing room'. We'll discover more shortly about the virtues of keeping yourself sweet smelling. But listen to what she says about it here at Chatsworth and we might wonder whether the duke and duchess had in mind fun rather than hygiene when they designed it.

> *There is a fine grotto – all stone pavement roof and sides. Within this is a bathing room, the walls all with blue and white marble, the pavement mixed – one stone white, another black, another of red-veined marble. The bath is entirely marble, white, finely veined with blue and is made smooth. It was as deep as one's middle on the outside, and you went down steps into the bath big enough for two people. At the upper end are two cocks to let in water, one hot, the other cold to temper it as persons please. The windows are all private glass.*

But were any of the treasures we marvel at today already in place? One of Chatsworth's many magnificent frescos adorns the ceiling of the State Dining Room. It was completed by the Italian master,

Antonio Verrio, six years before her arrival, and shows a series of semi-naked figures of both sexes. While he was staying at the house working on his masterpiece, Verrio had a row with the housekeeper, a Mrs Hackett. He got his revenge by portraying her as the central figure in his fresco, a malicious, black-gowned Fate with a pair of scissors cutting the Thread of Life, for ever after to be mocked and reviled by Chatsworth's high-ranking guests whenever they looked up from their dinner.

Fiennes hardly mentions it.

> *The dining room was delicately painted overhead.*

Nothing more. Perhaps this is another example of her restrained praise for – rather than outright condemnation of – naked limbs, or maybe she'd heard the story of Mrs Hackett and thought it inappropriate to ridicule a diligent servant so. She adds:

> *There were as many rooms on the other side which were not finished. They were just painting the ceilings and laying the floors.*

And that's probably the chief reason why she took less delight than we do today in the interior of this most splendid of England's stately homes. The place was only half built.

It's the gardens at Chatsworth that were her favourite.

> *Before the gate, there is a large park and several fine gardens with gravel walks and squares of grass. There is one garden full of stone and brass statues. The gardens lie one above another which makes the prospect very fine. Above these gardens is an ascent of 5 or 6 steps up to a green walk,*

The area she's talking about is on the gentle slope of the hill behind the house. A map drawn about this time shows the detail of what she describes.

The lawns, flowers, shrubs and the walks are all laid out in straight lines, right-angles and precise circles. In other words, the gardens reflect the regularity of the house's façade.

And there's more to it than that. Forcing plants into fixed regular patterns was all part of the new rationalism. In the Age of Reason, the natural world was regarded as some sort of terrifying wild beast that must be tamed and made to obey the will of mankind. Rationalists and their fellow-thinkers spurned the unruly and chaotic form which nature took when allowed to grow free, untouched by humans. Another visitor to Chatsworth about this time, a writer named Joseph Taylor, described the house and its gardens as 'a heaven from which one may survey the distant horrors of a hellish country'. Daniel Defoe in the mid 1720s wrote that the true wonder of Chatsworth was that it had been built in such a 'howling wilderness'. And Celia Fiennes herself could find little to admire here in nature's handiwork.

> *All Derbyshire is full of steep hills. Nothing but the peaks of hills as thick one by another is seen in most of the county. It's only hills and dales as thick as you can imagine. The surface of the earth looks barren.*

There's no evidence that the surrounding area would, back then, have somehow looked uglier to us than it does today. In fact, if anything the landscape would have been improved by the absence of electricity pylons, A-roads, motorways and windfarms – none of which are visible from Chatsworth itself. It's extraordinary that the Derbyshire Peak District – like all the other natural beauty spots which millions of us now adore – was once condemned as 'hellish', 'howling' and 'barren'.

This way of thinking was relatively short-lived. By the end of the eighteenth century, it was being turned on its head – Romantic

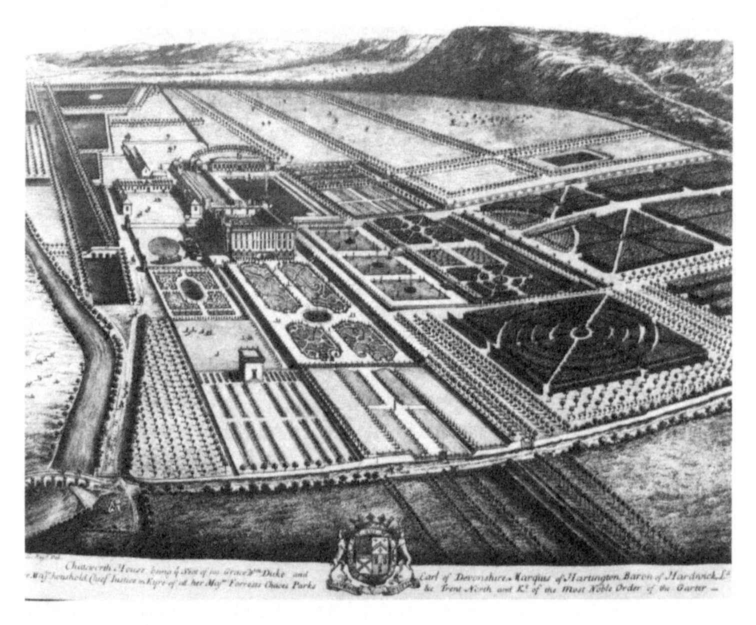

Chatsworth. 'There is a large park and several fine gardens with gravel walks and squares of grass.' Nature has been tamed into straight lines. (Wikimedia Commons)

poets and artists came to the fore, lauding the glorious wildness of unfettered nature. And in the same vein, 'Capability' Brown was redesigning formal gardens, turning them into naturalistic parklands of trees, lakes and rolling grass. And that's what he did at Chatsworth in the 1760s. And on this morning, as I look across beyond the house, all I can see is a gentle rise almost filled with woodland, as Brown had intended.

What Celia Fiennes describes then is a lost paradise from a now oft-forgotten age. She's especially fascinated by the way that water – the most slippery and elusive of nature's elements – has been tamed at Chatsworth in order to delight us mortals.

In the middle of each garden is a large fountain full of images, sea gods and dolphins and seahorses which are full of pipes which

> *spout out water. On a little bank stand blue balls 10 on each side, and between each ball are 4 pipes which, by a sluice, spout water across the steps to each other like an arbour or arch. While you are thus amused, suddenly there runs down a torrent of water out of 2 pitchers in the hands of two large nymphs cut in stone, which makes a pleasing prospect.*

And most to be applauded is beating nature at her own game, imitating her.

> *On each end of one walk stand two pyramids full of pipes spouting water that runs down one of them on brass which looks like rocks and hollow stones.*

But here's the *tour de force*:

> *There is another green walk and about the middle of it by the grove stands a fine willow tree. The leaves, bark and all look very natural, the root is full of rubbish* [i.e. soil] *or great stones in appearance. And all on a sudden, by turning a sluice, it rains from each leaf and from the branches like a shower, it being made of brass and pipes to each leaf, but in appearance is exactly like any willow.*

Today, the walkways are no longer the straight lines of Celia Fiennes' day. They straggle and twist among the trees giving sudden, unexpected views of the house. There's some water here still. A cascade, harnessed in a stone channel running straight down the hill for almost 200yds, reaches a wide path – also dead straight – between neat lawns. And alongside the house there's a lake with a fountain whooshing up higher than the roof of the house itself in an echo of the water gardens of yesteryear.

But there's something more. In the centre of a pond, there it is – the brass willow tree. Not quite, though. This one's a replacement built in the nineteenth century – the original had fallen into disrepair – and it's been moved across the park from where Fiennes was enchanted by it. Queen Victoria liked it too, she called it 'the squirting tree'.

Celia Fiennes' love of 'neat' gardens with their exact lines of regularly placed trees and shrubs may help account for her opinion about something else in England's plant life. In the late seventeenth century, there was one workplace revolution that was well under way. – the agricultural revolution.

The main improvement in farming productivity during the second half of the seventeenth century came from the introduction of crop rotation. When in previous ages farmers occasionally sewed a fresh crop in one of their fields, they began to notice that the plants were often stronger, more resistant to disease. By Celia Fiennes' time, rotating the type of crops across different fields year by year had become more and more common. We now understand the underlying reasons for this improvement. Certain plants – such as turnip roots for instance – restore nutrients to the soil, and crop rotation keeps down pests which can't then flourish on the same plant year on year.

It's relatively rare for her to tell us anything about farming methods, and it tends to be when something unusual strikes her. In Oxfordshire, for example:

> *The land in most part of this county is rich red mould and deep so they are forced to plough their ground 2 or 3 times for wheat and cannot use wheels to their ploughs. Its rich land and produces plenty of all things.*

However, at no point does she mention crop rotation. That's surprising, given her fascination with other methods of working such as coalmining. Why is that? It's possible that she sees farming – even though there's a new way of working – as traditional, old-fashioned, in other words it's not 'modern' which of course is what she finds praiseworthy. Or was crop rotation not yet a widespread practice across the country? This could be so. Historians now tend to veer away from the idea of a single agricultural revolution, and instead to identify a series of more gradual improvements in farming methods over several centuries.

Nevertheless, what she does observe is one of the necessary first steps that enabled crop rotation to take place. That was the enclosure of common lands. In medieval times, peasant farmers, who were tenants of the local landowner, had scraped a living from the soil alongside other peasants in the village. Together, they had divided up the village's common farmland into strips, with each farmer getting a roughly equal share of the good and the less productive land. Signs of this way of life survive to this day with the ridges and furrows – the old strips of farmland – which are a common sight in many parts of the country. The working lives of these medieval farmers were so interlocked that they set up local co-operative arrangements. The system had started to fall apart in Tudor times, when the lordly landowners began to drive their tenant farmers off the common land, and then enclose it with fences and hedges in order to create their own large farms. When Celia Fiennes travels the county, this move is well under way, and she notes it some thirty times, though usually it's just a passing reference. In Surrey, she observes, 'a fruitful vale full of enclosures,' and in Oxfordshire, it's 'a rich ground full of enclosures and looks fine'. And she sees them too in Devon and Kent.

The enclosure system had two effects. As well as enabling the increase in productivity with crops rotated around several fields on a large farm, it also had a damaging impact on the lower ranks of rural society. Driven out of their medieval co-operatives, many poorer farming folks couldn't find work as labourers with the local lord and were forced to seek a livelihood elsewhere. They began the exodus to towns and cities, where soon – a few decades after Celia Fiennes was writing – jobs would await them in mills and factories, or of course there was work below ground down the growing number of deep coal mines.

And the most likely explanation for her concentration on the enclosure of common land when she talks about farming is a reflection of the same view she had of the gardens in Chatsworth. Enclosures were another form of taming the wildness of nature, and this – in her mind and that of many of her contemporaries – was the role of humankind.

7

To Warwick

WHEN DISASTER STRIKES

There being no good accommodation for people of fashion, the country people being a clownish, rude people.

In the seventeenth century, chaotic danger and sudden death could lurk in the most innocent of settings. Uncertainty – with all the possibilities of destruction implied by that innocent word – was embedded in everyday life in a way that's difficult for us to imagine in twenty-first-century Britain. We may think we can understand because we too are no strangers to unexpected tragedy – road accidents, the ravages of Covid-19, and much else. But it's the unstoppable scale, speed and spread of danger in Celia Fiennes' time – from flood, fire and disease, to quote three examples – that put the threat then in a different category.

But not everything in life at the end of the seventeenth century was so unpredictable. The very backbone of society itself was fixed, according to unwritten, unchallengeable rules. There was a rigid class system, which – with few exceptions – meant that your station in life was determined not by your skill, talent, enterprise, intelligence or energy, but by a single unalterable, perhaps even God-given, factor – your birth and who your parents were. Dukes and duchesses begat privileged aristocrats. The children of parlour maids and farm labourers had no expectation – or opportunity – of rising above those humble stations.

It was as though people were compensating for the many unforeseen hazards that might suddenly hit. If they had to live with death-threatening unpredictability, then they would do their best to make the structure of society itself reliable, unchangeable.

When Celia Fiennes moves on from Chatsworth to visit Warwick, we see for ourselves these two extremes of everyday life in the late seventeenth century.

First, she tells us about the catastrophic devastation that had struck the place.

> *The town of Warwick by means of a sad fire about 4 or 5 years since had laid the greatest part in ashes.*

She's mistaken about the date. It was in fact just three years earlier. At two in the afternoon of 5 September 1694, a man was carrying a burning torch along the High Street. Before the days of matches, getting a light from your neighbour was often how you rekindled your own cooking fire. Was he careless? Was there a sudden gust of wind? We'll never know, but a spark flew off his torch. At a time when many houses were built of wood, thatch, lath and plaster, and were tightly packed together in towns, and when there was no question of help from a fire brigade, it's easy to imagine the result. It was the start of what became known as the Great Fire of Warwick. It blazed for six hours. We don't know how many people were hurt or killed before the fast-spreading flames were stopped by a line of stone-walled buildings. But the centre of the town was devastated.

Apparently, however, the people of Warwick wasted no time in rebuilding, as she tells us, and so something good had come from this terrible accident.

> [The town] *is mostly now new buildings, which are built with brick and quoined* [constructed at the corners] *with stone, and the windows the same. The streets are very handsome and the buildings regular and fine, not very lofty, being limited by Act of Parliament to such a pitch and size.*

Twenty-eight years earlier, the Great Fire of London had destroyed 80 per cent of the capital. That had prompted a new law laying down what materials could in future be used for buildings, their height, and the width of streets. At first the law applied only to London itself. But within weeks of the fire at Warwick, a similar ordinance was applied here, and, it seems from what Fiennes says, the builders complied to the letter with the new regulations.

Somehow the flames had penetrated Warwick's main church, St Mary's, despite it being built of stone, and she reports:

> *The ruins of the church still remain, the repairing of which is the next work designed* [i.e. planned].

Fortunately, the heart of the building seems to have been untouched, and she is able to admire a series of tombs topped with the effigies of their long-dead occupants. She is particularly taken by the monument to the 3rd Earl of Warwick. Her description is matchless.

> *The lines of his face and hands, with the veins and sinews, were so finely cast, and the very air of his countenance much to the life or like a living man. All is cast in brass and burnished very delicately so that it looks like gold. All his armour is very exact, with figures and images round the tombstone. Their garments are folded in differing shapes and with many wrinklings and gathers, which are very exact and the more to be noted being all in such a stiff metal as brass, and yet they look easy and natural.*

As it happens, these reclining statues are favourites of mine too. They date from the fifteenth century. Nowhere else have I come across such skilled stone craftwork. The colour of the faces and the clothing, though a little faded now, has survived enough to make you marvel at the dye they used so many centuries ago. The sombre features and rumpled gowns on these figures look so real that your fingers – like mine whenever I visit here – are compelled to touch them as though to check if there's still the warmth of life in them yet.

Before she leaves Warwick, she can't resist another grand house tour, with plenty more 'grass walks', 'noble halls' and 'fine paintings'.

Warwick Castle is a stately building. It is now the Lord Brooke's house.

On the morning I arrive here, there's a ten-minute queue of excited families waiting to buy £29 tickets at the gate. Warwick Castle is now owned by Merlin Entertainments – look no further than the company's name to find out what attracts today's visitors. It's a successful theme park for all the family.

This prompts the question: how does Celia Fiennes gain access to this private house, long before the idea of history as a lucrative backdrop for an entertainment empire? Unlike at other great houses she visits, the occupant is not a cousin nor any other relative who would as a matter of routine have invited her to stay. Though we can't be sure, the answer almost certainly lies in a shared history. The Lord Brooke that she mentions was Fulke Greville, the 5th Baron of that name. His great-grandfather had been a resolute Puritan like her own grandfather, and the two of them had been fellow conspirators – meeting at Broughton Castle – in opposition to the king. Fulke never witnessed their plot's conclusion. He was shot dead by a Royalist sniper at the Battle of Lichfield in 1643, six years before Charles I was executed. It's a fair guess, then, that – with this heritage in common – Celia Fiennes was welcomed here by the current Lord Brooke.

Today, when we're a lot more democratic about who we allow into such treasures of our heritage, I'm happy (for the moment at least) to follow the crowd, who seem to be heading around the side of the castle. Soon my vision is filled by what seems like a thousand

Effigy of the 3rd Earl of Warwick in St Mary's Church. 'Under his head is a roll of straw matting, being exceedingly natural cut in stone.' (Public Domain, Sjwells53)

people, variously chomping crisps, sucking drinks or licking chocolate covered ice creams, lounging on a grassy bank. The jousting is about to start.

When Celia Fiennes came here in the late summer of 1697, she – like today's visitors – seemed to have little interest in this place as one of the finest pieces of military architecture in the country. However, for her it isn't an entertainment venue, but another grand aristocratic home, to be admired, especially, as at Chatsworth:

> *... the fine gardens with good gravel and grass walks, squares of dwarf trees of all sorts and steps to descend from one walk to another.*

There are still gardens at Warwick Castle today, but not the ones she saw. And her remarks are significant. We know that in the early part of her century – seventy or eighty years before she came here – the then-Lord Brooke spent what in today's money would have been hundreds of thousands of pounds on laying out the gardens. They were described soon after by one visitor as 'most pleasant' with 'walks and thickets such as this part of England can hardly parallel'. However, they were dug up in the 1640s and replaced with defensive earthworks in preparation for attack during the Civil War. And the commonly held view is that they then remained as little more than an untended piece of waste ground until the great landscape gardener 'Capability' Brown transformed them in the late eighteenth century. But from Celia Fiennes' observations, we know that the gardens were not left neglected for 100 years, as has often been supposed.

Once inside the great castle, she begins her tour of the state rooms, telling us about 'a large parlour all wainscoted with cedar, which is full of fine pictures of the family'. The work was completed only twenty years or so before her visit. Two local craftsmen carried out the work. The style is Italianate, so the two men – named as Roger and William Hurlbutt – must have been highly skilled and knowledgeable.

What really catches her eye though is the state bedroom.

> *A bed chamber with good tapestry hangings. They are old, but so good work, so curious, all of silk, that the very postures and faces look extremely lively and natural, and the groves, streams and rivers look very well in it.*

She loves her art to be lifelike, and when I get up close to those tapestries, I can see what she means, though with our twenty-first-century eyes we might object that the figures look a bit fixed in unnatural poses. And the colours today may have lost a little of the vibrancy of 300 years ago. In the guidebook, Merlin have found a way to attract today's visitors to check them out for themselves. 'Urine was added to tapestries to stop the natural colours from running,' it says, adding, 'Men were even paid to drink large quantities of beer so that an adequate supply was available'.

My route to the state rooms lies across the vast courtyard of Warwick Castle, past a small crowd watching a bald eagle swoop down from the battlements to grab a chunk of meat from its trainer's gloved fist. Next there are small boys trying to throw toy rats through a hoop, and small girls waiting to go up the 'Princess Tower'. Forgive the sexist division – that's just the way it is here. They're all having a good time and making a noise about it. This morning, only a sprinkling of people are wandering past a sign that says STATE ROOMS, and I follow them through. Nobody seems to stop for longer than it takes to tap the button on the camera app of their mobile phones. The last room is the busiest. This is a shop, selling all you need from a full-size armour helmet to a fridge magnet.

I hesitate to ask, 'What would Celia Fiennes have thought of all this?' Hesitate, because it's hard to define how anyone would react if dumped in another age. But there are some safe bets. For a start, we can be sure she'd be shocked at what she would have regarded as the scantily clad mothers and young women – shorts or knee-length skirts – queuing in the shop to pay for the presents for their kids. Even her relatively liberal brand of Puritanism, as we've seen, would have been offended by flesh-revealing women's dress. Much as she might have made allowances in paintings given their skill and artistry, real live female 'nudity' would have been a different matter.

Then there are all those, what to her would have been, ill-behaved children, running around, throwing things about, and … and … having fun. In the late seventeenth century, the offspring of upper-class families were not permitted to play about or indeed enjoy anything outside the nursery. In fact, as we see from paintings of aristocratic infants at this time, the ideal child was regarded as a miniature adult, thoughtful, observant, polite. In all her diaries she makes little mention of children – other than in the occasional passing references. For example, in London, she speaks of 'free schools' with '3 large rooms to teach the children, with several masters'. The closest she comes to pointing out the unacceptable behaviour of children comes at King's College Chapel in Cambridge, where she writes of 'a gentleman that gave his estate to add to the revenues of the church, on a dislike to disobedient children'.

What she might have found most distasteful about Warwick Castle today would have been the crowds themselves: how herds of what she would regard as common people being permitted for a shilling or two (i.e. the seventeenth-century equivalent of £29) to invade this aristocratic haven. She's very aware of her own higher social class, and has three particular phrases to describe its members. At the village of Alford in Somerset, for instance, she remarks that there was:

no good accommodation for people of fashion, the country people being a clownish, rude people.

At the city of Bath:

there are chairs, as in London, to carry the better sort of people in visits.

At Hailes Abbey in Gloucestershire:

there is a pretty chapel with a gallery for people of quality to sit in,

and in Shrewsbury:

there are abundance of people of quality.

And her opinion of the worth of those who are not 'the better sort of people/of fashion/of quality' is clear in her account of parliamentary elections. As we shall see on her journey the following year, she praises England's constitution for its limits on who can vote or be elected so that 'none were chosen but the gentlemen of the shire living there, or else in the town the chiefs of their corporation that lived there'.

This does not make her a snob. It makes her a product of her own era. It was a time, for instance, when any idea that the vote should be extended to a wider section of the population was over a century into the future. What held society together was a dependable framework of rank and status. It would have undermined that structure to grant a share of power to those who were not wealthy or titled. This was the mainstream opinion of the period, and Celia Fiennes is in line with it.

However, there were some small signs that the social system might not be quite as rigid as it had been a few decades earlier. While Celia's grandparents' and parents' generations had all married into the families of viscounts, peers or baronets, her own sister, Mary, had married a commoner named Edmund Harrison in 1684. He was described as a 'Turkey merchant' of London. That meant he was part of a group of businessmen who traded with the Turkish Ottoman Empire and further afield in India. He made a lot of money, and – while he could not become a peer – his marriage to Mary Fiennes allowed him to move into what was regarded as 'good society'. So we see – by no means an upheaval in the class system – at least the first stirrings of social mobility, something that would soon become more common as the Industrial Revolution created a new middle class whom their 'betters' would be unable to ignore.

That's a far cry of course from letting every Jack and Jill off the streets see behind the scenes inside the home of those 'people of quality' in Warwick Castle. Country house tourism was another century or more away, though, as it happens, Warwick Castle was to be the ground-breaker. It was the first historic site in England to set itself up as a tourist attraction. By 1826, 6,000 visitors – mainly from nearby Birmingham and Leamington Spa – were viewing its bedrooms and dining halls each year. When the Earl of Warwick's housekeeper died in 1834, she was said to have left £30,000 in her will, solely earned from tips she got showing sightseers around.

But in the late seventeenth century, significant social upheaval was a long way off. In an age when, without warning, a whole town could be threatened by fire in single afternoon, the key was control – whether that meant elementary planning regulations, a straight line of trees in the garden, or everyone's rank in society. Chaos was a throwback to the past. Order was the future. That – in the Age of Reason – was the theory at least.

Celia Fiennes is loyal to the class system, as we would expect from a minor aristocrat in this period. But, as ever, given her independent spirit, she doesn't fit into simple generalisations. Much as she's aware of her own high social rank, and despite being in favour of a system that cut the lower classes out of the democratic process, she often ignores social divisions on her travels. One night she's savouring fine dishes at the table of an aristocratic relation, the next she's enjoying a flagon of ale in a scruffy inn. One day she's describing the work of labourers down a coal-pit, then within hours she's switched to detailing the décor of the great hall in some noble family's ancestral home. Time after time, she goes wherever her persistent curiosity takes her. Of course, it's her privileged position in society that allows her this freedom. No seamstress or chamber maid would have been accepted as widely as she was. Nevertheless, in the late seventeenth century it was unique for a high-ranking woman – or any woman – to behave like this. It's one of her many accomplishments that were unknown to most, if not all, of her peers.

And sometimes, when things go wrong, a bit of privilege can be a godsend – as she discovers when she heads off from Warwick towards London. She's aiming to get to Daventry by the end of the day, but the road is bad:

> *a very heavy way, and we could not reach thither being 14 miles. At about 11 miles we came to a place called Lower Shuckburgh – a sad village. We could have no entertainment* [i.e. lodgings and food].

For her, however, help is at hand.

> *Nearby on the top of a steep hill is Shuckburgh Hall, the seat of Sir Charles Shuckburgh.*

Luckily for her, she's spotted in her plight by a sympathetic resident of the place.

> *My Lady Shuckburgh was in her coach driving by us when in distress enquiring for lodging. She caused Sir Charles to come out to meet us. Seeing our distress, it being just night and the horses weary with the heavy way, he very courteously took compassion on us and treated us very handsomely that night, a good supper served 'in plate'* [perhaps, formally on the best tableware] *and very good wine and good beds. He shewed a generous, hospitable spirit to strangers. And, with a great deal of good humour, My Lady entertained us.*

Celia Fiennes is clearly touched by the treatment she receives. She doesn't often express an opinion – even a flattering one – on named individuals like this. And it's even rarer for her to be critical of a Lady So-and-so or a Mr Such-and-such. When she does give a name – a Mr Middleton or the Duke of Devonshire, for example – she's normally neutral in what she says about them. We glean nothing of their character.

Much of the time, her reporting is factual and objective. She keeps her opinions to herself. That's what she does at the next place we're going to visit with her. And it's surprising, because the spa town of Tunbridge Wells seems to represent everything about upper-class idleness and self-indulgence that she'd attacked so vehemently in the Introduction to her diaries. It's where the fashionable gentry of the day are starting to enjoy a new form of entertainment. But were they always quite as well behaved and innocent in their pleasures as Celia Fiennes seems to believe? They were not.

8

Tunbridge Wells

HUCKSTERS, HIGGLERS AND HIGH SOCIETY

The gentlemen bowl, the ladies dance,
or walk on the green in the afternoons.

From Shuckborough, she heads briefly to London, before setting off again, this time to the south-east.

> *I, being in Kent this year, shall insert something of Tunbridge Wells, whose waters I have drunk many years with great advantage.*

On the face of it, Tunbridge Wells doesn't seem like her kind of place. At the end of the seventeenth century, it was very different from Harrogate, where we saw her relishing the water as a 'quick purger', dipping her head under dozens of times, and remarking on the 'Papist' pilgrims at its springs. Tunbridge Wells, on the other hand, was less health centre by 1697 and more upmarket holiday resort. It was where high-ranking ladies and gentlemen came to show off how fashionable they were, disporting themselves on its leafy walks, and dancing and gambling in its ornate rooms. Not that they ignored the waters, but the salutary benefits of the springs weren't top on their list of Tunbridge Wells attractions. One visitor there in 1704 wrote, 'Those who repair thither for diversion ever exceed those who go thither for health.' It was the first of England's spas to make that switch.

Celia Fiennes then is in the minority. It's likely she favours it for the simple reason that it's handy for her – just 30 miles from her home, and it offers the kind of spa water she loves.

> *The waters are from the steel and iron mines, very quick springs, especially one well. There are two with large basins of stone fixed in the earth with several holes in the bottom by which the springs bubble up and fill it so it always runs over.*

Some folk, however, enjoy the health-giving properties of the water without actually going anywhere near the wells at all.

> *Many have it brought to their lodgings a mile or two off and drink it in their beds. Nay, some have it brought to London. They have the bottles filled in the well under the water and sealed down with corks, which they say preserves it.*

Tunbridge Wells didn't have a centuries-long reputation for miraculous cures like Harrogate and many other spas. Its fame dated only to 1606, when a 25-year-old nobleman, Dudley Lord North, out riding in the fields nearby, noticed a spring which had deposited rust-coloured marks around its edges. He suffered from tuberculosis or a similar disease, and he wondered if the water might help. He drank some, and – he claimed – was cured. On his return to London, North spread the word among his fellow aristocrats about the miraculous wells of Tunbridge. He was a close friend of the Prince of Wales, and was known at court for his love of poetry and music, as well as apparently being an outstanding athlete (which, if true, might give the lie to the suggestion he had TB or anything so serious). Soon, many of the most wealthy and mighty in the land, hearing of North's cure, were turning up at Tunbridge.

Over the next two decades, it became the vogue to spend the 'season' there, from midsummer's day to the end of September. The inhabitants of the town were slow off the mark in providing decent lodgings for their well-heeled visitors. In 1630, when King Charles I's wife, Queen Henrietta Maria came for six weeks, she and her attendants stayed in tents pitched on the Common. It was eight years later before the first hospitality buildings were constructed. Even by

1663, there were few lodging houses. In that year, when Charles II and Queen Catherine visited, while they occupied a fine house in the Mount Ephraim district, the royal retinue still had to camp out under canvas. In 1687, a devastating fire – just as we saw in Warwick – spread rapidly through the district around the springs. The charred ruins gave way to a construction boom, and, as Celia Fiennes tells us, the town had expanded.

> *They have made the wells very commodious by the many good buildings all about it for 2 or 3 miles as lodgings for the company* [i.e. the visitors] *that drink the waters.*

This had made the place even more attractive for her – as always, on the look-out for a bargain.

> *And they have increased their buildings so much that it's made them very cheap.*

New promenades had been constructed too.

> *These are all built with an arch or penthouse, some of which are supported by pillars like a piazza and are paved with brick and stone for the dry walking of visitors in rain.*

By 'penthouse', she doesn't mean what we would understand by it, a luxury top-floor apartment. According to the *Oxford English Dictionary*, a penthouse in the seventeenth century was 'a structure having a sloping roof' ('pent-' means leaning) 'forming a covered walk, arcade or colonnade, in front of a row of buildings'.

> *Elsewhere, they walk on clay and sand mixed together. They have been intending to make it gravel, which would be much better. All these conveniences are added by the visitors' contributions every year – that's the way it's been and always will be. At the lower end of the walk, on*

a broad space before you come to the walls of the wells, there is a large sundial set upon several steps of stone.

When she says all this building has been added by 'the visitors' contributions each year', she's talking about what these wealthy folk spend while in Tunbridge Wells, on lodgings, to local servants, for food and all else to keep them in the comfort they were used to. It was the prospect of this future income stream that had persuaded investors to put their money into new buildings.

And there are other – more spiritual – necessities, which guests pay for directly.

A chapel which has been built by the several collections of the visitors every year. It's a pretty place and cost a great deal of money, and every year there are contributions for the maintenance of a minister.

Different denominations are catered for:

At Mount Ephraim there is also a large chapel where the Presbyterians are preaching.

Because the season was so short, Tunbridge Wells near enough shut down when the weather turned cold, but not, we learn, the chapels:

They [the Presbyterians] *have a minister who by the collections of the visitors is also maintained all the winter to preach, as is the public chapel at the walks.*

One of the novel practices in high-society lifestyle at Tunbridge Wells of 1697 is how they organised dining. There's a new vogue: 'do it yourself' – up to a point anyway.

Tunbridge Wells in 1748, by Samuel Richardson. The promenades are alongside 'pillars like a piazza'. (*The Mirror of Literature, Amusement, And Instruction*, 1 August 1829)

> *All people buy their own provision at the market which is just by the wells. Flesh, fowl and fish in great plenty are brought from Rye and Deal* [both on the coast of Kent] *&c, this spa being on the road to London. Also the country people come with all their backyard and barn-door affords* [produce] *from their gardens and orchards, which makes the markets well stored and the provisions cheap.*

The wealthy visitors find it fun to do their own food shopping, something they wouldn't have dreamed of stooping to back home. It was a job for servants. But here on holiday the nobs are slumming it.

> *The gentry take it as a diversion* [an amusement], *while drinking the waters, to go and buy their dinners. Every day there's a market. It runs the whole length of the walk, which is between high trees for shade.*

The assumption must be that they'd brought their cooks with them, who back at the lodgings would prepare what their lordships and ladyships had picked out from the market stalls. Of course, to Celia Fiennes doing your own food shopping is nothing unusual. We've often seen her doing it, especially when there are bargains to be had. But it seems the fashionable shoppers at Tunbridge Wells are not as savvy as she is.

> *There are brewhouses for beer and bakers for bread, but some of them come from London and spoil the market by raising the price – there are the higglers and hucksters in a great number.*

'Higglers and hucksters' – a delightfully colourful phrase. The meaning of 'huckster' has changed little over the years. Back in Celia Fiennes' time it meant an itinerant market trader who to make a living would have needed to be assertive. And the term today – especially in the USA – describes a pushy, opportunistic salesman. The term 'higgler' has now dropped out of use. Back in the seventeenth century, it often described someone who bartered goods in the market, especially poultry and dairy produce. It's clear that she intended both as terms of mild abuse.

As well as food and drink, there were plenty of other items on sale to tempt visitors:

> *several apothecary shops* [and] *a row of buildings on the right side, which are shops full of all sorts of toys, silver, china, milliners and all sorts of curious wooden ware which this place is noted for.*

Visitors would have bought such items as souvenirs or gifts for those not lucky enough to be with them.

Keeping in touch with friends, relations and business associates is surprisingly easy, according to her. She explains that Tunbridge Wells has:

> *... a room for the post house. The post comes every day and returns while the season of drinking the waters is on, from London and to it – except Mondays none comes down from London, so on Saturdays none goes up. You pay a penny 'extraordinary'* [i.e. extra] *for it being brought from Tunbridge town which is 4 miles distance, that being a post town.*

The first mail service, available – in theory – to everyone, had been set up by Charles I in 1635, with the postage paid by the person receiving the letter rather than the one who posted it. For the next twenty years, the service was outsourced to private individuals. Then in 1655 it was put under direct government control, though for sinister reasons. Oliver Cromwell was in power and worried about underground anti-government conspiracies. He needed to know the rebels' plans in advance, so he put the post in the hands of his Secretary of State, John Thurloe, better known as the Spymaster General. Thurloe intercepted letters between known conspirators, read them, resealed them and sent them on, so the miscreants could be caught red-handed later. With the Restoration of the Monarchy in 1660, that system was abandoned, and the General Post Office was established. It was the foundation of the modern mail service. However, the fact that Celia Fiennes – thirty-seven years later – thinks it worthwhile emphasising that you could receive letters while staying in Tunbridge Wells, shows that the service was still far from regular in much of the country.

Tunbridge Wells today, like Harrogate, is no longer where visitors flock in any great numbers to 'take the waters', nor do the wealthy and titled come here anymore to look fashionable. The town's former image, however, has left its legacy in the everlasting joke about a mythical letter-writer to the *Times* who signs off 'Disgusted of Tunbridge Wells', the stereotype of someone who's strongly conservative, morally outraged and middle class – but hoping to be taken for a higher-ranker in society.

In its buildings, however, the town does still carry memories of its more glamorous past. What's known as the 'Pantiles', for instance, where lines of white neoclassical columns provide shaded walkways for those browsing today's shops and cafés, seems to parallel what Celia Fiennes describes in 1697. And there are hundreds of delicate, square-windowed houses with flat balustraded roofs topped with intricate stone urns or acorns – neoclassical architecture just coming into fashion at that time. But the disappointment for our investigation is that all these delightful structures – with the exception of the churches – were built during the century and a half *after* Celia Fiennes came here.

There's no doubt though that the historic look of the town draws visitors still – hundreds of thousands of them from all over the world, as I discover. Once I've managed to find somewhere to park, I stroll over to the Pantiles. It's a sunny day and I can hardly move along the promenade for the tables and umbrellas that have spread out from the lines of thin grooved columns to accommodate all the coffee-and-croissants consumers.

The café we can recognise today can trace its origins back to a time just before Celia Fiennes began visiting Tunbridge Wells. She tells us:

There are two large coffee houses for tea, chocolate &c.

These drinks were all relative newcomers. Not once in her journals does Celia Fiennes ever mention drinking any of them. Strange, given that she says so much about those other two beverages, beer and wine. Samuel Pepys in his diary made it clear that one of the newfangled drinks was still unusual in 1666: 'I did send for a cup of tee (a China drink) of which I never had drank before.' At first, tea was promoted as a medicinal aid, but by the time Celia Fiennes was visiting Tunbridge Wells, it was being sipped by the elite purely for pleasure, though it would be several decades before it became a byword for genteel afternoon gatherings. It was expensive: in 1660 one London merchant was advertising it at 6*d* 10*s*, that's the equivalent of several hundred pounds sterling in today's money!

Drinking chocolate was the real newcomer. In 1687, Sir Hans Sloane, later the President of the Royal Society of Physicians, ate some chocolate in Jamaica and declared it 'nauseous'. He tried mixing it with milk, liked it and brought it back to England where it caught on.

Coffee itself had arrived on English shores, in the same way as tea and chocolate, through the activities of the ever-growing number of businessmen who became rich by importing coffee and other newly sought-after luxuries. Though it first appeared here around 100 years before Celia Fiennes began visiting Tunbridge Wells, coffee took off only in the mid 1600s. A handbill – i.e. an advertising flyer – from 1652 declared:

> It is a most excellent remedy against the spleen,
> hypochondriac winds, or the like.
> It will prevent drowsiness, and make one fit for business,
> and therefore you are not to drink of it after supper,
> unless you intend to be watchful,
> for it will hinder sleep for 3 or 4 hours.
> It is observed that in Turkey, where this is generally drunk,
> that they are not troubled with the stone, gout, dropsy or scurvy,
> and that their skins are exceeding clear and white.
> It is neither laxative nor refrigerant.

The coffee house itself in the late seventeenth century was not the innocent venue its name might suggest to us now. Unlike Caffè Nero, Starbucks and the rest today, the seventeenth-century coffee house was the embodiment of sexual and social division, as well as a hotbed of subversive conspiracy, or so the government alleged.

The first establishment dedicated to serving the drink was established in Oxford in 1654. Twenty years later, there were 3,000 of them across the country. They'd soon developed into something more than where you met a friend while savouring the rich flavour of this new beverage. Coffee houses became debating chambers, places where you went to discuss and argue about the latest political, philosophical and religious ideas, as well as to pick up the latest news. The free-ranging expression of views which the coffee houses encouraged was considered so dangerous to the stability of the nation that Charles II even tried – but failed – to shut them down.

Most coffee houses were for men, and men only. Although a few were managed by women, often the only female customers to be seen were prostitutes touting for business. That was one reason why most respectable women were thus put off going inside.

In 1674, an anonymous pamphlet was widely circulated, entitled 'Women's Petition Against Coffee'. It declared: 'The excessive use of that new-fangled, abominable, heathenish liquor called *COFFEE* has eunuched our husbands, and crippled our more kind gallants, that they are become as impotent as age.' And it went on to spell out how their manliness had been stolen from them by coffee, 'For can any woman of sense or spirit endure with patience that when she approaches the nuptial bed, expecting a man that should answer the vigour of her flames, she on the contrary should only meet a bedful of bones, and hug a meagre useless corpse?' The pamphlet also attacked the coffee houses because they took a man away 'in times of domestic crisis when a husband should have been attending to his duties at home'.

Here we have an extraordinary fight-back by women excluded from cutting-edge political and religious debate. Except … we almost certainly do not. Instead, it's likely this is a spectacular and enchanting piece of seventeenth-century fake news. We now know that this so-called 'Women's Petition Against Coffee' was in fact written and distributed by supporters of Charles II and his campaign to ban coffee houses as subversive. The monarch regarded such places as breeding grounds for rebellion. The writer of the pamphlet – as likely as not, a man – was trying to make coffee houses unpopular by persuading customers that the drink made them impotent.

One group of coffee-house customers saw through it and hit back with their own pamphlet, called, 'The Men's Answer to the Women's Petition Against Coffee'. It claimed that, far from making them impotent, coffee made them better husbands by 'drying up' the 'crude flatulent humours' (i.e. what caused them to fart in bed). Besides, they added, 'The coffee house is the citizens' academy, where he learns more wit than ever his Grannum [i.e. grandmother] taught him.'

Recognising that the coffee house, in its current form, was out of bounds for 50 per cent of its visitors, the building developers of Tunbridge Wells saw a commercial opportunity. As Celia Fiennes points out, the spa had not one but 'two large coffee houses'. The first was for men only, and, incidentally, was also known as the Pipe Office, because customers could hire a pipe there and indulge in the newly introduced habit of tobacco smoking. But then, following the fire in 1687, a Ladies' Coffee House was built next to the Gentlemen's Coffee House. Inter-sex socialising was conducted outside in public view. Separate coffee houses for women were unusual. And there's no evidence that its customers in Tunbridge Wells mimicked their male companions and turned the place into a debating-chamber. Celia Fiennes tells us it has 'two rooms for the lottery and hazard board' and, if it's wet, there's another entertainment for the ladies to enjoy without the men:

> *there being music maintained* [paid for] *by the visitors to play in the morning while they drink the waters, and in the afternoon for dancing.*

Presumably the talk is what in the seventeenth century were regarded as more ladylike subjects. Even outside in the fresh air, it could still often be a divided society, as she explains.

> *There are several bowling greens about the wells, so the gentlemen bowl, the ladies dance, or walk in the green in the afternoons.*

So the story of the coffee house culture in late seventeenth-century England tells us a great deal about upper-class women at that time in their life away from domestic duties. Perhaps the strangest element in Fiennes' account is that it lacks any criticism or censure of this idle life.

There's one incident she describes during her time at Tunbridge Wells that's an even bigger puzzle. What she describes next looks like it should have been a total affront to the values of a Puritan lady of that time. While staying here, she takes a trip out.

> *I went from thence to Somerhill about 4 or 5 miles off. This is a seat of the last Viscount Purbeck. It stands on a hill in a good large park. There is an abundance of good sizeable rooms leading one out of another in vistos* [with views] *through the house.*

On the face of it, this sounds routine. Just another visit to the country house of someone she knows or has been introduced to. However, the 'Purbecks' had a dubious reputation.

Margaret Viscountess Purbeck was famed as a hostess, entertaining many noble and even royal guests at her house. She seems to have been the victim of what we would regard as a nasty smear campaign. Despite having a limp, she was said to love dancing. Her nickname was 'The Princess of Babylon' which was probably ironic because, according to one commentator, her looks didn't live up to those of the princess of that legend: her 'husband assuredly never married her for her beauty', adding, 'she had the shape of a woman big with child without being so'. The same writer claimed, 'she was made like the generality of rich heiresses, to whom nature seems just sparing of her gifts in proportion as they are loaded with those of fortune.' It's reported that her guests often laughed at her behind her back.

It seems, however, that some of the balls and other social events she presided over were not always as genteel as the spa routines that Celia Fiennes describes. In 1663, the French Ambassador after a visit to Somerhill, wrote that the waters of the spa were '*les eaux de scandale*, for they have nearly ruined the good name of the maids and the ladies' – that is, gentlewomen both single and married.

It's likely that any less respectable behaviour was down to her husband, John Villiers, rather than her. His title 'Viscount Purbeck' was based on an illegitimate claim – he was the bastard son of the last viscount. Villiers was a wastrel, who in the words of a contemporary, Lady Chaworth, 'makes what haste he can to consume his lady's fortune by gaming and all other extravagances'. He was killed fighting a duel in 1684. Such were the debts he left her that in that year, a large tract of land that she owned in the Mount Sion area of Tunbridge Wells had to be sold off to developers who built some of the houses that Celia Fiennes mentions.

Lady Margaret then married a man known as 'Beau' Fielding, who turned out to be even worse than Villiers. He was a bully who beat up women, and there's no reason to think that his wife escaped his abuse. His debts so sky-rocketed that she had to get rid of most of the estate. Lady Margaret died in the year following Celia Fiennes' account of her visit to the Purbeck home near Tunbridge, and the little that remained of her wealth was then soon frittered away by her son, also a betting man. Meanwhile, her widower, Fielding, was tricked into marrying a prostitute, before himself tricking the 64-year-old Duchess of Cleveland into a bigamous marriage.

It's hard to believe that Celia Fiennes knew nothing about these allegations and improprieties, and – assuming she did – would she really have wanted to be associated with the Purbecks? Perhaps she didn't believe the stories she'd heard. Or perhaps she felt they were none of her business.

And we may wonder, too, why, in her account of life at Tunbridge Wells, there's nothing comparable to what she said in the Introduction to her diaries, condemning 'laziness' in those women who pass 'tedious days' at a 'card or dice table'. The explanation may be that while she's content to offer general advice to her female peers on how they may improve their lives, she's not prepared to criticise a specific group, some of whom – like those at Tunbridge Wells – may be her friends or acquaintances. And we shouldn't forget that, exceptionally energetic as she is on her journeys, she herself takes a break every now and again to enjoy a pampered life at the luxurious home of some other aristocratic relative. There's nothing wrong with a holiday in Celia Fiennes' mind – so long as, in her case, there's plenty of hard work the rest of the time. But perhaps the most likely explanation for the objectivity of her account spa life is a loyalty to the upper class of which she's a member.

And so she's near the end of that summer's journey. She's clocked up an impressive tally of miles, counting trips she's done around the capital.

> *Add these to my Northern journey this year and that makes about 1,045 miles, of which I did not go above a hundred in the coach.*

That's a lot of miles side-saddle, an average of 15 miles a day, or if we take into account the many times she stayed at one spot for several days, in Harrogate or Hull for instance, then it's nearer 25 miles daily.

And so, as the weather turns colder and wetter in late autumn and the country roads become swamps, she settles into her London home for the winter. But Celia Fiennes being who she is, there's still a need to satisfy her boundless curiosity, now around the nation's capital. And the result for us is a no-holds-barred account of the brutal way that convicted criminals were punished in the late seventeenth century.

Interlude

JUSTICE, JAIL, THE NOOSE AND THE WHIP

His body is hung up in chains at a main cross-roads in view of all, to deter others.

Some parts of Celia Fiennes' diaries have a different tone from the pages where she writes about her travels around the country. They can seem less immediate. Not so much telling us what she witnesses at such-and-such a place on such-and-such a stage of her journey. They're more the result of observations over time. What she has to say in them, however, about life in the late seventeenth century is no less surprising, sometimes shocking even, to our twenty-first-century sensibilities. This is the case in her account of the punishments meted out to those found guilty in the law courts.

First, she tells us about the work of judges, juries and lawyers. She's critical of one of London's great courts of law, the Court of Chancery. This had jurisdiction over trusts, land law, the 'estates of lunatics', and the guardianship of infants. The court, she wrote:

> *... is so ill-managed that it admits of hearing, re-hearing over and over on the least motion of the contrary party, that will pretend to offer new reason for delaying judgment. By this, it accrues great advantage to the lawyers that have all their fees so continued many years, sometimes to the ruin of the plaintiffs and defendants.*

It was a problem not soon fixed. A century and a half later, delays in Chancery cases – often stretching for many years – were still the cause of such bitter complaint that in 1842 Charles Dickens made it one of the central themes of his novel *Bleak House*. 'Never can there come fog too thick,' he wrote, 'never can there come mud and mire too deep, to assort with the groping and floundering condition which this High Court of Chancery, most pestilent of hoary sinners, holds.'

When it comes to criminal justice, Fiennes reveals her admiration for the rights enjoyed by ordinary citizens. She gives special praise to the jury system.

> *Every free man of England comes, in due form of law, to demand his right to be heard by the judges and a jury of his own fellow subjects – his countrymen. They give their verdict in the matter as they think most just according to the statutes and laws. This jury are twelve men all sworn on the Bible solemnly to do justice, not out of fear, fraud or malice, favour or affection to injure any man.*

Her mention only of men jars with us today. But it's a reminder of the very limited role that women played in the judicial system – as in all public life – at the end of the seventeenth century. They certainly weren't allowed to be judges and lawyers, and women jurors would not be allowed to pass verdicts of guilty or innocent on an accused person for another 220 years. It was 1919 before they won that right, though it was another year after that before the plunge was taken and the first woman took her rightful place on the jury benches. On the receiving end of justice, however, women accused of a crime were brought to trial in Celia Fiennes' day alongside men, and to be fair to her, the terminology she chooses a little later is more gender neutral.

> *All persons are tried by those of their own rank, a commoner of England is tried by a jury of commoners.*

A verdict of guilty at the end of the seventeenth century was a promise of brutal and humiliating punishment, often to be witnessed by crowds of gloating fellow citizens. She writes:

> *The manner of criminals' punishment after condemnation, which, if it be for felony, is to be hanged. They are drawn in a cart from their prisons, where they had been confined all the time after they were taken, with their coffin tied to them and halters* [straps or ropes used for tethering horses] *about their necks.*

Over fifty offences, defined as felonies, were punishable by death. They ranged from murder, treason, rape, armed robbery and witchcraft to 'lying in wait with intent to put out an eye, disable the tongue or slit the nose'. The only relief in the otherwise merciless ritual of execution was the chance for a convicted felon to repent before a priest and so perhaps avoid the eternal fires of hell.

> *There is also a divine* [a priest] *that is always appointed to be with them in the prison to prepare them for their death by making them sensible of their crimes and all their sins, and to confess and repent of them. These do accompany them to the place of execution, which is generally through the City to a place appointed for it, called Tyburn. There, after they have prayed and spoken to the people, the minister does exhort them to repent.*

Tyburn was a small village just outside the western boundary of the City of London. The first execution there was recorded at the end of the twelfth century. By Celia Fiennes' time, a large, permanent gallows, known as 'Tyburn Tree', had been erected there with space for several hangings at the same time. There's no remnant of Tyburn today. The village has long since been swallowed up. The place of execution couldn't look more different, it's near the junction of Oxford Street and Park Lane, close to Marble Arch.

One of the big attractions for the huge crowds who flocked to Tyburn was to hear the accused's final words.

> *All at their execution have liberty to speak. And, in case they are sensible of and repent of their crimes, they do declare it and bewail it and warn others from doing the like. But if they are hardened, they persist in denying it to the last.*

She seems to discount the possibility that those who refuse to repent may have been wrongly convicted. If the condemned man confesses:

> *The executioner then desires the minister to pardon him.*

But none are spared the judgement of the court:

> *And so the halter is put on and he is cast off, being hung on a gibbet till dead. Then he is cut down and buried, unless it be for murder. Then usually his body is hung up in chains at a main crossroads in view of all, to deter others.*

It was often a long and painful death. Convicts didn't fall with a violent shock, so breaking their necks. Instead, they were left struggling at the end of the rope as they were slowly strangled. Sometimes, their friends and relatives speeded the end by clinging onto their legs and pulling them down. Hanging the corpse in chains in the case of murder, as she mentions, was more common in her day than at any other period. It was known as 'gibbeting'. The chains were in fact a loose iron cage in the rough shape of a human body. The mortal remains of the convicted killer, clasped in these irons, was suspended from a high wooden bracket somewhere prominent where it twisted and swayed in the wind, creaking and clanking, sometimes for years, as food for birds, maggots and insects, till only the bones were left rattling inside. The terror and shame of the condemned man's fate was meant to increase the deterrent effect of capital punishment.

A Hanging Day at 'Tyburn Tree'. (Wikimedia Commons)

And an execution without gibbeting was no guarantee of a dignified farewell either. If the body was not to be hung in chains, fights sometimes broke out over the corpse. On one side were thugs paid by surgeons who wanted to use it for teaching anatomy. On the other, were friends of the dead man, trying to take him away for burial.

Conviction for one class of serious crime meant an even more horrific prospect, with the brutality brought forward to while the condemned man was still alive.

> *For high treason they are drawn on a sledge* [rather like a piece of wooden fencing to which the condemned was tied while it was dragged along the road] *to their execution without any coffin. When hanged, they are taken down before quite dead, to be opened. They take out their heart and say, 'This is the heart of a traitor.' And so his body is cut in quarters and hung up on the top of the great gates of the City.*

To be hanged, drawn (that is to be cut open and have the heart or intestines pulled out) and quartered was rare when Fiennes was writing, though it didn't disappear completely in Britain until 1820.

Women convicted of treason suffered a different fate.

In case it's a woman which is a traitor, then she is condemned to be burnt.

Being burnt at the stake didn't always mean a slow, painful end as the flames consumed your flesh. If the culprit was lucky, she would lose consciousness as she was overcome by smoke, and often the executioner took pity on the woman and strangled her before lighting the fire. Burning at the stake was abolished in 1790 and was replaced by hanging, which by that stage involved a sharp drop and so a quick death.

Before she leaves the subject of the death penalty, Fiennes has one last category to mention: beheading. A quick death – provided the executioner was skilled – and a privilege for the upper classes. It was an altogether more dignified occasion.

If it be great persons and they obtain leave of the king, they may be beheaded, which is done on a scaffold erected on purpose in manner of a stage, and the persons brought in coaches with ministers. Then when they have ended their prayers and speech, they lay down their head on a block and stretch out their bodies. The executioner strikes off their heads with an axe or sword made on purpose. And such great persons, especially those that can pay well for it, have their heads sewed on again and so buried.

Reattaching the head afterwards wasn't usual. Charles I's corpse was reassembled like this in 1649, but it was more common to spear the head on a pike and display it on a bridge or at the gates of the city for all to see. In 1697, the very year in which we've just been following Celia Fiennes on her first great journey, Sir John Fenwick, a Jacobite rebel convicted of treason, was beheaded at Tower Hill. She notes:

> *The prison in London for great persons is the Tower, where are apartments for the purpose.*

The closeness of the prison to the execution site – both at the Tower of London – spared those of high rank the humiliation of a long final journey through jeering crowds. Fenwick was the last Englishman to be beheaded, but not the last person to suffer that fate. That honour – or shame – belonged to a Scot, another Jacobite, Lord Lovat on 9 April 1747, again at Tower Hill. Thousands came to watch him die, and when a wooden stand holding spectators collapsed, nine people were killed. It was said that Lord Lovat laughed.

For those convicted of lesser crimes, a different fate awaited.

> *There are in all the county towns, jails maintained at the public charge.*

There was one specialist variety of prison which she criticises as a soft option.

> *We have also prisons for debtors and some of which are privileged places, as the Kings Bench, the Marshalsea, and Fleet. Persons entering there cannot further be prosecuted. It's only for such as are debtors, and indeed it's a sad thing they should be so suffered* [tolerated] *and that there should be places of refuge for such.*

We often associate debtors' prisons with the nineteenth century, largely because Dickens wrote about the Marshalsea in several of his novels, and his spendthrift father spent several stretches there. But it's less well known that the institution thrived at the turn of the eighteenth century when Celia Fiennes was writing. Debtors held there who could afford to pay had access to a shop, a restaurant and even a bar, and could be allowed out during the day. But not all debtors were privileged in the way she indicates. If you didn't have any spare cash, you'd be crammed into a small room with dozens of others. A parliamentary committee in 1729 reported that 300 inmates had starved to death in the Marshalsea within a three-month period. It was demolished in the 1870s but go to Southwark just south of the Thames and you can still see a long brick wall there that once marked its boundary.

Another special category of prison meets more with her approval.

There are houses for correction of lesser faults, as Bridewell, to correct lazy and idle persons and to set them to work,

'Houses of correction' were places for the punishment and reform of the poor who'd been convicted of petty offences. The Bridewell, on the north bank of the Thames near Blackfriars Bridge was the first such institution, and by the late seventeenth century 'Bridewell' had become the generic name for such places. Among the offences that would land you inside, one was 'vagrancy', in other words rough sleeping – presumably those guilty of this were among Fiennes' 'lazy and idle persons'. Other crimes included 'nightwalking' (prostitution) and 'loose, idle and disorderly conduct' which could mean just about anything the City official, the beadle, didn't like. Over two-thirds of Bridewell prisoners were women, and most were single and had recently arrived in London. As well as being set to hard labour in the house of correction, many were whipped. The one consolation was that you'd probably be released within a few weeks. The theory was that a short, sharp shock might cure you of your idleness. Teaching you how to find honest work wasn't on the agenda.

But we must, as ever, be careful not to judge the practices of 320 years ago by the standards of today. Celia Fiennes' description

The Marshalsea Prison. (Edward Walford, 'Southwark: High Street' in *Old and New London: Volume 6* (London, 1878), pp. 57-75)

of the Bridewells' function – 'to correct lazy and idle persons and to set them to work' – is significant because it finds no fault with the system, and almost certainly implies approval. Her views about punishment were not extreme in the late seventeenth century and would have conformed to standard Puritan morality, which included the idea that hard work was a glory to God. Her own restlessness was testimony to that.

Punishment at this time was universally seen as having two functions: retribution, in other words judicially sanctioned vengeance, and deterrence, to instil fear in others who might contemplate crime. It was not until the 1770s that the idea of prison as a way to reform miscreants was recognised. Then came the beginnings of a new attitude that imprisonment and punishment might be used to change a convict from recalcitrant criminal to productive citizen. However, back in 1697, respectable members of society still usually condemned idleness. Those who mended their ways but stayed poor might be helped by a suitable charitable foundation. Then, if they were young and fit, they'd be set to some gruelling work in return for subsistence food. It was stick and no carrot.

And 'stick' is the right word, as she goes on to explain:

> *There are also stocks and pillories to punish them for their lesser faults. The pillory indeed is to punish perjured persons, which is a great crime. There is also whipping, some at a cart's tail.*

Both the pillory and the stocks were similar in the way that the convict's wrists and neck were locked in a wooden frame. The difference was that in the stocks, prisoners were seated, whereas in the pillory they were forced to stand. Both were set up in a busy street or open space, where crowds could gather. The offender would be pelted with rotten eggs and vegetables, bloodied offcuts from slaughterhouses, dead cats, mud, excrement, bricks and stones. It was not unknown for the culprit to be killed. Whipping involved being stripped to the waist and flogged as the offender was dragged along the street behind a cart 'until his' (or it could be her) 'back be bloody.'

To us today, Celia Fiennes' account of punishment might conjure up pictures of widespread state-controlled brutality. It's certainly true that if you were convicted of any one of fifty-odd crimes in 1697, public execution was the sentence. And if you committed lesser crimes, you could be whipped, pilloried or abused in a house of correction. However, that's far from the complete picture. None of these punishments was certain.

The Bridewell Prison. It had been rebuilt after the 1666 Great Fire of London. (Wikimedia Commons)

For a start, your chances of being caught were low. It's likely there was widespread violence and disorder at this time, hidden away in the woods and in the garrets and slums of the cities, which never reached the attention of the courts, so the perpetrators got off scot-free. There was nothing resembling a police force – that would have to wait another 130 years – to detect and arrest wrongdoers. Investigation and arrest – such as they were – was down to parish constables or so-called 'peace officers', who were poorly paid, corrupt men appointed by local justices of the peace or magistrates.

And then too there was little resembling public prosecutors. Victims often had to take the law into their own hands and try to bring a prosecution themselves. And how many would have the skill and determination to do that?

Then, even if you were apprehended and found guilty before the courts, there were still ways of wriggling out of due punishment. There were loopholes in the law that allowed many convicted of murder, other felonies and misdemeanours to escape judgement.

You could for instance claim 'benefit of clergy', a hangover from medieval times by which members of the Church convicted in a lay court then had to be handed over to the ecclesiastical authorities for punishment. The Church didn't allow 'spilling of blood', and murderous priests often suffered nothing more serious than being defrocked, sacked from the priesthood in other words. Over the centuries, some citizens with little connection to the Church also successfully started using benefit of clergy as a get-out. Celia Fiennes makes one reference in passing to this practice.

> *The spiritual courts and men will not pretend* [lay claim] *to use the sword of punishment ... They have left* [abandoned] *punishing the enormous crimes of their parishioners, nay of their clergy also.*

Because in earlier centuries it was only those in holy orders who were literate, anyone claiming benefit of clergy was required to read a passage from the Bible, usually from the 51st Psalm, which became known as the 'neck verse' since it could save you from hanging. But by Celia Fiennes' day, literacy levels had risen in the general population, so that many – though not the most disadvantaged, of course, who couldn't read – were able to evade the harshest punishments. The loophole continued in some form up to the 1820s. Why? It may have been a tacit recognition of the disproportionately cruel punishments available to judges. Or it may simply reflect the power of the Church. However, practices were introduced to cut down on its use. Thus, claiming benefit of clergy was often limited to first-time offenders. This, as she explains, was achieved by branding them.

> *For some crimes they are burnt in the hand or cheek as a brand of their evil, and if found again to transgress, that mark serves as a greater witness to their condemnation.*

The branding – a 'T' for theft, 'F' for felony or 'M' for murder – was carried out in the court itself at the end of the trial.

Benefit of clergy was not a men-only rule. A law passed in the early seventeenth century allowed women to take advantage of it, even though the concept of women priests was centuries off in the future. And a convicted woman might also be able to shelter behind another shield. If she was sentenced to death, she could claim she was pregnant, she could 'plead her belly'. She was then examined by what was called a Jury of Matrons, made up of women present in the court room. If she was found to be 'quick with child', i.e. if the movement of a foetus was detected, the Jury of Matrons could delay her punishment till after the child was born. Often then sympathy for the new baby meant the mother was pardoned.

The loopholes provided by benefit of clergy were also partly responsible for the growth of an alternative form of punishment: penal transportation. This was a combination of free enterprise and banishment. Merchants or ship-owners would choose those prisoners they thought they could sell as 'indentured servants' in the new American colonies, and they paid the cost of shipping them out there. The money they received on sale of the prisoners covered the shippers' outlay and left them with a profit. That changed with laws passed in 1718 and 1720, when the government began to pay the merchants to deliver the convicts to the colonies.

The result of these get-out rules meant that public executions were nothing like as common as they might have been. For instance, in London during the thirty years up to 1690, on average twenty-one convicts were hanged per year. Every few months there would be a 'hanging day' when typically half a dozen condemned prisoners were put through the humiliation and agony described by Celia Fiennes. Twenty-one executions a year out of a population in London at the time of half a million was not a large number when we consider the long list of capital offences.

It's often been suggested that the late seventeenth and early eighteenth centuries were a time of unprecedented violence, disorder and theft on the streets and byways of England, given that many were getting away with their crimes unpunished. Is that true?

There was certainly something of a crime wave during the 1690s, when Celia Fiennes was writing. For a start, during that decade the average number of executions in the capital rose from twenty-one to thirty-three per year. And there was a surge, for instance, in the number of robberies. It was a time of economic depression – caused by a series of poor harvests and disruption to trade during a Europe-wide war – and this may have pushed many of the poor into crime. Records also show a slight rise in the number of murders in London up from seventeen per year during the 1660s and 1670s to twenty-one annual homicides in the capital during the 1680s and 1690s. That's around 4.2 murders each year per 100,000 population, high by today's standards when the comparable figure is 1.2 homicides annually for every 100,000 people.

What we do know is that the government during the 1690s was sufficiently worried about the number of robberies to pass laws aimed at catching more offenders in the net of execution. A statute of May 1699 – the year after Fiennes' second great journey – made housebreaking and the theft of goods worth more than 5*s* (around £200 in today's money) from shops, warehouses, coach houses and stables a hanging offence. Did it have much impact? Between 1700 and 1710, the number of executions in London actually plummeted from thirty-three per year to eleven, a puzzling figure given that there were now so many more crimes for which you could be executed. At the same time, the average annual number of recorded murders in the capital after the new law came in also fell dramatically from twenty-one per year to eleven, which incidentally is around two per 100,000, hardly a tsunami of violence. Compare it with the USA's most violent city, St Louis, Missouri which in 2019 recorded 64.9 homicides per 100,000!

Does that mean the harsh new laws were at last deterring potential criminals from acts of violence? Or is there some other explanation? For instance, that the economy picked up, and fewer people were driven to a life of crime. But in all the figures we've just looked at, we can't ignore the ever-present fact that many crimes must have gone unreported. Corruption of officials, fear by victims, no police officers to bring perpetrators to court, wide legal loopholes favouring convicts, and faulty record keeping all playing their part. The true crime figures for the 1690s – as for all decades in this period – are likely to have been higher. But whether that means it was a time when crime was out of control is an unknown about which we can only speculate.

During her 1697–98 winter in London, Celia Fiennes must have known that she'd been lucky the previous summer not to have encountered armed criminals herself, out there on remote tracks in parts of the country where she was a stranger. Her luck would change during her next great journey.

Above left: Celia Fiennes' grandfather, William, 8th Lord Saye and Sele, a leading Parliamentarian during the Civil War. (From Broughton Castle, by permission of Martin Fiennes)

Above right: Her father, Nathaniel, a colonel in the Parliamentary army during the Civil War. Like his father, not an extremist for that cause. He died when Celia was 7 years old. She inherited the family's Puritan faith, though her attitude to the world was more liberal than her father's. (From Broughton Castle, by permission of Martin Fiennes)

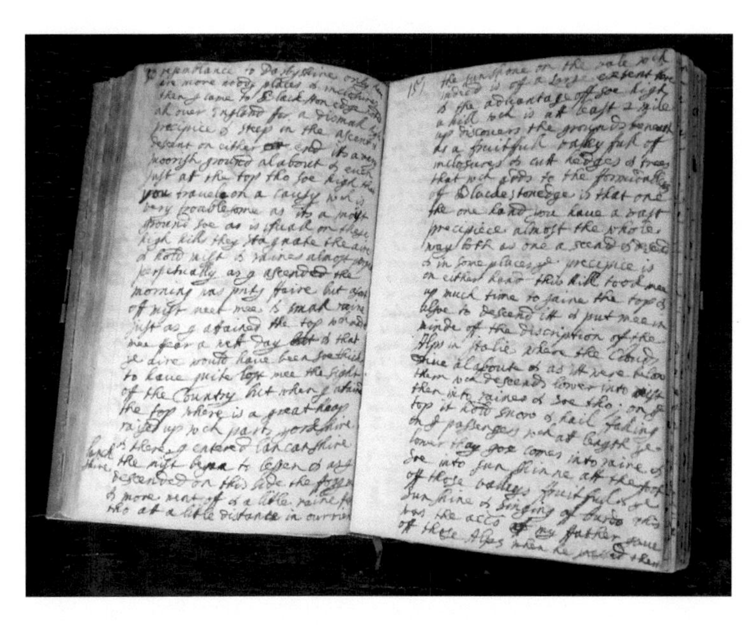

Celia Fiennes' diary in her own handwriting, now on public display at Broughton Castle, the Fiennes ancestral home. (From Broughton Castle, by permission of Martin Fiennes)

Riding side-saddle could look elegant enough in a long, flared skirt, as this painting by George Stubbs of the Countess of Coningsby shows. (Yale Center for British Art)

However, beneath the elegance, side-saddlers – as well as being uncomfortable on a long journey – could find themselves in a precarious position. Here, the rider seems to be strapped in place. But if the horse fell, she could end up beneath the animal with no chance of being thrown clear. (Wikimedia Commons)

St Robert's cave at the Knaresborough spa in Yorkshire. 'There is a little chapel cut out of the rock and arched and carved with figures of saints.' (From Roy's Blog)

'Kitchen scene' by an anonymous seventeenth-century artist. The proud chef is showing off delicious-looking meat, fish, fowl and cheese. As we discover from Celia Fiennes, vegetables were rarely on the menu except for the poor, who couldn't afford any better. (Rijksmuseum, Amsterdam)

While in Hull, she records, 'I was on board a new man-of-war… called the "*Kingston*"'. The ship can be seen in this painting by Samuel Scott (on the immediate right of the main vessel in the foreground) during an engagement off Cartagena eleven years after Celia Fiennes walked its decks. (Wikimedia Commons)

When she visits Chatsworth House in Derbyshire, the neoclassical façade is still under construction. 'It is formed with several large stone pillars carved.' (Public Domain, Rferroni2000)

As this seventeenth-century portrait shows, children from the high ranks of society in Celia Fiennes' time were expected to look and behave like miniature adults. Play or any kind of fun was not acceptable outside the nursery. (Public Domain)

Most coffee houses were for men only. They were where the latest political, philosophical and religious ideas were thrashed out, and the latest news could be picked up. Here the hostess is a woman, as was often the case. Note the mildly suggestive picture over the fireplace. (Wikimedia Commons)

Crowds at Tyburn gathering to witness the latest execution by hanging. Cartoon by William Hogarth, 1747. (Public Domain)

London's Monument to the Great Fire of 1666. 'This was set up in memory of God putting a check to the raging flame, which by the plots and contrivance of the Papists was lighted.' The belief that it was the result of arson by Catholics persisted for over a century after Fiennes' day. (Public Domain, Eluveitie)

Inside a tavern in the mid-seventeenth century, by David Teniers. 'Men, women and children all have their pipes of tobacco in their mouths, and so sit round the fire smoking, which was not delightful to me when I went down to talk with my landlady.' (Wikimedia Commons)

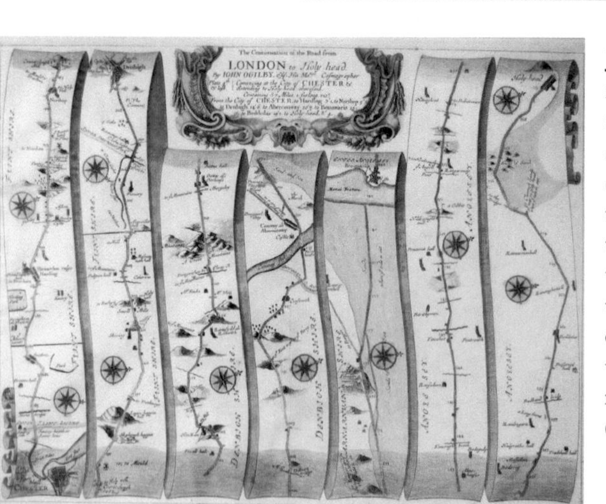

John Ogilby's strip maps, developed in the 1670s, at the time were a breakthrough in the detailed information they provided for the traveller. But they would have been of no use to Celia Fiennes on the many occasions when she left the main road to explore. (Wikimedia Commons)

In the pre-Romantic Baroque age, painters – like Nicolas Poussin above – sometimes relegated the natural world to little more than a backdrop to their main theme. In the same spirit, Celia Fiennes despised the 'inaccessible high rocky barren hills which hang over one's head in some places and appear very terrible'. (Art Institute of Chicago)

In Manchester she observes a 'weather glass'. The early barometer – seen here in 1690 behind its inventor Robert Hooke – was the earliest aid to more scientific weather forecasting. (Wikimedia Commons)

Here Claude Du Vall, who more than all others was responsible for the romantic image of the gentleman highwayman, is shown courting his lady victim. The artist, William Powell Frith, contrasts him in the painting with more thuggish robbers. The highwaymen Celia Fiennes encountered were in this latter category. (Wikimedia Commons)

The closest there is to a statue of Celia Fiennes. It's at No Man's Heath in Cheshire near where she was harassed by the two highwaymen. The monument was commissioned by local people in 1998 to commemorate the 300th anniversary of her visit here. (By kind permission of Ruth Shackleton)

'The fine and only thing in Plymouth town is the Citadel or Castle which stands very high above the town.' In this contemporary painting by Hendrik Danckerts, Cornwall lies across the estuary to the right. (Yale Center for British Art)

Her Second Great Journey 1698

1

To Ely then Westward (Part 1)

BEDS FOR THE NIGHT

I had frogs and slow worms and snails in my room.

There's one major city in all of England that Celia Fiennes knows well but tells us little about. Whereas she goes into detail about Hull, Nottingham, Tunbridge Wells and many other towns, there's another that we might have expected her to describe, criticise and praise as she does the others. That's the place where she lives: London itself. Not that she neglects it completely in her diaries. She doesn't. But she's very selective in the verbal pictures she paints for us of the small number of the capital's famous landmarks. Perhaps she felt that her readers would be familiar with London, so she need devote only a minimum of words to it. But the result is that we don't even know where exactly in the city she'd made her home. In recounting the start of what she describes as her 'Great Journey to Newcastle and to Cornwall' in 1698, all she says is 'From London to Albyns [a manor house near Romford] in Essex'.

Some detective work is needed. We know that on the death of her mother in 1691, she moved out of the family house in Newton Toney in Wiltshire and settled in the capital. That was where her sister, Mary, lived and it's probable that Celia either moved in with her, or else took a house near to her. The closest that she herself pinpoints the area is to tell us that it's 2 miles east of Kensington. That would put her in the square mile of the City of London itself, rather than, for instance, in Westminster, which by the 1690s was being absorbed into what we would call 'Greater London'. She herself observes in her diary:

> *London is joined with Westminster, which are two great cities.*

There are just four buildings in London that she describes. So let's start by looking at them for clues. She begins by telling us about:

> *… the Royal Exchange, a large space of ground enclosed around with cloisters and open arches where are built many walks and shops of all trades. The middle space below was designed and is used for the merchants to meet and to concert* [arrange by mutual agreement] *their business and trade and bills.*

As we've already remarked, her sister, Mary, had married a merchant, Edmund Harrison and they lived in London. He may well have wanted a home within a short walk of where he could do business with his fellow merchants at the Exchange. So, on the likely assumption that Celia would want to be close to her sister, somewhere near here might be the most likely spot for her home.

Can we be any more precise? Is there a clue in the other three London sites she chooses to tell us about?

The next one is the stone tower – known to this day as 'The Monument' – that commemorates the 1666 Great Fire of London, which had destroyed an estimated 13,000 homes and made around 70,000 Londoners homeless.

> *There is also a great monument of stonework. This is of a great height, 300 steps up, and on the top gives a view of the whole town. This was set up in memory of God putting a check to the raging flame, which by the plots and contrivance of the Papists was lighted.*

The extraordinary belief that Catholic activists deliberately started the Great Fire was widely believed in Celia Fiennes' time. She goes on to say:

> *There is a large inscription on it all around mentioning it.*

This inscription, which was not removed until 1830, read, 'Here by the permission of Heaven, Hell broke loose upon this Protestant city from the malicious hearts of barbarous Papists, by the hand of their agent Hubert, who confessed.' A parliamentary committee was even set up to look into the claim, and dismissed as 'very frivolous' the idea that Catholics had started the Great Fire. To no avail. Many Londoners still held it to be true.

The next site she mentions is only a stone's throw away, London Bridge, and she paints a picture of a structure very different from the one we know today.

> *The bridge is a stately building, all stone with 18 arches, most of them big enough to admit a large barge to pass. The bridge is so broad that two coaches drive abreast, and there are on each side houses and shops, just like any large street in the City.*

Finally, she mentions St Paul's Cathedral, still being rebuilt after the Great Fire. It was the most famous building in the City and no description of the capital would have been complete without it, so we might discount it as of no significance in our investigation.

But why – among all the other notable places she could have told us about in London – did she choose the Monument and London Bridge? Was it because she knew them well, perhaps because they were on her doorstep and were her local favourites? What adds strength to this theory is that the area around the Monument and the northern end of London Bridge is no more than 300yds from the Royal Exchange, so might well have been the spot where Celia Fiennes' brother-in-law, Edmund, would choose to live, close to his work.

1688 Map of London. 'Royal Exchange' [1], 'The Monument' [2], 'London Bridge' [3] and 'Laurence Pountney Hill' [4]. (Wikimedia Commons)

The next question is: are there still any seventeenth-century merchants' houses near the Monument?

Time to take a look.

I leave the car at a friends' house in Finchley, take the tube to Monument Station, and emerge into the daylight of London's financial district. There, across Canon Street, several narrow alleyways lead south towards the Thames. A street sign names the first of them as Laurence Pountney Hill. At no more than 8ft wide, it's just the sort of slender passageway we'd expect a seventeenth-century

London street to have morphed into. I've barely passed the marble and glass façade of the Bank of China on the corner before 50yds ahead appear white stucco and purple-red walls with long, square windows and what look like a couple of stone pillars, all typical of early neoclassical domestic architecture. A few yards down are two black gleaming doors, framed by intricately carved stonework with foliage and lions' heads. They're capped by stone hoods depicting cherubs who seem to be playing bowls. If we were to describe seventeenth-century merchants' houses, this is pretty much what they'd look like.

There's a date carved over the left door: 1703. A little bit late for the start of her 1698 journey. But still, it does show that this is the area where rich merchants settled in that period. And after all, much as we'd love to, we're not likely to find the exact house where she or her sister lived.

A few steps further on, there's a small square, and through the trees on the left, an even grander house – again a mix of stucco and brick with long, square windows. Its four storeys and small garden at the front are fenced by iron railings. It's crammed between two unbeautiful towering, modern walls, a defiant old lady jostled by giant thugs.

I press the bell outside its iron gate. There's no reply. But a quick smartphone search reveals that the house nowadays is 'enjoyed as a spectacular private residence, with the owner's City office just a short walk away'. Perfect then too for Celia's brother-in-law. Like many houses around here in the seventeenth century, it had been destroyed in the Great Fire of 1666, but ten years later it had been rebuilt pretty much in the form we see today. In the late 1690s, when Celia Fiennes set off, it belonged to a Samuel Clay, described as a 'gentleman merchant'. So though it wasn't where she or her sister lived, it is further evidence that this was the district favoured by successful merchants like Celia Fiennes' brother-in-law, and we may safely content ourselves with the thought her London home may well have been close to here.

Merchants' houses on Laurence Pountney Hill. (Public Domain)

We can't be sure of course. But if we picture her riding up the narrow thoroughfare of Laurence Pountney Hill on that morning in May 1698 when she started out on the second of her long journeys, the image won't be too inaccurate. And perhaps too, as she passed the elegant residences here, she might have allowed herself an inner smile of satisfaction that, unlike their female occupants, she would not be wasting her time in idle conversation over the card table, but instead would be exploring her country to its every extreme.

It's going to be a long trip this year. Her 1,100-mile expedition of the previous summer must have been a joy to her. Now she wants to be even more ambitious. She's 35 years old. There's no time to waste.

She sets off from her London home almost certainly in the month of May. Her route takes her north-east to Colchester, then parallel to the coast as far as Ipswich before turning inland to Norwich and Ely. The marsh lands here are especially treacherous.

> *The fens are full of water and mud. It's mostly low moorish ground on each side, defended by fen-dykes* [they're called 'dykes' to this day in eastern England], *which are deep ditches with drains.*

Ely itself is on an island and could be reached only across a causeway. As she discovers, it takes only a day or two's wet weather even in the warmer months to make the approach road very dangerous indeed.

> *The rains now had fallen so that in some places near the city the causeway was covered. And a remarkable deliverance I had. My horse, earnest to drink, ran to get more depth of water than the causeway had, for it was on the brink of one of these dykes. But – by a special providence which I desire never to forget and always to be thankful for – he escaped.*

We should not imagine that her thanks to the Almighty for saving her at Ely was mere ritual. Remember, it's almost certain that, like almost all her contemporaries, she couldn't swim. We can appreciate that the hand of Providence was much helped by Celia Fiennes' own skill as rider. And, as we'll discover later, the moment would come when neither skill nor Providence could keep her safe.

Ely, though no more than a small town according to the size of its population, is officially a city because of its cathedral, and its unusual architecture grabs her attention on arrival here. She stops and climbs to the top of its highest tower.

> *Ely Minster is a curious pile of building all of stone, the outside full of carvings and great arches and fine pillars in the front. When I was upon the tower, I could see Cambridge* [15 miles away] *and a great prospect of the country which by reason of the great rains just before was under water.*

You can still today see the spires and rooves of Ely's cathedral from all around the city, and I too make for it to get a closer inspection. It's an extraordinary sight. It looks like a fairy-tale castle – its towers tall and thin like arms raised in horror, with mournful, gaping niches and windows beneath Disneyesque castellations from which once a weeping maiden surveyed the land as she awaited the return of her heroic lover. Except of course it's a place of worship.

I'm staying for the night at the nearby Poets House Hotel. Perhaps its name was what set off my flight of fancy about the cathedral, or maybe the sight of the fairy-tale towers is what attracted a poet to this place that's now a hotel.

'Hotel' – in the twenty-first century, we never give the word a second thought. It's as embedded in the language as 'house' or 'office'. It's unlikely that Celia Fiennes had ever heard the word. It didn't make an appearance in the English language until seventy-two years after her 1698 journey. We owe its arrival here to a French school master named Pierre Berlon, who managed an assembly room in the High Street at Exeter. Monsieur Berlon was smart when it came to PR. In 1768 he put an ad in a local paper announcing that he had 'lately fitted lodgings, for the conveniency of those Gentlemen and Ladies who are pleased to honour him with their favours'. In 1770 he went one step further, describing his business as a 'New Coffee-house, Inn, and Tavern, Or, The Hôtel, In St. Peter's Church-yard, Exeter'. No doubt he felt that the Frenchness of the word would make the place sound exotic and refined, somewhere you might bump into the occasional *duc* or *comtesse*. He was right. Hôtels rapidly became popular, then lost their circumflex accent, and became commonplace until today when, whether your style is Claridge's or a Travelodge, your Google search is likely to start with a click on the word 'hotel'.

The words we use are powerful. They can tell us a lot about society. There were no hotels, nor even hôtels, for Celia Fiennes to stay at in 1698. The 'Gentlemen and Ladies' that Monsieur Berlon would later target with his ads were not yet doing much travelling around the country. Other than in spa towns, there was little demand for refined lodgings.

When she dismounts from her side-saddle in Ely after slogging her way through the fens, marshes and floods of East Anglia, almost anywhere – hotel or not – would have been better than where she ends up. Her lodgings for the night are a horror.

> *Though my chamber was near 20 steps up, I had frogs and slow worms and snails in my room, and suppose they were brought up with the faggots* [firewood]. *But it cannot but be infested with all such things, being altogether moorish, fenny ground which lies low.*

It's one of the worst overnight stops she has to suffer, and there are many more with varied inconveniences. In the Lake District, as we'll see shortly, she feels she's being ripped off.

> *My landlady ran me up the largest reckoning for almost nothing.*

Elsewhere the problem is more basic, and – we might think – more dangerous.

> *No sleep could I get, they burning turf, and their chimneys are sort of flues or open tunnels, so that the smoke does annoy the rooms.*

Sometimes the establishment's management are just plain neglectful – of Celia Fiennes' needs anyway. In Carlisle:

> *though I was in the biggest house in town, I was in the worst accommodation, and so found it, and a young giddy landlady that could only dress fine and entertain the soldiers.*

As she moves on west from Ely and reaches Derbyshire, she encounters a new category of discomfort. After a day labouring up and down steep hills, she stays at what was called an 'Entertaining House', where if you buy a meal, you get a bed for the night thrown in for free. Sounds like a good deal. However:

> *The beer they allow at the meals is so bad that very little can be drank. You pay not for your bedroom, and truly the other* [i.e. the food and drink] *is so unreasonable a price and the lodgings so bad, 2 beds in a room, some 3 beds and 4 in one room, so that if you have not company enough of your own to fill a room, they will be ready to put others into the same chamber, and sometimes they are so crowded that three must lie in a bed.*

And if that's not bad enough, in the same county she complains she can't get a good night's sleep.

> *There is no peace nor quiet with one company and another going into the bath or coming out.*

Of course, not all inns were unhealthy, noisy or over-priced. As we've seen, it could be fine food and uplifting conversation, or, at Bath for instance, she gives her lodgings five stars with the comment, 'They give you very good attendance'. But she never knows what to expect when she walks through the inn door.

However, not every overnight stay was fraught with uncertainty. Celia Fiennes has one very valuable ticket in her pocket that she can occasionally use to get an upgrade. That ticket was the Fiennes name. Her aristocratic status could sometimes give her an advantage that the average traveller could only dream of, and who can blame her for taking advantage of it?

As she crosses from Derbyshire to Staffordshire, she's about to call in at what may well have been her favourite house outside of her own home in London – to see someone with whom she must have had a close relationship.

> *Thence I went to Wolseley, 7 miles farther, to Sir Charles Wolseley, where I staid 6 weeks, it being my aunt, his Lady, who engaged my stay.*

We can almost hear her sigh of relief.

> *His seat stands very finely by the River Trent. There is also a moat almost round the house. The house is an old timber building, but with a large parlour and noble staircase with handsome chambers Sir Charles has new built.*

Sir Charles Wolseley, like many leading figures of the seventeenth century, had led a dramatic life. He grew up in a household that was strongly Royalist – his father, Robert, who'd been made a baronet by Charles I in 1628, fought on the king's side during the Civil War. Charles Wolseley, his eldest son, however, swung the other way. In 1648 at the age of 18, he married Anne Fiennes, the youngest daughter of Celia's grandfather, William Lord Saye and Sele. He could hardly have joined a family that was more strongly Parliamentarian. Following the execution of the king in 1649 and the Parliamentarian victory in the Civil War, Charles was unremitting in his praise for the victor who now ruled the land in place of a king. He wrote of Oliver Cromwell, that his 'personal worth … qualifies him for the greatest monarch in the world', and he was rewarded by being appointed to the Council of State. He served as an MP for Staffordshire and was then raised to the newly created Upper House. When the monarchy was restored in 1660, he faced the prospect of ruin, humiliation or worse. However, he managed to get a pardon from the new king, then retired from public life, and took up gardening.

During the weeks she spent with the family, Celia Fiennes explores the result of his retirement labours, and finds a personal connection.

> *There are green spaces and a fine green bank with box or philteroy* [possibly philodendron] *hedge cut round. There are fine flowers, tuber roses white and yellow. There was a fine senna tree that bears a great branch of yellow flowers* [probably the Golden Senna, also known as the Scrambled Egg Tree]. *There are several walks, one shady with high trees, which my aunt told me my mother liked to walk in, and so it was called her walk.*

The upheavals and strains in Sir Charles Wolseley's life were not entirely supplanted by his innocent love of spectacular-coloured flowers. In 1685, royal officials arrived at his gate and arrested him. He was accused of complicity in the Monmouth Rebellion, the uprising in the West Country aimed at overthrowing the king. He was interrogated, before being released. But more trouble was on the way.

His marriage to Celia's aunt, Anne Fiennes, had produced no fewer than seventeen children, ten daughters and seven sons. The eldest, Robert, who considered himself a poet, fought a duel in 1687 over what was described as a 'poetical quarrel'. He shot his opponent William Wharton in the thigh and Wharton died eight days later from the resulting infection. Robert was charged with murder and fled across the Channel. Six months later, royal agents pronounced that Sir Charles had now 'declared himself right and ready to serve his majesty in any capacity'. It seems he was now happy to go on record with whatever was needed for a peaceful family life. It was no coincidence that his son, Robert was then pardoned and returned to England.

Celia Fiennes clearly enjoys herself at the Wolseley family home.

> *There is a large lofty hall in the old fashion, a dining and drawing rooms on the one hand, and a little parlour on the other. The best rooms were newer, built with chambers over them, and a very good staircase well-wainscoted and carved with good pictures.*

And she finds herself taken around to call on other leading families in the local area.

> *This country is much for entertainments. In every house you must eat and drink.*

She even goes to the races.

> *Another day I went to Penkridge races over at Cannock Wood 7 miles, where were most of the gentlemen and ladies of the country, several coaches and six horses. There appeared only one horse to run for the plate which was a salver.*

It's not clear whether she means there was only one horse competing, or that only one horse stood any chance of winning. The old tradition had been to present the winner with a small bell. But the new practice was to award a silver plate, which was considered a more suitable trophy to decorate the mantlepiece of the triumphant owner.

All this entertainment – dare we say 'fun'? – is more evidence that energetic as Celia Fiennes is, she not above taking a break, and a not too Puritanical break at that. Sport – especially the races – would have been seen as wasteful wickedness by the more extreme members of her faith.

But her curiosity about the world beyond her upper-class circle can't be supressed for long. On one of her day trips out from her aunt and uncle's home, again at Cannock Wood, she observes a surprising crop – fern.

> *When it is at its maturity, which happens just before harvest or hay time, the whole country are employed in cutting it up and burning it in heaps for the sake of the ashes, which they make fine and roll up in balls. And so they sell them, or use them all the year for washing and scouring, and send much up to London.*

The ashes produced a strong alkali, used as a bleach, as well as potash which was an ingredient in soap-making. Soap, by the way, is mentioned only twice by her, once when it fails to do its job as a cleanser, and once when she sees it mixed with urine to treat wool.

And her investigations are not confined to the countryside. On one of her trips out from Wolseley to another grand house, the Earl of Chesterfield's Bretby Hall in Derbyshire, there seems to be a bit of tax avoidance going on.

> *I was in several bedchambers. One had a crimson damask bed, the other crimson velvet: this best was the bridal chamber which used to be called the Silver Room. When plate* [silverware] *was in nomination to pay a tax, the Earl of Chesterfield sold all the plate of the house, so that when the table was spread, I saw only spoons, salts and forks, but no plates or dishes and but few salvers.*

But the call of the road isn't far away. There's just time for one last bit of refreshment.

> *Then I returned into the hall and so into a cool room, in which was a fountain and where I drank a glass of wine, and so proceeded.*

She's taken us from the frog-ridden filth of Ely to the crimson damask bedspreads of Bretby.

But before we move on from this stage of her Great Journey, we're going to pause and investigate something which we today all know too much about. The physical health – or otherwise – of the nation. The word 'pandemic', which for us has become almost as commonplace in our language as 'tea' and 'biscuits', was unknown in Celia Fiennes' time. But deadly afflictions themselves were not. There were scores of such killers – many with names which we in turn don't recognise today.

2

To Ely then Westward (Part 2)

PANDEMICS

One of my sisters that died
at my grandmother's there of the smallpox

Today, when we worship cleanliness, when sanitiser and disinfectant have become our demi-gods, and handwashing, social distancing and sneezing into our elbows are the new rituals, it's hard to imagine life – and death – at the end of the seventeenth century. It was a time before anyone knew that we share our world with billions of tiny creatures we can't see, microscopic viruses and bacteria, many of which are hell-bent on making us ill or killing us. It would be centuries before these little murderers would come to light, and before any effective way would be devised to stop them doing their worst.

What, then, did people in Celia Fiennes' day believe caused disease? And beyond that, what did they think might protect them? In an age before provable, scientific evidence was available, the answers varied. Puritan Dissenters, for instance, held a wide variety of beliefs. Some preached that sickness and suffering were God's way of punishing humans for the original sin of Adam and Eve. Others believed more directly that those who contracted disease and came to an early death were being punished by God for their own misdeeds. A less severe belief was that suffering and illness were spiritually beneficial – they made humans humble and, above all, aware of their past sins. A common view, however, was that the body, which was vulnerable to sickness and death, was inferior to the soul, which was divine and immortal and destined to unite itself with God in Heaven after death.

The more practical theory – widely held to be true – was that illness was bred by what were called 'miasmas', meaning gases or foul air. We might think that this tallies with our own knowledge that respiratory infections – such as Covid-19 – are spread by droplets in the air, what we've learned to call aerosols, breathed out by people who've contracted the disease. But that wasn't so. In the seventeenth century, 'miasma' was a general term for any bad smell, whether from rotting food or sulphurous marshland.

So where does Celia Fiennes stand in this debate about the cause of disease? She doesn't discuss it directly, but before she leaves the city of Ely, she does hint at a theory. Ely, she says, is:

> ... *the dirtiest place I ever saw. It's a perfect quagmire, the whole city. Only just about the palace and churches, the streets are well enough for breadth. But for want of pitching* [paving], *they seem only a harbour to breed and nest vermin, of which there are plenty enough.*

She rages against the filth she finds there.

> *It is true, were the least care taken to pitch their streets, it would make the place look more properly a habitation for human beings, and not a cage or nest of unclean creatures. It must needs be very unhealthy, though the natives say much to the contrary, which proceeds from custom and use. Otherwise, to persons born in dry countries, it must destroy them, like rotten sheep, in consumptions and rheums* [tuberculosis, and any kind of cold or chest infection].

On the face of it here, she seems to be saying it's healthy to be clean. Ely is 'the dirtiest place I ever saw' and she adds, 'It must needs be very unhealthy'. We shouldn't jump to the conclusion however that she was somehow anticipating the lesson of the Covid crisis that frequent handwashing hinders the spread of infection. She was probably stating no more than a variation of the obvious: that drinking filthy water, deliberately or accidentally, is likely to make you ill. At the same time, her words are probably an echo of the miasma theory of disease. She condemns Ely's dirt as 'very unhealthy', because it encourages 'vermin'. There would undoubtedly have been rat and mouse droppings in the dirt, which ties in with the belief that one of the sources of the miasmas was human and animal waste.

But it's perhaps surprising that she complains so much about Ely and rarely makes similar criticisms of other towns and cities. After all, apart from walking or the occasional sedan chair, there was only one source of transport power – horses. Thousands of them, all leaving their offensive trademarks in the street alongside open sewers full of human waste and butchers' offal. That state of affairs was the norm in England's growing cities. So it's a puzzle that she doesn't put other towns in the same low cleanliness rank as Ely.

She certainly seems to value keeping herself clean – as did others of her social rank. As we saw, when she visited Chatsworth House in Derbyshire, it had a newly constructed marble bath.

> *It was deep as one's middle on the outside, and you went down steps into the bath, big enough for two people.*

And it wasn't just for the upper classes, as we heard at her lodgings in that same county.

> *There is no peace nor quiet with one company and another going into the bath or coming out. It's what makes so many strive to be in this house because the bath is in it.*

It seems there was a vague idea around at this time that there was a connection between washing your body and staying healthy. As we've already seen, Celia Fiennes – like so many of her social status at that time – valued the water of spas to keep herself healthy, not only by drinking it, but often by bathing in it. Time after time she praises the water for warding off and curing illness and other bodily disorders.

Personal hygiene had long been regarded as a worthy habit – though it had little to do with staying healthy. Apart from the obvious reason for washing yourself at least among the upper classes (i.e. that otherwise friends would turn their noses up at you and tell you to go away), cleanliness was also said to be ordained from Heaven. In 1605, Sir Francis Bacon wrote, 'Cleanness of body was ever deemed to proceed from a due reverence to God.' In Celia Fiennes' day, some Puritans taught that a clean body was the hallmark of morality, of respectability. It's pretty obvious where that idea came from. Someone with dirty face and filthy clothes was untrustworthy, might be about to beat and rob you, and was of the lowest class. Then later, in 1778, the Methodist John Wesley first preached what became a famous saying: 'Cleanliness is next to Godliness.' Until the nineteenth century then, it seems personal hygiene had a stronger connection to a righteous way of life than to halting the spread of disease.

One of the biggest puzzles in reading Celia Fiennes' diaries is how little she has to say about the reverse side of good health, about the cruel impact of sickness and disease on people high and low. She lived in an age when illness was rampant and 10 per cent or more of the population died every year from some affliction or other. Today that figure averages less than 1 per cent.

One of her few mentions of sickness concerns her own family. On a visit to Reading, she tours several churches.

In one lies buried one of my sisters that died at my grandmother's there of the smallpox. Her monument of white marble stands up in the chancel.

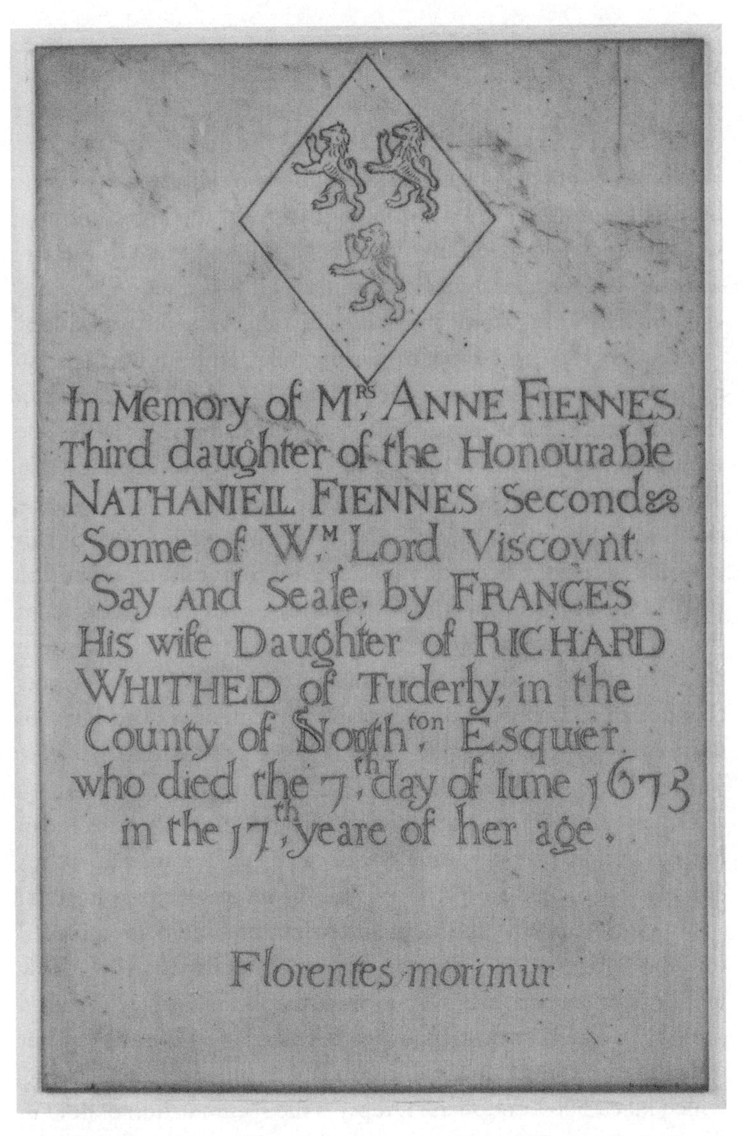

Memorial plaque to Anne Fiennes, Celia's younger sister. (Copyright the Rector and Churchwardens of St Giles-in-Reading)

What she sees is the memorial to Anne Fiennes, which is still there today in St-Giles-in-Reading Church. Anne was Celia's elder sister by three years. She died in 1675 at the age of 16.

Symptoms of smallpox included a high fever, chills, weakness, pain, headache, vomiting, and a rash of pustules over the body. Just how widespread smallpox or any other killer illnesses were in the late seventeenth century is difficult to estimate. However, we do have one extraordinary set of records from which we can draw some conclusions.

Between 1657 and 1758, data were collected from every parish in London on the number of people buried according to Church of England rites – that was five-sixths of the population – as well as the supposed causes of their deaths. The results were recorded in what were known as 'Bills of Mortality'. I say 'supposed' causes because there were few reliable ways of diagnosing most illnesses in this period. The record-keepers often resorted to itemising symptoms. In 1698, for instance, our current year with Celia Fiennes, the record shows 'Vapours in the Head' killed off four Londoners, and seven perished from 'Lethargy'. Sometimes, it seems, the data-collectors abandoned all precision. For example, they dumped the cause of death for 1,023 citizens in the catch-all 'Aged and Bedridden', while fourteen were simply listed 'Found dead in the Streets, &c'.

Other causes might not make much sense to most of us today, but – as I've discovered – some at least can be unfathomed by today's clinicians. I turned to a schoolfriend of mine, a retired hospital consultant, Alan Wilkinson, for some enlightenment. He pointed out that, for instance, when the Bills of Mortality for 1698 show 409 Londoners perished from a 'Stopping in the Stomach', they'd probably suffered from strangulated hernias, bowel tumours or gut inflammation. How about 'Dropsy and Tympany', for example, which killed 508 Londoners? Dropsy is the accumulation of fluid in the legs which could, for instance, be due to heart failure, for which there was no treatment at that time. 'Tympany', which implies a swollen stomach shaped like a drum, would probably have been caused by a bowel obstruction.

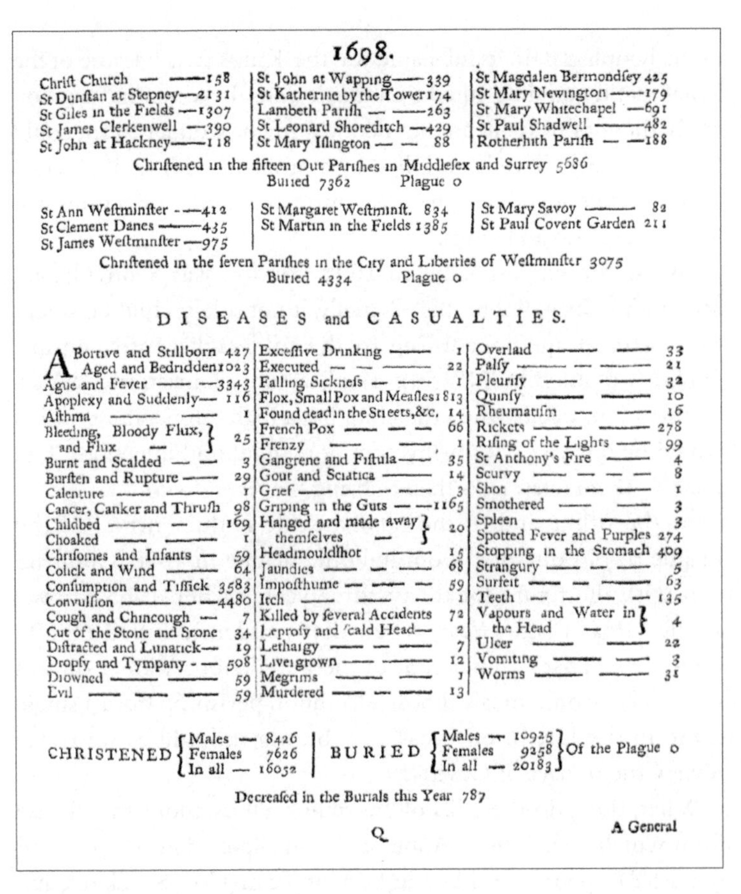

1698.

Chriſt Church	158	St John at Wapping	339	St Magdalen Bermondſey	425
St Dunſtan at Stepney	2131	St Katherine by the Tower	174	St Mary Newington	179
St Giles in the Fields	1307	Lambeth Pariſh	263	St Mary Whitechapel	691
St James Clerkenwell	390	St Leonard Shoreditch	429	St Paul Shadwell	482
St John at Hackney	118	St Mary Iſlington	88	Rotherhith Pariſh	188

Chriſtened in the fifteen Out Pariſhes in Middleſex and Surrey 5686
Buried 7362 Plague 0

St Ann Weſtminſter	412	St Margaret Weſtminſt.	834	St Mary Savoy	82
St Clement Danes	435	St Martin in the Fields	1385	St Paul Covent Garden	211
St James Weſtminſter	975				

Chriſtened in the ſeven Pariſhes in the City and Liberties of Weſtminſter 3075
Buried 4334 Plague 0

DISEASES and CASUALTIES.

Abortive and Stillborn	427	Exceſſive Drinking	1	Overlaid	33
Aged and Bedridden	1023	Executed	22	Palſy	21
Ague and Fever	3343	Falling Sickneſs	1	Pleuriſy	32
Apoplexy and Suddenly	116	Flox, Small Pox and Meaſles	1813	Quinſy	10
Aſthma	1	Found dead in the Streets, &c.	14	Rheumatiſm	16
Bleeding, Bloody Flux, and Flux	25	French Pox	66	Rickets	278
		Frenzy	1	Riſing of the Lights	99
Burnt and Scalded	3	Gangrene and Fiſtula	35	St Anthony's Fire	4
Burſten and Rupture	29	Gout and Sciatica	14	Scurvy	8
Calenture	1	Grief	3	Shot	1
Cancer, Canker and Thruſh	98	Griping in the Guts	1165	Smothered	3
Childbed	169	Hanged and made away themſelves	20	Spleen	3
Choaked	1			Spotted Fever and Purples	274
Chriſomes and Infants	59	Headmouldſhot	15	Stopping in the Stomach	409
Colick and Wind	64	Jaundies	68	Strangury	5
Conſumption and Tiſſick	3583	Impoſthume	59	Surfeit	63
Convulſion	4480	Itch	1	Teeth	135
Cough and Chincough	7	Killed by ſeveral Accidents	72	Vapours and Water in the Head	4
Cut of the Stone and Stone	34	Leproſy and ſcald Head	2		
Diſtracted and Lunatick	19	Lethargy	7	Ulcer	22
Dropſy and Tympany	508	Livergrown	12	Vomiting	3
Drowned	59	Megrims	1	Worms	31
Evil	59	Murdered	13		

CHRISTENED		BURIED		
Males	8426	Males	10925	Of the Plague 0
Females	7626	Females	9258	
In all	16052	In all	20183	

Decreaſed in the Burials this Year 787

Q A General

The Bill of Mortality for London, 1698. (British Library reprint from 1759)

There was 'French pox' (sixty-six deaths), meaning syphilis; 'Quinsy' (ten), tonsillitis; and 'St Anthony's Fire' (four), a skin infection. And the most exotically and mysteriously named 'Rising of the Lights', which was listed as the killer of ninety-nine Londoners and was croup or obstruction in the windpipe. And what about 'Evil', fifty-nine victims? Not, as we might think, witches who perished from their own curses, but scrofula, a tubercular infection of the lymph glands. Its full name was the 'King's Evil' because of the belief that it could be cured by a touch from the king. And how on earth, those of us (who are not dentists) might wonder today, could 135 Londoners have been killed by a problem with their 'Teeth'? Simple – but appalling – because untreated dental infections can lead to abscesses and sepsis.

By far the biggest killer in 1698 London was 'Convulsion', accounting for 4,480 deaths – 'chiefly, if not solely, children under two years of age', according to the mid-eighteenth-century publisher of the Bills. 'Not surprising', says my clinician friend Alan. 'Convulsions occur when the child has a high temperature, which would be the case with many common childhood infections. And there were no treatments then to bring the fever down.'

At the other end of the fatality scale is this entry: 'Of the Plague 0.' No one died from bubonic plague in 1698. Compare that with the figure for thirty-three years earlier, 1665, known as the Great Plague Year, when that pandemic killed 68,596 Londoners. That's 16 per cent of the population. A killer on this scale today would mean almost 11 million perishing from a single cause in the UK in one year! A sobering thought as we today review the impact of Covid-19.

What, then, do the Bills of Mortality tell us about the disease from which Celia's sister, Anne died – smallpox? The 1698 record states 1,813 people perished in London from 'Flox, Small Pox and Measles'. A breakdown of statistics for these three illnesses in later bills shows that smallpox accounted for 95 per cent of them. If we scale up these figures for the population of England as a whole, we get a figure of around 21,000 deaths from smallpox in one year. And remember that there wasn't just a bulge of deaths from the disease over a few months. If you lived at the end of the seventeenth century, you faced the same odds of being killed by it every year of your life. Not everyone who caught the disease died. Seven out of ten survived, but they were likely to spend the rest of their lives with a face and body disfigured by scars, while many were left blind.

There was no effective treatment, cure, nor yet a vaccine for smallpox. Physicians prescribed remedies ranging from swallowing a boiled mixture of herbs, to bloodletting and exposure to red objects! One doctor told smallpox-infected patients to leave the windows open, draw the bed sheets no higher than the waist, and drink plenty of beer (safer than water of course), a rare piece of good sense which might at least have cooled the sufferer down and helped reduce the fever.

The first inoculation against smallpox became available in Britain twenty-three years after Celia Fiennes visited her sister's memorial. The procedure – called variolation – aimed to give you a mild case of the disease and hence immunity. This was achieved by blowing a smallpox scab up your nose or by scratching your skin with the blood from someone who had the disease. But it was a risky process. You could end up with a serious, even fatal, dose of smallpox and you might pass it on to others. Those hazards apart, many people didn't like the idea anyway. Some believed inoculation was interfering with God's will. Others, in an age when large families were normal, even regarded a killer disease as a good thing, since it helped control the size of the population. And although the world's first effective and safe vaccine against smallpox was discovered by Edward Jenner in 1796, major outbreaks of the disease continued into the twentieth century.

As well as Anne, Celia had two other older sisters, Frances and Elizabeth, and they too had died before reaching adulthood. We don't know the cause of death for either of them, nor how old they were. Celia Fiennes herself lived to see her 80th year, and her younger sister Mary died at 74. The contrast between the two groups of sisters tells us a great deal about life expectancy in the late seventeenth century. The average age to which a new-born baby might expect to live was around 38 years. But that's misleading. Exclude children from the calculation and the average person lived into their fifties or sixties. There was a high rate of childhood mortality.

The risks infants faced were many, varied and nasty. Thirteen per cent of children in the second half of the seventeenth century died before their first birthday. Nine per cent were dead before they reached one month. And life was little more promising for older children. Take, for instance, the Norfleet family from Faversham in Kent, contemporaries of Celia Fiennes. John and Katherine Norfleet had seven children, all of whom died before they were 11. Furthermore, John's brother, Thomas and his wife Elizabeth, who had eight children, lost all but one of them before they were 7 years old.

Many children at the time succumbed to diseases which are easily treatable or have been wiped out today. Diarrhea would have been responsible for many deaths, as well as scarlet fever, smallpox, whooping cough, flu and, as we've mentioned already, 'convulsions'.

Children were also prone to accidents, the like of which are almost unheard of today. William Coe, from Mildenhall in Suffolk, who kept a diary between 1693 and 1713, recounted the accidents that befell his eight children. Two of them almost choked to death on pins in their food, another was burned when the cap the child was wearing was set on fire by a candle, one was struck in the eye by an oak rail, another lad was hurt when boiling hot fat spilled on his 'frock' (presumably he was an infant), while one of his siblings was accidentally stabbed with a pointed tool. The list of mishaps among the junior Coes goes on: one careless child was found hanging by the neck from a hall window, one fell into scalding water, a third was pierced through the cheek by a cow's horn, and the last one was thrown from an open coach on a rutted road and was almost crushed to death by a passing wagon. From what we know, it seems that such misfortunes were common occurrences for vulnerable youngsters who'd not yet learned to avoid the many traps that lay in wait for them.

It's also significant that neither of the families we've cited here were from the lower ranks of society where we might expect ignorance and poverty to put a child's life more at risk. Thomas Norfleet was described as a 'yeoman', which at this time commonly meant the lord of the manor, and William Coe was a 'gentleman farmer' who owned 100 acres and took a leading role in his community. The Fiennes family, of course, sat in the top-most ranks, and, as we've seen, of the five daughters only two – one of whom was Celia – made it to adulthood. But the most spectacular and shocking example must be Queen Anne, who acceded to the throne in 1702. She had eighteen pregnancies. Thirteen of them ended in a miscarriage or stillbirth. Of the other five, four died as babies and the last one perished at the age of 11. Childhood mortality seemed not to discriminate between poor and privileged. It was almost as though the early years were a cruel proving ground. Survive disease and disaster, reach your twenties, and you might look forward to another thirty or forty years of life.

There was at least one group who were the unfortunate exceptions to this rule, and they were mothers.

As she moves on from Ely, Celia Fiennes stops at the town of Turvey near Northampton. There she visits the local church, as she often does, and notes the elaborately carved figures on the memorials to the Earl of Peterborough's family.

> *One in a widow's dress, all marble finely gilded and painted, on a bed with rolls of mat, very natural, at the head and feet. There was another – the lady died in childbed, the child by her.*

Research into tombs and records of the time show that the mother died in twenty-five to thirty births out of every thousand. And this is almost certainly an underestimate, not taking into account those who perished soon afterwards from infections and other perinatal complications. So, given that five or more children were born in most families, then as many as 20 per cent of women who became pregnant the average number of times were likely to die.

And to fight all this death and disease, there was of course no health service, no local GP surgeries. There were places called 'hospitals', as she points out when she reaches Leicester on this stage of her journey.

> *There are two hospitals, one for old men, the other women, 24 in number. They are allowed 2s:8d per week, candles, fuel, oatmeal, butter and salt.*

A 'hospital' was not what we would understand by the word, it was more like a care home supported by charitable donations. And Leicester was no exception. She sings the praises of such establishments in nine different towns across the country. At least something positive, then, if you managed to survive for half a dozen decades.

It's clear that at the end of the seventeenth century you needed at least two things on your side in order to live to a grand old age: luck and an exceptionally strong constitution. As Fiennes discovers while still in Leicester, it was a big help if you had a resilient DNA. The genes carried by some families seemed to give them outstanding longevity. At St Martin's Church, she notes:

> *Here, I saw Herrick's tomb, who was a mayor of the town, and was married to one wife 52 years in all, during which time he buried neither man, woman nor child, though most times he had 20 in his family. His age was 79, and his widow 97 at her death. She saw 142 of her posterity together.*

What a remarkable family the Herricks were!

So, given that sickness and early death were such a common part of life in late seventeenth-century England, why did Celia Fiennes say so little about them on her journeys? There could be a number of explanations.

First, perhaps she considered it improper and unrefined for a lady of breeding like herself to discuss such things, that it would be in poor taste. This seems unlikely. There are several examples of women from the upper classes at this time writing about their sickness symptoms in graphic detail. Mary Rich, Countess of Warwick, for instance, who died in 1678, recounted with precision the ups and downs of her own illnesses. And, of course, Fiennes herself doesn't hesitate to tell us about one of the most delicate of subjects, how water at the many spas she visits is a 'quick purger', a fast-working laxative.

Or was she squeamish? That too seems to be an inadequate explanation. Consider her encounter with a couple of corpses when later she visits Newcastle.

> *I went to see the Barber Surgeons Hall, which was within a pretty garden walled in, full of flowers and greens. There I saw the room with a round table in it, railed round with seats or benches for the conveniency in their dissecting and anatomising a body, and reading lectures on all parts. There were two bodies that had been anatomised. One the bones were fastened with wires. The other had had the flesh boiled off, and some of the ligament remained so the parts were held together by its own muscles and sinews that were dried with it. Over this was another room in which was the skin of a man that was taken off after he was dead, and dressed, and so was stuffed – the body and limbs. It looked and felt like a sort of parchment.*

Note that she seems to have 'felt' the dried skin herself.

Another possible explanation might be that her Puritan upbringing somehow made it unacceptable to dwell too much on the widespread misfortunes of sickness and death that afflicted humanity. Would it imply a cruel side to God? But there's nothing to indicate such a view in all her writings.

Where, then, do her own beliefs fit? And will the answer give us any clue to why she glosses over sickness and disease? Most of her references to her own religious beliefs come when she has a narrow escape and praises God's intervention to save her. We saw that, for instance, when she was almost thrown from her horse at Ely, but was rescued 'by the good hand of God's Providence, which has always been with me, ever a present help in time of need'.

But her most revealing discussion of her faith is in a conversation with the landlady at her lodgings when later she visits Truro in Cornwall.

> *She was but an ordinary plain woman, but she was understanding of the best things – the experience of real religion and her quiet submission and self-resignation to the will of God in all things.*

This seems to be the basis of Celia Fiennes' own belief. She adds:

> *Indeed, I was much pleased and edified by her conversation, and the pitch* [perhaps 'importance'] *of the soul: her resignation to the will of God, and thankfulness that God enabled and owned her therein. And, therefore, to him we must address for help in this or any duty he calls us to, both in the use of what means he appoints, as also for success and blessing on it.*

These, then, were the three strands to her faith – that God helps the (presumably) godly when they most need it, that He holds unruly nature in check, and that whatever befalls us we must resign ourselves to the will of God. Do any of these beliefs, or all of them together, explain why she might have avoided writing about people who were ill or dying? Far from it. In fact, the reverse could be true. She might have felt empowered to write of such matters, confident that whatever we suffer is in the end part of God's great plan.

So if neither refined taste, squeamishness nor religious belief explain her reluctance, could the reason have something to do with experiences in her own life? Perhaps the suffering and demise of her sister Anne or of her other sisters who were all taken away at such an early age made the subject of disease and death too painful for her to discuss. She never tells us anything about these very personal matters. So it's all conjecture. We'll just have to accept it as one of mysteries of her character.

3

To Wales

NOT GETTING LOST

I observe the ordinary people
can scarce tell you how far it is to the next place.

There is something of the English nationalist in Celia Fiennes. She stresses that her two lengthy journeys in the summers of 1697 and 1698 are to discover more about her own country. And she states in the Introduction to her diaries that travelling around England would 'add much to its glory and cure the evil itch of overvaluing foreign parts.' She's now heading for Wales, not exactly 'foreign parts', but what she says about her visit there tells us as much about English attitudes towards the Welsh as about the Welsh people themselves.

Her route west takes her via Newcastle-under-Lyme to Chester.

> *The town is mostly timber buildings. The trade and concourse of people to it is chiefly from the intercourse* [commerce] *it has with Ireland – most take this passage. And also the intercourse with Wales, which is parted from it and England by the River Dee which washes the castle walls.*

In medieval times, Chester had been a significant trading port, but by the late seventeenth century the Dee Estuary was silting up, so preventing larger ships from reaching the town.

Her route from there into Wales poses particular dangers to those not familiar with area.

At the end of the town, just by the castle, you cross over a very large and long bridge over the River Dee, which has the tide come up much beyond the town. You enter Flintshire and so I crossed over the marshes, which are hazardous to strangers.

But help is at hand for a well-connected woman.

Therefore, Mr William Allen – who was the mayor of Chester at that time and gave me a very civil treatment, being an acquaintance of my brother-in-law, Sir Edmund Harrison – ordered his son and another gentleman to ride with me to Howarden.

Then comes her one and only – brief – taste of Wales and its people (beware: insult alert).

At Holywell they speak Welsh. The inhabitants go barefoot and bare-legged – a nasty sort of people. Their meat is very small here. Mutton is no bigger than little lamb, what of it there is was sweet. Then I passed through Flint town. It's a very ragged place - many villages in England are better. The houses all thatched and stone walls, but so decayed that in many places are ready to tumble down.

Was Wales really so poverty stricken? Were its people as objectionable as her language suggests? This does sound like prejudice, racism even. But as ever, we should be wary of judging those in the past. What's important to us as historians is to understand *why* people spoke and acted as they did.

Part of the explanation for her damning language may lie in recent history. During the earlier part of the seventeenth century during the Civil War, Wales – with the single exception of Pembrokeshire – had been enthusiastically Royalist, and many troops of Welsh infantrymen crossed the border to fight in the king's army. So, the fervent Parliamentarianism of her own family may go some way to account for her dismissal of the folk of Flintshire as 'a nasty sort of people'.

She seems to speak as though Wales was a separate, foreign country. But that wasn't so. It had come under direct English rule under the Tudors. In earlier history, the Normans had regarded it as a largely unconquerable mountain wasteland and had set up a series of semi-independent marcher territories along the border to keep the Welsh at bay. Edward I had invaded and annexed Wales at the end of the thirteenth century. It was Henry VIII who formalised the relationship in 1536 with an Act of Union. This required Wales to send MPs to Westminster and stated that English must be spoken in Welsh courts. Henry was himself of Welsh blood. His ancestor was one Owain ap Maredudd ap Tudur ap Goronwy ap Tudur ap Goronwy ap Ednyfed Fychan, who – luckily for English school children in history classes ever since – decided to go for a simpler surname, and the Tudor dynasty was born.

By the time Celia Fiennes came here, Wales was growing more prosperous. Farming and cattle herding were the most common occupations. But the Welsh were also exporting increasing amounts of wool and cloth, and Fiennes makes an important observation about other flourishing industries in Flintshire, the Welsh county she's visiting.

> *There are great coal pits of the cannel coal that's cloven in huge great pieces.*

Cannel coal – also known these days as oil shale – commanded a high price for home-heating. She explains why.

> *It burns as light as a candle – set the coals together with some fire and it shall give a snap and burn up light.*

It had other value too. Its appearance and texture are nothing like ordinary coal.

> *Of this cannel coal they make saltcellars, stand-dishes* [presumably ornamental dishes] *and many boxes and things which are sent about*

and sold in London. It's very finely polished and looks much like jet or ebony wood, for which one might easily take it when in boxes &c &c. I bought some of them for curiosity's sake.

Her description of the way it was excavated indicates much deeper mines here than the bell pits she's described elsewhere. The Welsh, it seems, were ingenious in the way they brought the coal to the surface and how they tackled the perennial problem of draining the inevitable floods at the bottom of the pit.

They have great wheels that are turned with horses that draw up the water and so drain the mines which would else be overflowed so they could not dig the coal. They have also engines that draw up their coal in sort of baskets like hand barrows which they wind up like a bucket in a well, for their mines are dug down and sometimes it's pretty low before they come to the coals.

And cannel coal isn't the only mineral that the Welsh exploit.

In this country are quarries of stone, copper and iron-mines and salt hills.

This objective account of Welsh industry – all apparently conducted with great efficiency and much hard work – is at odds with her earlier condemnation of the Welsh people. It almost seems that her remarks about them being 'lazy', 'nasty' and living in 'decayed' conditions were formulaic, an expression of a common English prejudice of the time that she had to get out of the way before her curiosity and detailed observation take over, producing a more accurate picture of the Welsh and their working lives. But the subject of her nationalistic attitude – and whether it amounts to my-country-right-or-wrong chauvinism – is one we'll return to shortly when she visits Scotland.

Her crossing back into England turns out to be more hazardous than the outward journey.

> *I forded over the Dee when the tide was out. The sands are here so loose that the tides do move them from one place to another at every flood, so that the same place one used to ford a month or two before is not to be passed now, for as it brings the sands in heaps to one place, so it leaves others in deep holes which are covered with water.*

As she explains, a route that was thought relatively safe could soon become lethal.

> *Many persons that have known the fords well and have come a year or half a year after, if they venture on their former knowledge, have been overwhelmed in the ditches made by the sands which are deep enough to swallow up a coach or wagon.*

It's impossible today to know exactly where she crossed the estuary. The route I take is the A548, as boring as any A-road anywhere in the country – until suddenly ahead of me, rising several hundred feet into the sky, is a stunning piece of gigantic sculpture. It's a suspension bridge. It's half a mile long, and yet its architects have managed to support the road it carries by swooping lines of cables from only two huge legs, one on each side. It spans much more than the river itself. It also takes us over hundreds of acres of flat barren land with the occasional mounds of grass, along with many ponds, survivals of the sandy, waterlogged marshes that Celia Fiennes describes. And it strikes me how often she describes floods and bogs which hinder her route and are a threat to the safety of travellers, in a way that's unthinkable nowadays. What's changed is obvious to anyone crossing the River Dee as I am today. The river itself has been canalised, its course widened and straightened, and embankments have been constructed on each side to stop the tidal waters flooding into the surrounding land. So here are two pieces of civil engineering –

Today, a spectacular bridge over a straightened and a canalised River Dee speeds the traveller between England and Wales. Celia Fiennes 'crossed over the marshes, which are hazardous to strangers'. (Image by Dronepics.Wales)

massive bridges and containment of rivers – undreamt of when she was on her great journeys.

Even today, of course, Britain can be hit by dramatic inundations that can suddenly devastate hundreds of homes. But when that happens, it's big news. In 1698, floods and mile after mile of waterlogged land were normal. The solution then was to avoid building on the flood plain, and to accept the risks. If you needed to travel, as here, between north Wales and Chester, then you recognised you'd have to ride across shifting quicksand, and just pray that you'd reach the other side.

For Celia Fiennes, human help is also at hand.

I had two guides to conduct me over.

Even then, she isn't safe.

> *It was at least a mile I went on the sands before I came to the middle of the channel, which was pretty deep and with such a current or tide which was falling out to sea together with the wind, that the horses feet could scarce stand against it.*

Hiring a local guide is something she often has to do and, as she recounts, they weren't always up to the job.

> *You are forced to have guides as in all parts of Derbyshire. The country here about is so full of moor or quagmires and such precipices that one that is a stranger cannot travel without a guide, and some of them are put at a loss sometimes.*

Getting lost was a daily problem for the traveller almost anywhere across the land. As well as employing a guide, there were three other possible means of staying safe and on the right road. You could refer to a map. You could look for a signpost. Or you could resort to that eternal solution – stop and ask someone. There were problems with all of them.

Let's start with maps. Celia Fiennes must have had access at least to some kind of general road map, otherwise she wouldn't have been able to plan her journeys. There were a few such maps available at the time (like the one overleaf). They showed the relative positions of major towns and cities with lines to indicate where main roads linked them. Such a map would do no more than enable her to identify the approximate location of a few key objectives – where a relation lived who might accommodate her for a night or two, or a particular town that she wanted to explore.

Late seventeenth-century road map. (Public Domain)

Though she makes no mention of maps in all her diaries, it's hard to see how she could have decided where to aim for without something like this. But such a map would have been useless once she was up on her horse and off on her travels. It told you nothing about when to turn left or right on some remote track or local road, which of course was the majority of the time outside towns.

There was one accurate set of maps available at this time which could help, though that too had its own snags. In 1675, a man named John Ogilby – an ex-dancing master and theatre director – had published his *Britannia*, an atlas covering 7,500 miles of England's highways with a few travellers' tales thrown in. Ogilby was the first cartographer to use a standard definition of the mile, so his maps were a great leap forward. However, they looked nothing like a modern AA road atlas – they were laid out in strips (see lower image on page 6 of the colour section). So long as you stuck to a main road, that was fine. You started at the bottom left corner of the sheet, and followed the road up to the top, before picking it up again at the bottom of the next strip, on up the page again, and so on. However, if on your travels, you wandered accidentally down a side road, an Ogilby strip map gave you no clue how to get back onto the main road. And of course, if you were Celia Fiennes, often exploring the byways of England, his maps would not always have been much use. If she did make use of such maps, then it's surprising she never once mentions them in her diaries.

How else then would she usually have found the route to her next destination? What about signposts? In most of the country, that wasn't much use. In all of the 600 and odd pages of her travel diaries, she mentions only once coming across fingerposts. It's on this stage of her journey as she rides north from the Welsh border through Lancashire.

They have one good thing in most parts of this principality – or County Palatine it's rather called – that at all cross-ways there are posts with hands pointing to each road, with the names of the great town or market towns that it leads to, so that strangers may not lose their road and have to go back again.

Her description makes it clear that these signposts were a rarity. Up to then, the only comparable aid had been provided by a few crosses pointing the way which had been erected centuries earlier by monasteries in the most lonely parts of the land for the benefit of travellers, lost on the moors or mountains, and who might perish. Otherwise, there was nothing until just one year before she spots the finger-posts of Lancashire. In 1697, a law had been passed which decreed that in the more remote regions, where two or more paths intersected, the local parish surveyors were to erect guideposts. It was the birth of the modern signpost. But in 1698, except here in Lancashire, it was too soon to be of much help to Celia Fiennes.

Finally, to avoid getting lost, there was plain old asking the way. This must have been an everyday routine for her, not worthy of being recorded most of the time. But – and oh, how little some things have changed – folk weren't always too good at giving directions. It was a problem right across the country. In Suffolk:

Generally, the people here give so bad a direction that passengers are at a loss what aim to take: they know scarce 3 miles from their home. And meet them where you will and enquire how far to such a place, they mind not where they are then, but tell you the distance from their own houses to that place.

In Cornwall, they're more interested in asking you questions rather than helping you.

The people here know but little from home, only to some market town they frequent, but will be very solicitous to know where you go, and how far, and from whence you came, and where is your abode.

And in the north of England, she often gets misleading advice from locals.

> *I observe the ordinary people, both in these parts of Yorkshire and in the northern parts, can scarce tell you how far it is to the next place, unless it be in the great towns. And they do not esteem it uphill unless it's as steep as a house or precipice.*

All in all, it's a wonder she didn't get lost more often. Especially on the next stage of her journey. She's about to tackle the far north.

4

The Lake District and Scotland

BARREN HILLS AND SLOTHFUL PEOPLE

They live in so nasty a way …
that one has little stomach to eat or use anything.

If we could time-travel, and were really riding alongside Celia Fiennes, day in, day out in her company, there might be times when conversation would get a bit tense, with common ground in our discussions hard to find. But, of course, what would hold us to stick with her would be our desire to understand how very different from ours were the values and views of people who lived 320 years ago. Not to mention our admiration for a woman who – though we didn't always agree with her – was so much her own person. Her trip to the Lake District and Scotland are among the most extreme examples of when touchy arguments might have broken out over supper in the evening.

From Lancaster, she rides 20 miles north to Kendal.

Most of the way was in lanes.

Not like my 'lanes' on the M6 before I branch off at Junction 36. Most of us will know Kendal as the jumping off place for what's regarded by many as the most beautiful and spectacular scenery in England. We'll probably have sighed at the sight of Scafell Pike, Helvelyn and their giant neighbours, craggy hillsides delicately painted with a thousand shades of green and golden brown. We'll have pulled out our phones to capture perfect images of Ullswater, Coniston Water and Windermere so we can WhatsApp them to friends not lucky enough to be with us in this rural paradise. The Lake District has been admired and loved by the English for centuries. William Wordsworth wrote hundreds of lines in praise of its landscape, which, he said, 'seems to send its own deep quiet to restore our hearts'. The English Lakes, he wrote, are simply 'the loveliest spot that man hath ever found'. Though we can't match Wordsworth's poetic talent, most of us will have felt our hearts lifted by the untamed but somehow perfectly composed combination of mountains and lakes stretching endlessly into the distance.

And what does Celia Fiennes make of the Lakeland's beauty a century or so before Wordsworth praised it? The first thing is that she barely seems to notice it. Her main concern is the hazardous road surface.

> *These great hills are so full of loose stones and shelves of rocks that it's very unsafe to ride down them.*

When she does stop to explore, she finds her surroundings quite threatening.

> *As I walked down at this place, I was walled on both sides by those inaccessible high rocky barren hills which hang over one's head in some places and appear very terrible.*

Her route takes her from Kendal to Ambleside at the head of Lake Windermere, then along the banks of Ullswater before she heads north-east to Penrith. In other words, she's skirting the eastern edge of the Lake District. Even that route would give most of us enough of a taste of the spectacular scenery to tempt us to explore further west. Not Celia Fiennes. When she reaches the northern tip of Ullswater, she's had enough.

> *Hereabout we leave these desert and barren, rocky hills. Not that they are limited to Westmoreland only, for had I gone farther to the left hand into Cumberland, I should have found more such, and – they tell me – far worse for height and stoniness about Whitehaven and Cockermouth.*

Of course, part of her lack of interest in, or sometimes disdain for, the spectacular scenery may be to do with her overriding worry about the uneven, dangerous tracks she has to travel. But that can't be the whole story. Plenty of us today struggle up rocky mountain paths so we can enjoy the view from the top. It's significant that one of the things she does admire around here is the farmland.

> *At the end of this Ullswater is a fine round hill, which looked green and full of wood, very pleasant with grass and corn, very fruitful.*

The counties of Westmoreland and Cumberland, she says, 'have very good land and fruitful, but they equally partake of the bad' – the 'bad' being those 'terrible … rocky hills'. What we're reading here is a common opinion of the natural world in the late seventeenth century, a view based on both philosophical and religious foundations. The sprawling natural world with its unpredictable crags, barren moors and hostile forests, was best tamed by farming or by neatly planted gardens, as we saw at Chatsworth. She sums it up in a comment about the countryside near Kendal.

> *The lands in the enclosures are rich.*

It was a fundamental belief in the Age of Reason that the natural world was chaos, a threat to the ordered world of humanity. It was our job to control it. Thus mountains, for example, were hated as infertile deformities, little better than the earth's rubbish dumps. And this attitude was also in part underpinned by a religious belief. It's one that she herself subscribes too, as we see,

Scafell Massif in the Lake District. It's not hard to see why Fiennes loathed such inhospitable-looking mountains. It wasn't just a fad of fashionable philosophy. Danger and discomfort were a traveller's daily worries, and a road through bleak hills could mean both. (Public Domain, Doug Sim)

for example, when she observes the threatening power of a lake in Derbyshire.

> *That water I saw was strange, so deep and large, and looked like would swell so as to cause a bursting out of the earth. All these things shew the great wisdom and power of our blessed Creator to make and maintain all things within their own bounds and limits, which have a tendency to work ruin on the whole frame of the world, if not bridled by God's command.*

It was held that there was a purpose to all God's works, and the sole usefulness of mountains was to supply rivers and lakes with water. In fact, on her trip to the Lake District, waterfalls are the only natural phenomenon she does pick out to enjoy.

Many little currents of water from the sides and clefts trickle down to some lower part where it runs swiftly over the stones and shelves in the way, which makes a pleasant rush and murmuring noise, and like a snowball is increased by each spring trickling down on either side of those hills, and so descends into the bottoms, a moorish ground in which in many places the waters stand, and so form some of those lakes as it did here.

But again, she has no admiration for the surrounding mountains.

I observed the boundaries of all these great waters are those sort of barren, rocky hills which are so vastly high.

Celia Fiennes, in her opinion of nature, is very much of her era. And it can be quite shocking in the twenty-first century. It shows how what we may think of as fundamental, timeless values, such as the beauty of wild landscape, is in fact neither fundamental nor timeless.

But it's not all about the landscape – barren, rocky hills with a bit of pleasant trickling water. Before she leaves the Lake District, she does manage to have some fun near Ambleside.

I rode through a fine forest or park, where were deer skipping about and hares, and by means of a good greyhound I did a little coursing. But we being strangers could not so fast pursue it in the grounds full of hillocks and ferns, and so it escaped us.

It's another example of her relatively liberal brand of Puritanism. Many of that faith would have frowned on what amounted to sport – she was not hunting out of necessity to feed herself. And there's something even more intriguing. What she's doing may well have been illegal. Laws passed in the seventeenth century restricted hunting on private property to the landowner and his sons. Does she know that? Or has the landowner turned a blind eye? And who lent her a greyhound?

Soon she's back on the road. From Penrith, she heads north to Carlisle. She writes:

> *You enter over the bridge and double gates which are iron grates, lined with a case of doors of thick timber. The walls of the town and battlements and towers are in very good repair and look well. I walked round the walls and saw the river which twists and turns itself round the grounds.*

The castle is less well preserved.

> *There remain only some of the walls and ruins of the castle, which does shew it to have been a very strong town formerly. The walls are of a prodigious thickness and vast great stones. It's moated round and with draw bridges.*

Carlisle has been caught in the middle of many violent north–south disputes since Roman times. Back then it marked the northern boundary of a great empire. The castle and walls which Celia Fiennes observes were first built by the Normans, and the city had changed hands and was fought over by warring Scots and English armies countless times during the next 600 years. Some stretches of the fortified walls can still be seen today. They've been part-demolished and part-restored several times since Fiennes was here. I make for what is the best-preserved bit around the castle and find there a glowering structure of brick and stone. What she did not know was that the harshest challenge to these fortifications was yet to come, forty-six years after her visit to Carlisle. In November 1745, Jacobite forces loyal to Bonnie Prince Charlie would capture the town after a brief siege of the castle.

It's drizzling with rain as I head for my night's lodgings, the Crown and Mitre, a tall, red-brick piece of Edwardian pomp, and after checking in, I go to see if anything remains of what she saw in the city centre.

There is a large marketplace with a good cross and hall.

The place today turns out to be the architectural opposite of the castle. There are no dark, towering structures, but an open square, its cobbled ground curling around a dozen sapling trees, surrounded by low, welcoming buildings, modern on one side, selling the brands you find in any town centre these days, more ancient on the other. The prize among these older ones is a long, pink stucco, nineteenth-century affair with a small clock tower on top. This is the Old Town Hall, erected in 1668, and much as Celia Fiennes saw it thirty years later. In front of it is her market cross. It had been placed there only sixteen years before she rode into town. A shining brass plaque at its base is inscribed 'JOSEPH REED MAYOR 1682'.

From Carlisle our route lies north to the limit of England – and beyond. I've forgotten how the English countryside once clear of the Lake District National Park is more gentle rolling hills than spectacular mountains. The A7, the main trunk road to Edinburgh, isn't a trunk road as in a multi-laned motorway, but one of those fast-but-narrow routes that soon leave you (well, me, anyway) frustrated and cursing at the end of a queue trapped behind an eighteen-wheeler and trying to work out what 'Delivering Sustainable Distribution' written on its rear means.

I pull into the Marchbank Hotel forecourt and take out a map. Am I in Scotland or not? The hotel is apparently right up against the border. Pass it and I'll be in Scotland. I look for a sign as I drive on, a big 'Welcome to Scotland' perhaps. Nothing. And the flat green landscape with occasional woods now I'm clearly in Scotland is much the same as it was on the English side north of Carlisle. The houses and cottages, often neatly painted white, could be rebuilt in the English Lake District and not look out of place.

And when Celia Fiennes made the same journey in 1698, she wasn't suddenly stepping over a threshold into some very different, darker world either. The Scottish borderlands in the late seventeenth century had little in common with the Highlands of Scotland to their north – not only by reason of their geography, but also according to their culture, religious faith, language and politics. The Highlanders, for instance, were likely to be much fiercer in their opposition to English interference than were the Scottish borderers. They – in many ways – were closer to the English. For instance, they traded freely with their neighbours to the south. Fiennes sees them crossing to England over the river that marks the border.

> *Men, women and children take off their shoes, and holding up their clothes, wade through the rivers when the tide is out.*

They buy Lake District produce.

> *Kendal Cotton is used for blankets, and the Scots use it for their plaids.*

And dwellings in England hadn't been much different.

> *The houses were but a little better built.*

Nevertheless, her crossing into Scotland is much more of an event than mine. In fact, it's not without its dangers. She has to ford two rivers. There's the Esk:

> *which is very broad and hazardous to cross even when the tide is out. It leaves a broad sand on each side, which in some places is unsafe, and made me take a good guide who carried me about and across some part of it here, it being deep in the channel.*

And then the Sark, where she makes a rare observation about the wildlife.

> *On the sand, before the water was quite gone from it, I saw a great bird which looked almost black, picking up fish and busking* [shifting about restlessly] *in the water, it looked like an eagle and by its dimensions could scarce be any other bird.*

I asked a friend of mine, Nigel Robbins, who's a keen ornithologist, what kind of bird he thought it might be. 'It was most likely a Sea Eagle, also known as a White-tailed Eagle,' he told me. 'By 1916 they were extinct in the UK and have only been successfully reintroduced since 1985. The juvenile is a uniform dark brown – appearing black at a distance and in certain lights. It has a 2-metre wingspan and does indeed splash around in shallow waters for fish or trying to drown ducks. It was listed in an Act of Henry VIII's in 1534 with a bounty of 4*d* for its corpse.'

Despite all the similarities in the late seventeenth century between the English and the Scots close to the border, Celia Fiennes – to put it mildly – does not take to them. She immediately bursts forth with an undiluted disdain for the folk she encounters. First, it's their laziness. (Proud Scots might want to skip the next dozen extracts.)

> *All here about, who are called 'Borderers', seem to be very poor people, which I impute to their sloth. Scotland, this part of it, is a low marshy ground where they cut turf and peat for the fuel, though I should think the sea might convey coals to them.*

We might think it unfair of her to criticise them for not buying English coal when they've got their own local fuel. Next, the women come in for her special condemnation.

I see little that they are employed in besides fishing, which makes provision plentiful, or else their cutting and carving turf and peat, which the women and great girls bare-legged do. They lead a horse which draws a sort of carriage, the wheels like a dung-pot [we may guess what this is, though difficult to imagine as a wheel]. *These people though with naked legs are yet wrapped up in plaids, a piece of woollen like a blanket, or else riding hoods – and this when they are in their houses. I took them for people who were sick, seeing 2 or 3 great wenches as tall and big as any woman sat hovering between their bed and chimney corner, all idle doing nothing.*

And what about their homes?

The houses look just like the booths at a fair. They have no chimneys. Their smoke comes out all over the house, and there are great holes in the sides of their houses which lets out the smoke. There is no room in their houses other than those that go up to the thatch and in which are 2 or 3 beds, even their parlours and buttery. And notwithstanding the cleaning of their parlour for me, I was not able to bear the room. The smell of the hay was a perfume ['by comparison', I think she means] *and I rather chose to stay and see my horses eat their provender in the stable than to stand in that room, for I could not bring myself to sit down.*

They even manage to spoil good food here.

My landlady offered me a good dish of fish and brought me butter in a lairdly [probably meaning suitable for a laird] *dish with the clap bread, but I could have no stomach to eat any of the food they should order. So, I bought the fish she got for me which was full cheap enough, nine pence for two pieces of salmon, half a one near a yard long, and a very large trout of an amber colour.*

She's got plans for that fish later. Then at last, something she likes.

> *Drinking – without eating – some of their wine, exceeding good claret, which they stand conveniently for to have from France. And indeed it was the best and truest French wine I have drank this seven year and very clear … it was very fine.*

But then it's back to complaining.

> *I went up to their church which looks rather like some little house built of stone and brick such as our ordinary people in a village live in. The doors and the seats and pulpit were in so disregarded a manner that one would have thought there was no use of it. But there is a parson who lives just by, whose house is the best in the place.*

It's a problem where to stay for the night.

> *Therefore, for the most part, persons that travel there go from one nobleman's house to another.*

The usual solution for her of course when there are no decent lodgings – at least that's how it is south of the border for a lady of quality like herself. But – alas – here, even if you manage to stay with the topmost echelons of Scottish society, you're no better off – or so she's been told.

> *Their houses are all kinds of castles, and they live great though in so nasty a way as all things are, even in those houses, that one has little stomach to eat or use anything, as I have been told by some that has travelled there. And I am sure I met with a sample of it enough to discourage my progress farther in Scotland. Their miles are so long in these countries, they made me afraid to venture, lest after a tedious journey I should not be able to get a bed I could lie in.*

And she finishes by telling us again what she believes to be the fundamental problem in Scotland.

I attribute it wholly to their sloth, for I see they sit and do little. I think there were one or two at last did take spinning in hand – in a lazy way.

There's only one thing for it. She's been in Scotland for no more than a handful of days, but now it's back south over the border.

Thence I took my fish to carry it to a place for the English to dress it.

Celia Fiennes' attack on the Scots during her brief visit to the country is unprecedented in her diaries. There are plenty of times in England when she complains about the idleness of folk she meets, or about dirty houses and of course near-impassable roads, the inedible food at some lodgings, or a neglectful landlady. But nowhere else does she throw out these accusations in such a tirade against one set of people. It's close to being a rant. And then there's her highly unusual and bitter attack on those of a similar rank to herself, the Scottish nobility, who – she says – live 'in so nasty a way'. The only times she uses this word 'nasty' in all her diaries (except to describe a rainstorm once) is about the Scots and the Welsh, and never about folk in England, however much she may disapprove of their behaviour. She almost seems to be saying, 'There you are! Idleness. Nastiness. Typical of the Scots!' The passages I've quoted from the Scotland entries in her diaries sound like racial prejudice. Is that a fair accusation?

However, her description of the poverty she found in Scotland – leaving on one side for the moment her accusations about slothfulness and nastiness – may well be accurate. The economy in the Scottish borderlands in 1698, like much of the rest of Scotland, was indeed suffering.

Scots in the latter part of the seventeenth century had been the victims of a series of harsh economic blows delivered by war, English oppression and famine. For most of the century, Scotland was in a position of semi-independence from England. Both countries in theory recognised the same king but had different laws and parliaments. And the confusion about the extent to which Scotland was subservient to England was a recipe for conflict between the two.

The relationship became more complicated following the restoration of the monarchy in England in 1660 with the end to Oliver Cromwell's rule. Many Scots now found themselves at odds with the newly strengthened Anglican Church. The Scottish Covenanters (Presbyterians) were being forced to accept bishops and all the hierarchy and ritual of the English Church. For the next twenty-five years, the Covenanters suffered brutal persecution, and three rebellions were suppressed. During intermittent invasions by the English, Covenanters were hunted, tortured and executed in a period known as 'the Killing Times'. The Glorious Revolution of 1688–89, when the Protestants William and Mary came to the throne, launched a new round of fighting. This time there was an uprising by the Jacobites, supporters of the dethroned king, James II.

All these wars and rebellions had a profound impact on the Scottish economy, with the destruction of crops and the disruption of markets. Some improvement in living conditions during the 1680s was then knocked back in the following decade by a series of failed harvests, known as the 'Seven Ill Years', the time Fiennes is writing about. The result was severe famine, starvation for many and a rise in abnormally premature deaths.

So Celia Fiennes' description of the poverty in the Scottish borderlands may not be far from the truth. But what about her lack of sympathy for the people here who're the victims? She targets them for being uncouth and immodest and repeats her judgement that the foul conditions they live in are all their own fault for being so lazy. Of course, sloth and bare legs, as we've seen, are much despised by her wherever she finds them, whether in England, Scotland or Wales. As a restless Puritan gentlewoman, they're contrary to her own nature.

Should we therefore conclude that it's just in her character to condemn laziness and that there's no nationalist chauvinism in her attack on the Scots? Is Celia Fiennes xenophobic or not?

She's certainly an English patriot. As we've noted before, in the Introduction to her diaries, she writes that travelling around England would 'add much to its glory and cure the evil itch of over-valuing foreign parts'. And she certainly has an unalloyed loyalty for King William and Queen Mary. She frequently uses epithets such as 'glorious', 'good', 'hero', 'wise' when writing of them, and she spells out the reasons for her admiration of the monarchs.

> *Ever glorious King William and Queen Mary, his royal consort, jointly on the throne of these kingdoms, whom no time can ever obliterate the memory of, their being England's deliverers in God's hands from popery and slavery.*

You'll by the way notice she says, 'on the throne of these kingdoms', a reference to England and Scotland – in theory at least – sharing monarchs at this time.

But she's not a my-country-right-or-wrong chauvinist. As we see time after time, she doesn't hesitate to criticise English institutions or her fellow citizens if they don't conform to her view of Christian morality, industriousness or good government.

If she does seem to be biased against the Scots, she'd not be alone in her time. There was a long tradition in English literature of regarding the Celts from Scotland, Ireland and Wales as savages. It went back at least to medieval times, and in the reign of Elizabeth, for instance, the antiquarian William Camden characterised the Scots as a wild and barbarous people who 'drank the blood out of wounds of the slain'. When the Scottish Jacobite uprisings began, Whig politicians in England tapped into the tradition of belittling and despising the Scots and turned it into anti-Scottish propaganda. It might be that Celia Fiennes is in line with this Whig anti-Jacobite movement – that would hardly be surprising given her religious faith and political sympathies. So her dislike of the Scots may be because she sees them as a troublesome thorn in the side of the Protestant, post-Glorious-Revolution England of William and Mary, although she certainly doesn't ever spell that out.

Her visit to Scotland in 1698 comes just before a period in Anglo-Scottish history which managed the trick of combining fundamental change with more of the same old prejudice. Just nine years later, in 1707, came the Act of Union which was designed to bring together Scotland and England as a single nation. However, many Scots wanted independence and took up arms in a series of fierce rebellions culminating in the Jacobite uprising of 1745. With defeat at the Battle of Culloden, many Scottish highlanders were hunted down and killed, and whole clans were destroyed. Disdain for – and mockery of – the Scots was stepped up. Dr Johnson, towards the end of the century, was quoted as saying, 'The noblest prospect which a Scotchman ever sees, is the high road that leads him to England!' And in his ground-breaking dictionary, he defined oats as 'a grain, which in England is generally given to horses, but in Scotland supports the people'.

We might, then, perhaps see Celia Fiennes' attacks on the Scots in this context. Though not an extremist in her views, she was still reflecting a common prejudice of her time. We don't have to applaud that in order to understand where her bias came from and how it reflects a stage in a long story of bigotry.

And before she leaves the district close to the border with Scotland, there's a reminder that her criticism of those she meets is most certainly not reserved for the Scots. Just across in England, at the little town of Haltwhistle, she bemoans the dreadful treatment she receives.

> *There was one inn, but they had no hay, nor would get any, and when my servants had got some elsewhere, they* [the landlord and landlady] *were*

> *angry and would not entertain me. So I was forced to take up in a poor cottage which was open to the thatch and no partitions but hurdles* [like a piece of fencing] *plastered. Here I was forced to take up my abode, and the landlady brought me out her best sheets which served to secure my own sheets from her dirty blankets. But no sleep could I get, as they were burning turf, and their chimneys are sort of flues or open tunnels, so the smoke does annoy the rooms.*

Perhaps she's not quite so anti-Scottish as we might have thought. She doesn't trust anyone, be they English, Scottish or Welsh, to provide clean sheets – she brings her own. People can be as rude and dirty in England as anywhere else.

5

Newcastle to Manchester

READY FOR A REVOLUTION

I could see all about the country,
which was full of coal pits.

Celia Fiennes' likes and dislikes, and what sparks her curiosity, are often – as we've seen – in line with the dominant philosophy of her time. But given her independent spirit, there's also a personal twist to the way she sees her country and its people. Fashionable thinking at the end of the seventeenth century that God had made humans the masters of the world, and it was our role to bring untamed nature to heel, fitted well with her character. The human energy and inventiveness needed for that job are the very qualities she admires most. They match her own restlessness and curiosity, the attributes that spur her on to undertake her great journeys.

It's midsummer and starting to heat up as she approaches Newcastle along the north bank of the Tyne.

> *The river looked very refreshing, and the cattle coming to its sides and into it where shallow, to cool themselves in the heat. This afternoon was the hottest day I met with, but it was seasonable being in July.*

Again, as we discovered in the Lake District, water seems to be the only natural phenomenon she enjoys. After all, it can be more than a hazardous obstruction, it's also a resource that we – and our animals – need in order to survive.

As she rides closer to the town, she's greeted by a sight which tells of both an ancient past and a very different future. A means of transport almost as old as humankind, carrying a cargo which will soon change the economic and social course of the country.

As I drew nearer and nearer to Newcastle, I met with and saw an abundance of little carriages with a yoke of oxen and a pair of horses together, which are to convey the coals from the pits to the barges on the river. There are little sort of dung-pots – I suppose they hold not above two or three cauldrons.

Coal dominates the area.

This country all about is full of this coal. The sulphur of it taints the air and it smells strongly to strangers. Upon a high hill 2 miles from Newcastle, I could see all about the country, which was full of coal pits.

By the late seventeenth century, coal had already been a source of heat in Britain for well over 1,000 years. The north-east, especially around Newcastle, was almost certainly the first part of England where coal was mined in abundance. The Romans burned it in their fires and it was a common fuel throughout the Middle Ages. In the thirteenth and fourteenth centuries, as the population began to grow, mining became more widespread. The pits she talks about would have been the shallow basins – bell pits – we came across in Derbyshire.

There's a specific type of coal here.

This is sea-coal, which is pretty much small though some is round, yet not like the cleft coal.

By 'cleft coal', she probably means coal that's been split off in chunks from a coalface. Originally, 'sea-coal' was so called because it was found washed up on the beaches around Newcastle. But the term, it seems, then started to be applied to all coal in the north-east, even if it was mined miles inland. She explains its benefits.

> *This is what smiths use, and it cakes in the fire* [i.e. turns to coke] *and makes a great heat. The small sort is as good as any – if it's black and shining, that shows its goodness.*

Certain types of coal can be heated to a high temperature in order to burn off impurities. The result is coke, which can then be used to produce – as she says – 'a great heat'. In 1709, just eleven years after she visited Newcastle, Abraham Darby became the first to use coke in a blast furnace, and so revolutionised iron smelting. It was a significant first step in the Industrial Revolution.

The power that would soon turn the wheels of factory machinery and railway locomotives would be generated by the steam engine and that would need coal – lots of it. And so, when during the following centuries deep mines became possible, there were at one time or another close on eighty of them here in a single 10-mile stretch along the River Tyne. A dozen or more were clumped around the one village of Heddon. And that's where I'm heading next as I drive along the Hexham Road – almost certainly the route that Celia Fiennes took to approach Newcastle and where she saw so much activity in 1698. Heddon-on-the-Wall, to give it its full title, is close to the old Roman boundary.

Given the near obliteration of the Britain's coal industry in the 1980s, I'm wondering what vestige of the old way of life might remain here. The answer is – not much. Scanning the fields round about, I eventually make out – where two giant electricity pylons stand close together amid the greenery of trees – a hillock, black, dirty and incongruous – an old slag heap surely – and near it a half-demolished building. And that's it.

The words 'Newcastle' and 'coal' have long been inseparable workmates. The phrase 'Coals to Newcastle', for instance, meaning any ludicrous suggestion of giving someone something which they already have in abundance.

In her diaries, Celia Fiennes' observations reveal a significant fact about the city. In 1698, Newcastle was not some second-rate town-in-waiting, ready to take off once the Industrial Revolution arrived. Instead, its economy was already flying high, as she explains.

> *It's a noble town. It most resembles London of any place in England. Its buildings lofty and large, of brick mostly or stone. The streets are very broad and handsome and very well pitched.*

We might today see her use of London as the measuring stick by which this northern town may be judged as a case of metropolitan elitism. Nevertheless, by the second half of the seventeenth century, Newcastle was widely considered the leading town in the kingdom after the capital. And what's more, London's growing population was dependent on Newcastle, whose ships brought them the fuel they needed to heat their buildings.

And this wealth has been turned to the advantage of its citizens' health.

> *Many of the streets with very fine conduits of water in each, always running into a large stone cistern for everybody's use. There is one great street where, at the market cross, there was a great conduit with two spouts which fall into a large fountain paved with stone. It held at least 2 or 3 hogsheads* [between 150 and 225 gallons] *for the inhabitants.*

By the late seventeenth century, the town had become a flourishing national and international trading centre – and in the streets of market towns across the North Sea in Flanders, Denmark and Norway, you could find traders from Newcastle hard at it, selling and buying.

She tells us:

> *The quay is a very fine place and looks itself like an exchange* [i.e. a market], *being very broad and so full of merchants walking to and again. And it runs for a great length with a great many steps down to the water for the conveniency of landing or boating their goods, and is full of cellars or warehouses. The harbour is full of ships – those above 2 or 300 tonnes cannot come up quite to the quay. It's a town of great trade.*

A map of Newcastle from the late seventeenth century shows that the main quay was alongside the Tyne bridge leading south. And today the road there is still called 'Quayside'. But, as I discover driving along it, the name is the only reminder of the bustling loading and unloading of ships that Celia Fiennes saw here. There's now a wide promenade alongside the water – joggers and fast-walkers dodging around strollers – with takeaways and cafés on the opposite side to serve the office workers. Fiennes has put her finger on why this quay didn't survive – the river wasn't deep enough here for the bigger ships to be able to dock. Newcastle and the north-east are still served by one of the country's main ports, though it's now some 7 miles east along the Tyne closer to the sea.

It can be hard for us today to understand that the words 'coal' and 'prosperity' were once linked in what looked like an unshakeable marriage. When Celia Fiennes visits Newcastle in 1698, the city has become the wealthiest coal port in the country.

We shouldn't imagine, however, that with the arrival of the Industrial Revolution, Newcastle sat back and relaxed, having done all its work. Far from it. As the country grew, prospered and changed – not always for the better – Newcastle took a lead. Its role in the Industrial Revolution would not be confined to providing the fuel. George and Robert Stephenson established the world's first purpose-built locomotive works here. Then Newcastle added shipbuilding to coal and railways, and so formed the industrial base of Britain's prosperity and global strength in the eighteenth and nineteenth centuries.

Her account of the wealth and industry of Newcastle and its surrounding area is a reminder that the Industrial Revolution was not always the sudden 180-degree shift in society that the word 'revolution' implies. The north-east described by her shows us that industrialisation and wealth creation was already under way in the late seventeenth century.

She takes one last view of the city as she crosses the river south to Gateshead.

> *There is a fine bridge over the Tyne River with 9 arches, all built as London bridge.*

And she climbs a nearby hill.

> *As that gave a large prospect of the town and whole country about on that side, so this gives as pleasing a sight of the whole river and ships in the harbour.*

From Gateshead, she rides to Chester le Street – 'a little market town' – and from there she can see her next city stop, Durham, 5 miles away.

> *The city stands on a great rise of ground and is a mile and half in length, the middle part much higher than the rest.*

What strikes her is the medieval feel of the place, a contrast to Newcastle.

> *The cathedral and castle, which is the palace, with the college and all the houses of the doctors of the churches are altogether built of stone, and all encompassed with a wall full of battlements above the walk,*

'There is a fine bridge over the Tyne River with 9 arches, all built as London Bridge.' (Summerhill)

And although she finds much to praise about the place – 'clean and pleasant buildings, streets large, well-pitched' – at one of its seven churches, she discovers something that marks down the city in her ever-constant Presbyterian estimation.

> *In the vestry, I saw several fine embroidered capes. I saw one with the whole description of Christ's nativity, life, death and ascension. This is put on the Dean's shoulders at the administration of the Lord's supper, and at several more ceremonies and rites retained from the times of popery. Here is the only place that they use these things in England. There are many papists in the town, popishly affected, and daily increase.*

It's an example again of her more liberal brand of Puritanism. Yes, she disapproves of the growing number of 'papists' so 'popishly affected' but notice that – while she disapproves of the designs on the capes – yet she praises the fine embroidery work that went into producing them. It's a rational, tolerant opinion – compared with the violent opposition of Civil War times – consistent with the mainstream spirit of the age.

What she doesn't tell us about Durham is that the city wasn't entirely free from the influence of coal. The surrounding district was rich with pits, and the city's bishops through their ownership of land had profited from mining for centuries.

Thence to Darlington. It's a Monday, a busy day.

> *A great market of all things, a great quantity of cattle of all sorts, but mostly beefs.*

And on to the North Riding of Yorkshire. Richmond – noted today by tourists from across the world for the splendour of its Georgian architecture. That came after Celia Fiennes. In 1698 it is in a dilapidated state.

> *I must say it looks like a sad shattered town and fallen much to decay and like a disregarded place.*

The wool industry which helped bring wealth to the town is evidently not yet well-established.

It is a different story in the third major town she then visits on this stretch of her journey.

> *Leeds is a large town, and good houses all built of stone. Some have good gardens and steps up to their houses and walls before them. This is esteemed the wealthiest town of its size in the country. Its manufacture*

is woollen cloth – the Yorkshire cloth in which they are all employed and are esteemed very rich and very proud. They have provision so plentiful that they may live with very little expense and get much variety.

The woollen industry had been the heart of England's prosperity in the Middle Ages. English sheep had provided a product that was exported all over Europe – it was still doing so in Celia Fiennes' day. And just as Newcastle's coal was the source of pre-Industrial Revolution wealth as well as being at the heart of industrialisation, so Leeds's wool did much the same. The difference being that whereas coal would drive the machinery, wool – in its spinning and weaving – would be the beneficiary of the steam-powered engines that would be devised over the following century. And her account of Leeds makes clear that the town is already, in her words, 'very rich' from the textile industry in the late seventeenth century, before the age of mass production which the Industrial Revolution would deliver.

But it's not just the industry and prosperity that attracts her to Leeds. It's apparently the only place in Yorkshire where a local tradition survives that promises to satisfy her appetite for a bargain and for something else.

A tankard of ale is always a groat [four pence] – *it's the only dear thing all over Yorkshire. Their ale is very strong, but for paying this groat for your ale, you could have a slice of meat either hot or cold according to the time of day you call, or else butter and cheese gratis into the bargain.*

Alas, that's how it used to be in most of Yorkshire, not anymore.

And though they still retain the great price for the ale, yet make strangers pay for their meat, and at some places at great rates, notwithstanding how cheap they have all their provision.

However, the special offer still exists in Leeds – on just one day a week.

> *There is still this custom on a market day at Leeds. At the 'Sign of the Bush' just by the bridge, anybody that will go and call for one tankard of ale and a pint of wine and pay for these only, shall be set to a table to eat with 2 or 3 dishes of good meat and a dish of sweet-meats after.*

But she's arrived on the wrong day!

> *Had I known this and the day which was their market, I would have come then, but I happened to come a day after.*

Somehow, though, she still manages to get a good deal.

> *However, I did only pay for 3 tankards of ale and what I ate, and my servant's meal was gratis.*

As she rides on further west, she pauses to tell us about her crossing of Blackstone Edge. This gritstone escarpment, rising to 1,500ft above sea level, forms a natural wall between Yorkshire and Lancashire. Its crags and rocky paths are a favourite with hillwalkers and rock climbers today. And, consistent with her loathing for wild landscape, the best bit is once you get back down off the hillside.

> *This hill put me in mind of the description of the Alps in Italy, where the clouds drive all about. And though on the top it holds snow and hail falling on those who pass, at length the lower they go, comes into rain and so into sun-shine – at the foot of those valleys, fruitful, the sun-shine and singing of birds. This was the account my father gave of those Alps when he passed them, and I could not but think this place carried some resemblance in a little proportion to that.*

Her father, Colonel Nathaniel Fiennes, had died when she was 7. So this must have been one of her few memories of him and clearly one that stuck in her mind. He'd crossed the Alps as a young man on a visit to Geneva.

My route over Blackstone Edge is via the M62, and I'm struck by how remote we often feel today from our surroundings when we travel the country. For Celia Fiennes, the narrow winding tracks that she rode over hills, through woods, across marshes and down valleys, meant she was absorbed into the landscape. We, on the other hand, often choose speed as our priority and that means one six-lane motorway is much like another. When we travel in the twenty-first century, we've often lost the constant and immediate feel for our natural surroundings that Celia Fiennes experienced in 1698.

And so to Manchester. For me, it's an hour or more's drive from the outskirts before I get anywhere near its centre. Today, of course, we think of Manchester alongside Leeds and Newcastle as one of the great conurbations of northern England, and given that Celia Fiennes tells us the other two had thriving economies in the late seventeenth century, we might expect her now to launch into a description of Manchester's industrial energy and trading competence. She doesn't. Not that she denigrates the place.

> *Manchester looks exceedingly well at the entrance – very substantial buildings. The houses are not very lofty but mostly of brick and stone. The old houses are timber work,*

Ever with a sharp eye for the unusual, she's drawn to a collection of oddities in the church library.

> *There is a long whispering trumpet, and there I saw the skin of the rattle snake 6 foot long with many other curiosities, the anatomy of a man wired together, a jaw of a shark; there was a very fine clock and weather glass.*

This 'weather glass' is probably an early barometer. Meteorological forecasting was just starting to emerge from an age when folklore ('Red sky in the morning, shepherd's warning') was the best you could do. The barometer had been developed in the late seventeenth century by the physicist Robert Hooke. He began linking its readings to weather patterns. On 16 January 1690, he observed, 'a most violent storm or hurricane which blew down trees, houses, chimney &c. It blew down part of my parlour chimney, untiled much of my long garret, broke windows &c. The Barometer was very low.'

There's no mention in her diary of Manchester's textile industry, which had started to grow in previous decades, encouraged by the community of Flemish weavers who'd settled here earlier in the century. But compared with Leeds and Newcastle at this time, Manchester was still a small market town. Its era of great wealth and expansion would have to wait for the invention of the spinning jenny which would start the process of automation, and for the canals and then the railways to provide convenient and soon much faster means of transport, a time in the later eighteenth and the nineteenth centuries when Manchester would march at the head of the Industrial Revolution.

Her account of the northern cities of Newcastle, Durham, Leeds and Manchester tells us that, although industrialisation began before the so-called 'Revolution' in Leeds and especially in Newcastle, it did not do so everywhere. Some cities – even Durham, which was surrounded by rich coalfields – retained their medieval origins, and Durham still does to this day. Others, and Manchester is the chief example, didn't see dramatic growth in their economies until the steam engine arrived to jack up the rate of industrial output. The same was true of Liverpool. She has even less to say about it than she does about Manchester.

The original town was a few fishermen's houses and now is grown to a large fine town. It's a very rich trading town.

She doesn't expand on that comment. Given her ever-observant eye, it seems that the great gateway to Britain's colonies and overseas markets that we recognise in Liverpool's history was still a few decades away.

In summary, there was no single pattern to economic development in the lead up to what we've come to call the Industrial Revolution. It's the example of Manchester, which played such an important role in the Industrial Revolution, that sometimes has made us – mistakenly – think that the massive economic and social changes of the eighteenth and nineteenth centuries were the sudden results of new inventions. What Celia Fiennes teaches us is that it was often a more gradual process which was already well under way in Newcastle and Leeds when she saw them in 1698.

Her visit to Manchester tells us not only about the progress of industrialisation in the late seventeenth century, but also about a social issue of the time – education. She remarks on a school in the town.

> *Just by the church is the college which is a pretty neat building with a large space for the boys to play in, and a good garden walled in. There are 60 Blue Coat boys.*

'Blue coat' was the name given to charity schools, maintained by donations from local people. They were usually run by religious organisations. Literacy levels in the population of England at large had improved during the seventeenth century, though from a very low starting point – it's estimated that two-thirds of people were illiterate back then. In Celia Fiennes' time, there was an enthusiastic move to spread general education. In the year we're travelling with her, 1698, the Society for the Promotion of Christian Knowledge was founded with the aim 'to promote and encourage the erection of charity schools in all parts of England and Wales'.

You'll have noticed that at Manchester's Blue Coat School, she writes only of 'boys' attending the school. No mention of education for girls. That had been the usual practice for centuries. In Tudor times, educating girls to the same standard as boys had been considered unseemly. At the end of the sixteenth century, for instance, Lady Dorothy Newdigate expressed a wish in her will that her sons should be brought up 'in good learning' and her daughters in 'virtuous and godly life'. Some limited change was on the way by Celia Fiennes' day. Girls as well as boys attended the establishments set up by the Society for the Promotion of Christian Knowledge. In 1704, its schools in London and Westminster, for example, had a total of 1,386 boys registered and 745 girls. The inequality in numbers, however, isn't the whole story. In 1706, it's recorded that boys there were taught 'to write a fair legible hand, with the grounds of arithmetic to fit them for apprentices or service', while girls, having been taught to read (not to write), then learned 'to knit their stockings or gloves, to mark, sew, mend or make their clothes'. Schooling for girls at the same level and in the same subjects as boys in the late seventeenth century was regarded as unnecessary. A woman's job was to improve the lot of her children and especially of her husband.

That principle extended to the higher ranks of society. While she's in Manchester, Fiennes observes another teaching establishment.

> *Here is a very fine school for young gentlewomen as good as any in London, and music and dancing and things are very plentiful here.*

It's the same story in Shrewsbury. Again, she approves of the syllabus.

> *Here is a very good school for young gentlewomen for learning work and behaviour and music.*

The first moves towards gender equality in education are not usually recognised until decades after Celia Fiennes made her great journeys. In the mid-eighteenth century, Elizabeth Montagu helped found the Blue Stocking Society, which brought like-minded, forward-thinking women together to promote their education. Then towards the end of the century, Mary Wollstonecraft, from a middle-class London home, expounded a revolutionary philosophy – that women were the equals of men, and only seemed inferior because they were not given the same schooling. The only hint of these ideas in Celia Fiennes' day is usually reckoned to be a book entitled *A Serious Proposal to the Ladies for the Advancement of their True and Greatest Interest*, written in 1694. Its author, Mary Astell, made the – limited – argument that better education would help women to make more measured decisions in the choice of a husband.

But despite her praise of schools which teach young gentlewomen 'music and dancing', Fiennes expresses what, for her time, is a radical idea about the need for women to improve their lives through study. In the Introduction to her diaries – probably written a few years after her great journeys – she writes:

> *I shall conclude with a hearty wish and recommendation to all, but especially my own sex, the study of those things which tend to improve the mind and make our lives pleasant and comfortable as well as profitable in all the stages and stations of our lives, and render suffering and age supportable, and death less formidable, and a future state more happy.*

It's not necessarily an argument for better schooling for all women. But it is a recognition by her that women as much as men can benefit from studying and observing the world around them. For this – if for nothing else - Celia Fiennes should be remembered.

6

Cheshire to Shropshire

HIGHWAYMEN!

With bundles about them
which I believe were pistols.

Novelists who don't flinch from a cliché have been known to hint that something bad is soon going to happen, with the words 'It all began peacefully enough'. We're supposed to guess that it won't last.

Sometimes though, reality mimics the cliché. For instance, when Celia Fiennes leaves Lancashire and rides south into Cheshire.

> *I went a very pleasant road, much of it on the downs, mostly champion ground, some few enclosures. I went by Dunham Massey, the Earl of Warrington's house, which stands in a very fine park,*

And this pleasant fineness is followed by something she loves even more: the chance to investigate local industry.

> *I passed over two or three stone bridges across little rivers to Northwich. It's not very large, and is full of salt-works, the brine pits being all here and about. The town is full of smoke from the salterns.*

A 'saltern' is a salt-works. The Cheshire area was known for its salt-water springs. This brine was collected in large containers made either of ceramics or later of iron, in which the water could evaporate leaving behind the salt crystals. The process of evaporation couldn't be left to the sun given normal English weather, so a fire was lit beneath the containers. Hence the smoke that she witnesses.

Before the invention of refrigeration, salt was of vital importance. It was the only way to preserve meat and fish. I need to find out more. And so, abandoning my own less than perfect start to the day (i.e. the dreaded M6, delays, minor outbursts of road rage), I take advantage of a sudden spurt in the speed of my fellow drivers, swing off at Junction 20 and head for the village of Marston just outside Northwich. It's home to one of the few museums in the country that tells the history of the salt industry. It turns out to be a modern glass and brick barn close by the remnants of an old salt-works.

I tag along with a retirees' club outing from Chester on a tour. The first thing we learn is that salt has been produced in Northwich and its neighbours, Nantwich and Droitwich ('All the -wiches make salt', as Celia Fiennes puts it) since Roman times. There have always been two ways of using it to preserve food: dry salting, where you rub it into your beef or lamb, or if it is fish, you put thick layers of salt between each slice, and wet salting, where the food is immersed in brine.

Everyone needed salt. There was so much money to be made out of it that in 1693, five years before Celia Fiennes came to Northwich, the king had decided to get a piece of the action for the royal coffers. He brought in a new tax on the producers of it. So valuable was salt that there was even a brisk trade in smuggling it.

When she visits Cheshire, the area is seeing a resurgence of prosperity, and she tells us why. The best type of salt was rock salt, and up to the 1690s, most of it was imported to England from western France. But then, Northwich and the others started to produce it much more cheaply. She explains what's happened.

> *They have within these few years found in their brine pits a hard, rocky salt that looks clear like sugar candy. They call it rock salt. It will make very good brine with fresh water to use quickly. They carry it to the waterside in Wales by the rivers that flow with the tide.* [This is probably the wide Mersey Estuary, no more than 12 miles from Northwich] *And so they boil these pieces of rock in some of the*

> ***salt water when the tide is in, which produces as strong and good salt as any others.***

It turns out that she had a personal connection with Northwich rock salt. During the winter of 1705–06, an obscure legal case was brought before the House of Lords concerning a dispute over a piece of land here which was rich in salt. The name 'Cecilia Fiennes' (note the extra 'ci' – 'Cecilia' is believed to be her birth name) is listed as one of the Appellants. She held a mortgage on the land. We know nothing more. Whether it was her visit here and her understanding of the potential riches of rock salt that persuaded her to invest her money in it, or whether it was a decision by a financial adviser, remains a mystery.

From Northwich, she heads south towards Whitchurch in Shropshire. She's precise about her route.

> ***Then to Beeston Wood and came by Beeston Castle on a very high hill, the walls remaining round it, which I left a little on my right hand just at the foot of the hill.***

This identifies her route as what today is Chapel Lane. The castle is now an English Heritage site, and I have to stop outside its stone gatehouse, as several families make their way from the field that's been converted into a car park and cross the road in front of me. English Heritage claim that Beeston is 'one of the most dramatic ruins in the English landscape'. During the Civil War, the castle witnessed a tale of betrayal, cowardice, death and bravery enough to fill a BBC boxset. It had lain derelict until, on 20 February 1643, a Parliamentary force moved in, repaired some of the walls and prepared for the inevitable Royalist onslaught. But it came in an unexpected way. On 13 December, nine soldiers loyal to the king crept into Beeston by night – possibly aided by a traitor in the castle garrison. The Parliamentary governor of the castle, Captain Thomas Steele, was so unnerved by what had happened that he surrendered without a fight on condition that he be allowed to march away to safety. Safety, however, he did not find. Cromwell had him put on trial for his failure to defend the castle. He was found guilty and was shot. Meanwhile, the Cavaliers who'd taken over the castle were themselves now besieged by the Roundheads. They held out for twelve months until they ran out of food and had no choice but to run up the white flag. In 1646, Cromwell gave orders for Beeston Castle to be partly demolished so it could no longer play a role in the war. And it's in this ruinous state that Celia Fiennes sees it fifty-two years later.

Immediately south of the castle, Chapel Lane makes a sharp left bend. But there's a footpath that goes straight on, and, as anyone who's studied old maps knows, this means you're almost certainly looking at the route of the original, ancient road. A sign tells me it's called the Sandstone Trail. It's likely Celia Fiennes' route would have been along here. I park at the Sandstone Café, lace up my walking boots, stick a bottle of water in a pocket and set off. At first there's a shoulder-high stone wall on the right, the track is no more than a yard wide, and I have to keep grabbing my all-weather brimmed hat to duck beneath the branches on the left. If this was the ancient road that she took, it's become overgrown in the centuries since. There's no way horse-mounted travellers or a coach could navigate it now. Then suddenly after a quarter of a mile or so, it changes. It's still a walking track by twenty-first century standards, but it widens out as it enters some wood.

'Yes!' I can't stop myself calling out to no one but myself. I'm excited because this must be pretty much what it would have been like when she rode this route. The track winds through tunnels of leafy light. Occasionally, I come to a small glade, then just as suddenly the trees close over my head again and I seem to be in semi-darkness. But it remains a good 3 or 4 metres wide. Would Celia Fiennes have felt that a wood like this was a dangerous place? Would she have hurried to reach the safety of the next village? Probably not. By now she'd rode for over 2,000 miles and was no stranger to remote, enclosed country roads. Why should there have been anything to worry about now?

But it was at this spot (or somewhere close by like it) that she faced what must have been the most terrifying experience during all her thousands of miles on the road. She takes up the story.

> *Here, I think I may say, was the only time I had reason to suspect that I was engaged with some highwaymen. Two fellows, all on a sudden, from the wood fell into the road. They looked trussed up with great coats, and, as it were, bundles about them which I believe were pistols.*

Now, Celia Fiennes is not one to exaggerate or to over-react. If anything, as we've seen, she tends to underplay dramas on her exploits. She continues:

> *But they dogged me, one before, the other behind, and would often look back to each other, and frequently jostled my horse out of the way, to get between one of my servants horses and mine.*

The robbers seem nervous.

> *They would often stay a little behind and talk together, then come up again.*

We can only guess that they were weighing up whether her servants were beefy enough to be able to resist a hold-up. She tells us that the robbers' suspicious activity continued for 'three or four miles'. If we assume that her party were travelling at a brisk walking pace, then the episode lasted more than half an hour.

In the end, she has a lucky let-off. It happens to be harvest-time and it was market day in the next town down the road.

> *The providence of God so ordered it that there were men working in the fields, haymaking. And it being market-day in Whitchurch, as I drew near to it in three or four miles, I was continually met with some of the market people. So the men at last called each other off, so left us and turned back.*

Now, we may think that this encounter doesn't sound life-threatening, and as attempted robbery goes, we might even see it as all a bit amateurish and nothing much to worry about. But that was far from the case, and I'll explain why.

Let's start with this word 'highwaymen', which – as we've seen – she herself uses. It may seem an odd term to describe the two men she encountered. What it often calls to mind in many of us today is something like the following tale. And by the way, this was widely reported as fact in books and pamphlets at the time.

One day in the late 1660s on Hounslow Heath, west of London, a gentleman-highwayman holds up a coach at pistol-point. It's carrying a nobleman and his lady. The woman is determined to show she's not afraid and takes out her flageolet – a small wind instrument similar to a recorder – and begins to play. The highwayman just happens to have his own flageolet about his person and joins her in a duet. They hit it off so well that he then asks her to dance with him on the heath, the accompanying music being provided by gentleman robber's singing. Afterwards, he escorts her back to her seat in the coach and points out to her husband that he's not paid for the entertainment. Though the nobleman has some £400 with him, the highwayman – in tribute to the lady's grace and gentility – lets him off with a payment of £100, and promises to advise his fellow robbers that the noble couple should in future be allowed to pass in safety.

The robber in this tale was Claude Du Vall, and the legend of the romantic highwayman probably owes most to him. He gained the titles of 'the true gentleman of the road' and 'an eternal feather in the cap of highway gentility'.

For all Claude Du Vall's romantic-sounding name, he came from a lowly background. By 1666, he'd turned to robbery and was working the heaths and woods just north of London – the very area, as we've seen, that Celia Fiennes had to negotiate whenever she travelled out of the capital. But Du Vall was no run-of-the-mill criminal. He'd cultivated a reputation for fashionable dressing, nice manners with the ladies, and for a gentle approach to his trade, avoiding any violence. So the story went anyway, though quite how he managed to persuade his victims to part with their cash and not laugh in his face if they were confident he wasn't going to hurt them, isn't clear.

Du Vall's career of genteel crime lasted just three years, and his downfall was less than romantic. He was arrested while drunk in a London pub, known variously as the Hole-in-the-Wall and Mother Maberley's Tavern in Covent Garden, and he appeared before Judge Sir William Morton charged with a string of robberies. The story then goes that such was his reputation as a charming rogue that the cream of society tried to bully the judge into releasing him. It was said that the ladies of the Court organised a campaign to get him freed. Even King Charles II gave his support and called on the judge to grant Du Vall a reprieve. Justice Morton threatened to resign, and after a brief stand-off, the king gave way.

And so, on 27 January 1670, Du Vall was hanged at Tyburn. He was 27. Several biographies were soon produced lauding his life. They related how the crowd at his execution, including a number of ladies of quality wearing facemasks, wailed and wept to see their hero perish. A grand funeral followed at St Paul's Church, Covent Garden. It's said – though not confirmed – that he was buried beneath the central aisle with this epitaph:

Here lies Du Vall, reader.
If male thou art,
Look to thy purse.
If female, to thy heart.

Du Vall wasn't alone. There were others, equally fabled for their good manners and kindly ways, such as 'Swift Nick' Nevison, Captain James Hind and, from a few decades after Celia Fiennes was on the road, Dick Turpin.

Clearly many of the tales about these gentleman criminals were fiction that appealed to the romantic tastes or political beliefs of the reader. But there's almost certainly a grain of truth in the sandpit of myth. So what do we know as facts about the road robbers of the late seventeenth century?

When Fiennes was making her great journeys, highway robbery was reaching its peak. Following the Civil War fifty years earlier, some Royalist-supporting English gentlemen, whose cause had been defeated and who'd fallen on hard times, turned to stealing at gunpoint on remote roads. A celebrity cult grew up around them. The trend continued when the Catholic James II was ousted in 1688 and succeeded by the Protestant rulers, King William and Queen Mary. Celia Fiennes of course adored the country's new monarchs. But support for a Catholic kingship did not disappear overnight, though those who supported it had to be circumspect. The continuing legend of the Royalist highwayman – the rebel operating in the shadows – fitted that political viewpoint. Many were former gentleman soldiers who wanted to see the now-exiled James II restored to the throne.

Most highwaymen – the ones in the records – during the period when Fiennes was on her travels, bore little resemblance to Du Vall and his kind. Some favoured organised gangs. In 1674, in Yorkshire, a highway robbery was committed which couldn't have been further from the image of non-violent, polite 'relieving' the victims of their cash. A mob of around twenty robbers set upon fifteen butchers who were travelling to Northallerton Fair. The butchers fought back and seven of them were killed while three of the robbers perished too. The gang must have had inside knowledge of the spoils. They stole the huge sum of £936. But the parish officers – the nearest there was at that time to anything resembling a police force – followed

James Hind, highwayman. A picture of genteel elegance rather than common thuggishness. (Wikimedia Commons)

them, and a second battle ensued that night, in which four more of the thieves were killed. The other thirteen were imprisoned in York Castle, and before they were all hanged, two of them claimed they'd ridden with Du Vall himself. That might have been a tale to try to win for themselves some of the sympathy which 'gentleman' Du Vall commanded.

And we know of other brutal road crimes. In 1691, a gang of highwaymen killed three local people near Barnet, close to the north-west outskirts of London. And one observer records how in 1693 five highwaymen operating on the road between Rochester and Gravesend in Kent carried out a series of robberies, in which nine innocent people were murdered. And as for the romantic treatment of the fair sex, consider the fate of a woman who was held up by William Cady on Finchley Common in 1687. He called her a whore, then demanded her wedding ring. To keep it from him, she managed to swallow it. Cady was furious. He tied up her husband, and then shot the woman in the head. He proceeded to cut her open and removed the ring from her stomach. He met his end at Tyburn in 1687, not praying or making a contrite speech, but cursing. He was 25.

Celia Fiennes' experience looks to be in a different category completely. Her highwaymen were neither genteel celebrities nor psychotic killers. They seem to be nervous chancers. Armed with guns – if her assumption about the bundles they carried is correct – but uncertain whether they'll meet any resistance. That was likely to be typical, because most road robbers knew that the biggest threat they faced was from their victims themselves or from some other armed traveller happening on the scene. Provided they could be sure that no one there was going to pull out a pistol and shoot back, the robbers could be fairly confident they were safe. You have to remember, as we saw earlier in Fiennes' account of crime and punishment, that before the days of police forces – unheard of for another 150 years – the robbers' chances of being arrested and brought to justice were slim. That had another effect. Except in the rare circumstances that there was a diarist like Celia Fiennes involved, then the only hold-ups we usually know about are where the culprit was caught, tried and hanged. Then we might have a record of the court case. But of course that didn't happen often. And this was an age when, apart from a few rumour-filled pamphlets, there were nothing like newspapers around to report unsolved crimes. And no Office for National Statistics was counting every last stabbing and shooting, and publishing the numbers.

It's likely there were hundreds if not thousands of highway robberies in the late seventeenth century that neither we today, nor indeed most people back then, ever got to hear about. Celia Fiennes' highwaymen would have been local ruffians, nervous and disorganised, and hoping they'd meet no resistance. Their edginess would be no reassurance either. You could be shot in a moment of panic and the perpetrators would be off and away, never to be heard of again.

Her account, then, of what happened in the woods on the way to Whitchurch was almost certainly the norm of highway robbery in the late seventeenth century. It's the true story of the highwayman – of frightening, usually unreported crime committed by small-time violent thugs any time of the day or night, anywhere on England's thousands of miles of country roads away from the nearest town. She was lucky to escape.

Her encounter with the highway robbers raises the question of how many servants, or others, travelled with her on her two great journeys. As we heard her say, the highwaymen 'frequently jostled my horse out of the way, to get between one of my servants horses and mine'. Because she doesn't put an apostrophe in the word 'servants', it's not clear whether she means 'one of my servants' horses', i.e., more than one servant, or 'one of my servant's horses' which would imply that there was one servant who had charge of a spare horse, entirely plausible on long, difficult journeys.

The subject of servants is not one she ever addresses directly. We're dependent on a few passing references. Several times she does clearly state that she has more than one attendant with her without any further detail. Often it's to do with the treatment she receives at some inn. In Leeds for instance, 'I did only pay for 3 tankards of ale and what I ate, and my servants were gratis.' So were they men or women? Several times she's more specific. In Northumberland where the road was steep, she watches 'as my man rode up that sort of precipice'. And later when she crosses the Tamar Estuary into Cornwall and the ferry stalls in the strong current, she tells us, 'I set my own men to row also'. So on that occasion there was more than one. And in Derby, we did get a quick glimpse of what may have been the norm, when she complains about the price of meals, saying, 'My dinner cost me 5*s* and 8*d*, only 2 servant men with me'. It's fair to interpret this as a complaint about how expensive the food was for only two servants and herself – rather than 'only 2 servant men', implying she usually had more than two with her.

What about maidservants? She mentions female attendants only once. When taking the waters at Bath, she tells us that the women guides at the spa help you take off your bathing dress 'and in the meantime, your maids fling a garment of flannel made like a night-gown with great sleeves over your head'.

But this is not on either of her great journeys of 1697 or 1698. It's when she's much younger on a trip out from her mother's home at Newton Toney in Wiltshire. Maids are never mentioned in her account of either of her major travels round the country. So if she never takes a maidservant with her, why would that be? It's possible she may have felt that having young women with her for thousands of miles on the road would be an unnecessary worry, so decided she could do without them. A couple of trustworthy men, however, would have been useful to look after the horses – it's likely she would have had at least one spare mount and at least one packhorse to carry luggage – and, of course, two burly blokes would be an invaluable protection in case of threats of violence, as we've just seen.

And, of course, what we tend to forget – because she never touches on the subject – is that there must have been one especially valuable part of her luggage. Money. A lot of it. Long before the days of credit cards or high street ATMs, she would have needed to be carrying a huge amount of cash not only to pay for lodgings and meals, but also for reshoeing horses, ferry fares, paying guides, and buying the odd gift. If we allow, say, a modest seven or eight shillings a day for 150 days, that would be somewhere around £50 or £60 which she would need at the start of each of her great journeys. In today's money that could be the equivalent of £20,000 to £30,000. Bank notes wouldn't arrive on the scene for another 100 years, so it would have to be carried in coins. The most common were the smallest denominations: the farthing, halfpenny and the silver penny. But there were larger ones including pound coins. It's possible she had some arrangement to borrow money from the several relatives she calls on. But even if that were the case – and there's no evidence of it – much of the time she would still need to have plenty of ready cash on her. This would have made her especially vulnerable to being robbed. Any thief seeing a clearly well-heeled, probably aristocratic, woman on the road, would know that there would be rich pickings to be had. So this meant it would be important to have servants with her who could double as bodyguards. A strong argument that two male attendants were probably her norm.

There are also times when she has company from members of her own class. She makes several references for example to calling in to see people who are known to someone travelling with her.

> *From Coventry to Warwick going to see an acquaintance of our company.*

And she uses the same phrase in Cambridge.

> *Here we are entertained by some of our company's acquaintance.*

It's rare that she does identify 'our company'. For instance, on the road south from Gloucester.

> *From thence I went in company all this while with my cousin Filmer and family. We came to Nympsfield after having ascended a very steep narrow and stony hill.*

But by the time she's travelled 50 miles or so from Gloucester, it's no longer 'we' but now:

> *Here I passed by Babington, the Duke of Beaufort's house.*

The Filmers were the family of her cousin Susannah, who'd married a prominent London lawyer, Thomas Filmer, and they had two daughters. As we saw earlier when she left London, they lived at Amwell in Hertfordshire just north of the capital. So this reference is a puzzle, because the Filmers' home is nowhere near Gloucester, it's 130 miles to the east. They can't have travelled all the way up to Scotland with her and back, because there are many incidents and events where she would have told us about them. The most glaring example is the frightening experience with the highwaymen – the Filmer family were clearly not part of that. It's much more likely that they'd been staying somewhere with friends or relations in the Gloucester area, and arranged to meet up with Fiennes and ride with her for a spell.

We can't be sure who was with her for most of her travels, but all the evidence is that while she might occasionally have had companions from her own rank in society, she is never without two manservants. From time to time, as we've seen, she would employ a local guide, if one was available, to avoid getting lost. But always she's in charge. She chooses which direction to take, whether that's up rocky hills, through marshy lowlands or crossing rivers. It's her decision where they stop for the night. She's the leader throughout the many excitements and perils along the way. No other woman at this time could match that.

Before we move on from the road to Whitchurch where she came up against the two robbers, there's something we must see at a place there called No Man's Heath. This humble village has done something which neither London, nor Newcastle, not Ely nor Chester, nowhere else has done. It's honoured this remarkable woman and her achievements. In the middle of the small village green in No Man's Heath stands a stone block, on one side, the moulded image of a woman wearing a high hat with brim in a sweeping curve, and a horse peering shyly at her from round the corner. It was commissioned by local people in 1998 to commemorate the 300th anniversary of her visit here. The inscription reads, 'Celia Fiennes passed through this place on her great journey 1698'.

7

Whitchurch to Worcester

POLITICS: FOLLY, FACTION AND WICKEDNESS

Those that would be Parliament men
spend prodigious sums of money to be chosen.

One of the things we've learned about Celia Fiennes is that she is a very private person. Certain things of course make her cross: badly repaired roads, laziness, getting ripped off when buying food or drink, rude or neglectful landladies. But she would no more discuss the intimacy of her feelings in her diary than she would tell us about her emotional relationships with friends or family. So in the first days after her terrifying encounter with the highwaymen, we've no way of knowing how she feels, whether she's shocked or nervous or whether she can just brush it off and get on with her journey. When she reaches Whitchurch, only a couple of miles down the road, she seems remarkably calm.

> *Here are two very fine gardens. One belongs to an apothecary, full of all fruits and greens. The other was at the Crown Inn where I stayed. It was exceeding neat with orange and lemon trees, myrtle, striped and gilded holly trees, box and phillyrea* [a shrub of the olive family].

Perhaps she took refuge in nature to still her nerves. Or perhaps she was determined not to let those thugs get the better of her. It is notable that on the next 50 miles or so of her journey – apart from saying that 'The miles were long and the wind blew very cold' on the way to Shrewsbury – all seems idyllic. The town itself meets with her approval, especially the abbey gardens.

> *Every Wednesday, the ladies and gentlemen walk there, as in St James' Park, and there are abundance of people of quality live in Shrewsbury, more than in any town except Nottingham.*

Those 'people of quality' again. We can almost hear her thoughts: 'Not those nasty lower-class thugs with pistols.' Then, after calling in at her favourite aunt and uncle's house at Wolseley, she heads south.

Just beyond Wolverhampton, she mentions staying at an inn called the Seven Stars, and I've found on TripAdvisor that there is indeed still a pub of that name in the same spot, at Sedgley. But my hopes of finding an ancient hostelry – thatched roof, low oak beams, or maybe a neoclassical façade and cobbled coach entrance, or anything old-looking at all – are dashed as soon as I reach the car park. I'm sure it's a fine pub, but brick, slate roof and a bit of wood cladding – circa 1970? – are definitely not the sight that would have met her eyes as she dismounted that day in 1698.

Beyond there, it's suddenly a very different story. No more about innocent flower gardens or strolling 'people of quality'. It's something which enflames her, perhaps more than anything else on either of her great journeys. It's a problem that affects the well-being of the whole nation. The corrupt state of England's treasured democracy.

> *All the way from the Seven Stars, where we stayed, to Ombersley* [a distance of 19 miles], *the road was full of the electors of the Parliament men to be chosen from the Knights of the Shire.*

That year was a parliamentary election year in England and Wales. Much as we might complain today about our politicians, there's not much about the electoral system back then that we'd recognise – or applaud. As her reference to 'Knights of the Shire' hints, much of the process for choosing members of the House of Commons was –

literally – medieval. From around the end of the thirteenth century, the practice became established that as well as barons, bishops and abbots being invited to the council, or *parlement*, that advised the king, a few men (no women of course) from the next level down should also help make decisions of national importance. So each county now sent two knights of the shire, while each town, or borough, supplied two burgesses. Fifty years later in 1341, these commoners were split off from the Lords to form their own chamber. The definition of who had the right to choose members of the House of Commons was laid down in 1429: the franchise was limited to men who owned land outright which was worth at least forty shillings a year – a significant sum. That was only 3 per cent of the population, mainly a few men who were the wealthier landowners or merchants.

At the time that Celia Fiennes was writing, that system hadn't moved on for over 250 years, and it wouldn't even begin to do so for another 134 years, when the Great Reform Act of 1832 began – very cautiously – to extend the franchise. One of the starkest injustices of the system in Celia Fiennes' day came from its failure to recognise that since medieval times some villages had become towns, and that some towns had shrunk. Hence, Leeds, Birmingham and Manchester didn't have a single MP between them, whereas the hamlet of Dunwich in Suffolk – a major port in the Middle Ages which had been all but destroyed by storms in the fourteenth century – still got to elect two MPs in 1698 with an electorate of no more than a handful. London was almost the only city where the system was fair, according to the standards of the day that is: 8,000 men voted for four MPs.

The campaigning that Celia Fiennes encounters on the road to Ombersley was for the county of Worcestershire to choose its two 'knights'. She points to what had become a major problem. Those out on the campaign trail:

> ... *spake as they were affected* [i.e. according to the impact on them of candidates' policies], *some for one, some for another. And*

> *some were larger in their judgments than others, telling their reason much according to the good liquor's operation. And of these people all the public houses were filled, so that it was a hard matter to get lodging or entertainment.*

'According to the good liquor's operation' – an ironic phrase perhaps, to indicate that it was often how much beer and wine a candidate splashed out on at election time rather than his politics that won over the votes. She'd seen it before, back in Durham.

> *There was great striving in the choice of the Parliament men, which I had the trouble of in most of my journeys - the random they made in the public houses.*

'Random' in the seventeenth century had its original meaning, 'a rush or a scramble without care, consideration or control'. At Boroughbridge in Yorkshire, she had a different word to condemn the chaos.

> *Here I met with the clutter of choosing Parliament men.*

We can almost hear the anger in her words.

> *There is such bribing by debauching by drink and giving money, that instead of the Parliament men which used to be chosen to be the country's representatives and servants, to whom they allowed so much a day for their expenses, now those that would be Parliament men spend prodigious sums of money to be chosen. Some to serve for knights of the shire have spent £1000 and £1500, and for corporations and boroughs in proportion.*

Bribery by 'treating' electors with alcohol and fine food was common. Even candidates who deplored such practices had to swallow their scruples or risk losing the vote. In 1695, Sir Edward

Abney campaigning in the borough of Leicester complained that the result would depend 'upon the suffrage of the unstable vulgar. Last night I treated most of the companies of trades of this town, visiting all of them myself at ten several houses [i.e. taverns] where I entertained them.'

Many MPs were unhappy with this corrupt practice, and there were repeated attempts to stamp it out. In 1696, Parliament had passed the 'Treating Act' which specifically forbade 'the payment of money for votes, and the provision of food and drink to electors'. But, as Celia Fiennes' account demonstrates, two years later the new law was being widely flouted. It continued to have little impact. In 1701, a bill was introduced in Parliament 'to prevent bribery and corruption at elections'. It was rejected. Similar proposals were debated by MPs in 1702, 1708, 1709, 1710 and 1711. They all failed. And in 1721, one disgruntled candidate in Stafford complained that 'so many worthy persons are eating and drinking themselves into the good opinion of their electors who cannot but value them according to their abilities that way'.

The bribery and treating to food and drink only worked because of the way votes were cast. There was no secret ballot and wouldn't be for another century and a half. Each voter's name and address along with the name of the candidate he chose were recorded in a 'Poll Book'. This was often printed afterwards, so each elector's preference became public knowledge, and if he'd been bribed or leant on to vote a certain way, it was easy to check if he'd kept his word, and otherwise, he'd know there could be nasty consequences.

The candidates themselves were drawn from an exclusive social group. It was an unwritten convention that any potential 'Knight of the Shire' should be a prominent local landowner – the broader his acres, the higher the regard in which he was held. And not only were most candidates drawn from the leading landed gentry, choosing

Despite the many attempts to stamp out corruption, parliamentary candidates were still bribing voters by 'treating' them in 1755, as Hogarth's cartoon 'An Election Entertainment' shows. (Wikimedia Commons)

who should and who shouldn't stand often fell to the same, small, charmed circle. To become an MP representing a shire, you had to enjoy the backing of some of the more substantial county gentry. And local landowners didn't limit their influence to choosing candidates for the county. They often managed to manipulate elections in nearby towns as well. In most boroughs, the merchants who lived there weren't rich enough to influence who would and who wouldn't stand as an MP. Again, the one exception was London, where the merchant princes of the great trading companies were the leading lights in electoral politics.

Though Celia Fiennes objects to manipulating the vote by 'treating', she has no problem with what we would see as an undemocratic stitch-up. There's never the slightest hint in her writing that she believes it could be possible for women to have the vote. That would have been unthinkable in 1698. And she reveals her late seventeenth-century upper-class prejudice and applauds the system that puts legislative power in the hands of a small number of elite men. Or rather – she applauds the underlying principle.

> *This was an excellent constitution, when kept to its order, that none were chosen but the gentlemen of the shire living there, or else in the town the chiefs of their corporation that lived there.*

But her comment also tells us that the local landed gentry did not have a monopoly on the choice of MP. And that's a problem for her. She believes it's only by 'living there' in their constituencies that MPs can carry out their duties.

> *By this means, they are fully instructed what is for the wealth and good of each place they serve for, and so can promote designs for its advantage and trade and represent its grievances to be redressed. They also know the strength and riches of the nation and so can with a more equal hand lay the taxes on all answerable to their ability.*

So, she believes it's a good thing to have the upper classes in power – but only so long as they're locals who understand local issues. She condemns the election of outsiders.

> *They care little for the good of the nation, being for the most part perfect strangers to the places they serve and consequently all its circumstances.*

And she launches a savage attack on such MPs.

> *To their shame it must be owned, many – if not most – are ignorant of anything but the name of the place for which they serve in*

> *Parliament. How then can they speak for, or promote their good or redress their grievances?*

The whole country would benefit if these MPs just took the trouble to:

> *know and inform themselves of the nature of the land, the genius of the inhabitants, so as to promote and improve manufacture and trade suitable to each, and encourage all projects tending thereto.*

And it was by bribery and treating that these strangers managed to muscle in. Thus, for example, in 1701, New Shoreham in Sussex suffered exactly the abuse that makes her so irate. There were protests about the tactics used by a Mr Nathaniel Gould, who had 'come down from London, and ordered the public crier of the said borough to give notice with his bell, to all the votes men to come to the King's Arms to receive a guinea a man to drink Mr Gould's health; by which and other corrupt practices, he procured himself to be elected and returned.'

Celia Fiennes' objection to these corrupt MPs who've bought their way into the House of Commons is not just that they're ignorant of their constituents' and the nation's needs. Once in Parliament, she says, they have only one aim: to milk the system for their own benefit.

> *They come in* [get elected] *with design to be bribed by the Court or anybody that has any business before them, so they may be reimbursed and may gain more. Indeed, it's their own gain they mainly aim for and pursue, tending to the enlarging as well as securing their privileges.*

And she claims that some of these elected villains are even exploiting parliamentary privilege to evade bankruptcy.

The nation is so corrupted with hopes of preferment at Court or being screened by their privileges from paying their debts, which is thus: during the sessions, or forty days before or after, such as are in Parliament cannot be arrested or troubled for money they owe. The reason at first was well grounded, in case a troublesome person had money due and might find such a one at the Parliament House, and might lay him in prison and so hinder the business of the nation. But this is abused. And how can those that are worth little or nothing be good disposers of the kingdom's treasure or privileges, or stand up for them?

The parliamentary privilege she refers to, that an MP couldn't be arrested or imprisoned as a debtor, had its origins centuries earlier. The right of a Member of Parliament to be free from any arrest had been claimed as early as 1340. Over the centuries, it became usual for it to apply only in civil and not criminal cases. And in 1697, it was resolved 'that no Member of this House has any privilege in case of breach of the peace, or forcible entries or forcible detainers [i.e. abductions or kidnapping]'. The new law did nothing, however, to stop bankrupt MPs from exploiting their position to evade their creditors.

One of the most frustrating elements of Celia Fiennes' account of voting is that she tells us next to nothing about the issues at stake in parliamentary elections at this time. Clearly not every vote was cast on the basis of which candidate bought you more beer. And the gentry, mayors and corporations had party allegiances, political ideologies, economic interests and religious faiths that would push them to favour one man or another as their representative at Westminster.

The years immediately following the Glorious Revolution of 1688–89 and an end to a Catholic monarchy inclined to authoritarianism saw the birth of party politics as we might begin to recognise them. It was a period known as 'the rage of party'. Many from the upper classes, who, as we've seen, called most of the shots at election time, were divided into two well-defined groups, the Whigs and the Tories. The Whigs, who were moderate descendants of the Civil War Parliamentarians, advocated the supremacy of Parliament and championed toleration for Presbyterian Dissenters. The Tories, with a distant line back to the old Royalists, inclined more to support the monarchy and they upheld the supremacy of the Anglican Church. It's pretty certain that Celia Fiennes would have supported the Whigs. But we can only guess. Neither the word 'Whig' nor 'Tory' crops up even once in all her diaries.

Despite the fresh emergence of political parties in the country, we shouldn't imagine that by the end of the seventeenth century the House of Commons had clearly demarked government and opposition benches. Ministers were appointed by the monarch and the Royal Court, but in order to carry out their policies they had to have support in Parliament. The House of Commons that was elected in 1695 was made up of 257 Whigs and 203 Tories, with another 53 MPs who were either independents or switched between the two sides, and the 1698 election result was broadly similar. But these figures were not necessarily a guide to how members would vote. On occasion, MPs from the two parties came together to oppose measures put forward by the king's ministers. Celia Fiennes' remark, quoted already, that some members 'come in with design to be bribed by the Court or anybody that has any business before them', shows the kind of tactics that could be used by the government – or its opponents – to win votes in the Commons.

From Ombersley, she rides on south for 6 miles to the great cathedral city of Worcester, and she's just in time to see the county's election result declared.

> *We entered Worcester town next day just as the ceremony of the election was performing, and so they declared it in favour of Mr. Walsh and Sir John Pakington.*

The florid careers of these two gentlemen, elected to represent the county of Worcestershire, tell us a great deal about English parliamentary democracy at this time. Mr William Walsh, though not a knight of the shire in name, certainly was by ancestry. The family were lords of the manor of Abberley in Worcestershire. His father had fought on the Royalist side in the Civil War and lost much of his wealth as a result. William himself was described in 1698 as 'an ancient gentleman of the county, a well-bred man and a great poet, but his estate reduced to about £300 a year, of which his mother has the greatest part'. It's likely that he was one of those who – as Celia Fiennes says – stand for Parliament 'with design to be bribed by the Court … it's their own gain they mainly aim for'. Despite his family's Royalist connections – which might have made him a Tory supporter – he decided the Whigs were now a better bet, and in 1693 he wrote to a leading Whig in the county asking for 'patronage', essentially financial support. The Whigs at this time tended to line up with government ministers appointed by King William. And, four years after Fiennes saw him returned for Worcestershire, in 1702, Walsh was rewarded for his support by being appointed Gentleman of the Horse, a position at the Royal Court which required not much work for a handsome salary of £256 a year.

Sir John Pakington – the other MP whose election she witnessed – had a quite different story. Though his family, like Walsh's, had been firm supporters of the losing side in the Civil War, unlike Walsh, Pakington had held onto his vast fortune. He liked to boast that he was so rich he couldn't be bribed. He was first elected to Parliament in 1690 as a stalwart Tory with a reputation as a vocal critic of the Court. He peppered his speeches with dire warnings about the dangerous direction the country was taking after the Revolution of 1689. He was a staunch supporter of the elaborate rituals and formality of high church Anglicanism, considered by many to be too close to Roman Catholicism. Pakington fought a long and bitter battle against the Bishop of Worcester, William Lloyd, whom he regarded as low church. The two attacked each other with venom. Pakington got Parliament to condemn the bishop as 'malicious, unchristian and arbitrary'. The churchman in turn accused the baronet of acts of debauchery and support for the Catholic Jacobite cause. Pakington was still fighting his corner in 1705 – this was after Queen Anne's accession to the throne – when he marched into Worcester town centre with 'a banner carried before him, whereon was painted a church falling, with this inscription: "For the Queen and Church, Pakington"'.

Before she leaves Worcester, Celia Fiennes visits the cathedral. It's one of my favourite historic sites. It dominates the city, and today you can see its four-pinnacle tower on the road from more than a mile away. Once inside, you see two lines of elegant columns on each side of the nave that lead your gaze to a surreal height where the criss-cross ceiling of stone ribs dwindles into the distance somewhere away at the east end. But it's not only the majestic architecture that I love in Worcester's cathedral, it also contains a supreme piece of history's irony – and it's related to the very subject we've just been investigating with Celia Fiennes: the abuse of political power. In the holiest position that any mortal could have in any cathedral, before the high altar, she spots it.

> *The cathedral is a lofty magnificent building. The choir has good wood carved and a pretty organ. There is one tombstone stands in the middle of the choir by the rails on which lies the effigy of King John.*

She's at the foot of the sacred steps in the middle of the chancel. It's the final resting place of the man who has often been judged the most evil of all England's monarchs. The Victorian historian J.R. Green said, 'Hell itself was defiled by the fouler presence of King John.'

So how did it happen that a ruler commonly regarded as so villainous should be awarded such a holy and honoured memorial? It's all down to Thomas Cromwell, the brains behind Henry VIII's throne. Cromwell needed propaganda to support the king's decision to end the Pope's control of the English Church, and he knew that King John too had fought a similar battle against papal authority, defying the pope for six years. So Thomas Cromwell ignored John's reputation as a despot who oppressed his subjects, and in 1529 he ordered his remains to be dug up and reburied before Worcester's high altar within a high-sided tomb, better befitting a Tudor hero.

Now, given that when Celia Fiennes came here in 1698, it was an accepted, orthodox principle that the Pope had no role in England's religious affairs, we might be forgiven for thinking that King John would still be a popular figure in the country. But he wasn't. The violent political upsets of the mid-seventeenth century had intervened to change allegiances. While Parliamentarian Presbyterians may have seen the Pope as the official enemy, they also recognised that the more immediate threat was homegrown. An English monarch who believed in the 'Divine Right of Kings' – Charles I – and Magna Carta, the great charter of liberties, which had brought King John to heel, was now seen as the weapon that Parliament could use in the same way against this king. It played a central role in justifying his trial and subsequent execution in 1649. And so King John too was put back in his place amid the ranks of most-hated monarchs. However, it seems no one got around to doing anything about his impressive monument in Worcester Cathedral, where to this day it still proudly occupies the most holy position in this house of God.

Celia Fiennes – though unconcerned by the reverence paid to John – acknowledges in her diaries the importance of Magna Carta in parliamentary democracy.

Our kingdom is governed by laws made and established pursuant to the first constitutions and Magna Carta, from which is derived all the charters full of privileges for each Corporation in the Kingdom, suitable to their customs and wellbeing of each. These laws are made and are not truly authentic if not enacted and passed by our three states which are King, Lords and Commons.

She believes this constitution makes us the envy of other nations – provided, that is, both monarch and people act within the law.

Our Magna Carta or fundamental laws of the land, which Constitution is by all the world esteemed the best if kept, and when the King exerts not his prerogative beyond its limits to the oppressing his people's privileges, nor the people become exorbitant and tumultuous in the standing or running up their power and privileges to cloud and bind up the hands of the prince.

This in essence was the agreement made between king and Parliament in the Glorious and Bloodless Revolution of 1689. She observes that provided both sides – rulers and subjects – stick to their side of the deal, mutual respect, prosperity and peace will follow.

So the King might always reign in his people's hearts by love as well as over them, and they yield duty and obedience to him, that should preserve them in all their privileges and trade, which would procure us honour and admiration from the whole world, and continue us too great for enemies to invade or molest us, and so great as to have all seek to be our allies.

And in case we might think she's being naïve and idealistic, she brings us back to the real – not so perfect – human world.

> *Alas! It's too sadly to be bemoaned that the best and sweetest wine turns soonest sour. Some by folly, faction and wickedness have endeavoured our own ruin.*

There is hope, however. For her, it lies in her faith.

> *And were it not for God's providential care and miraculous works, we should at this day be a people left to utter despair, having only the aggravating thoughts of our once happy Constitution to lament its loss the more.*

She may not have discussed the minutiae of policies and issues being debated on the hustings at election time or on the floor of the House of Commons, but Celia Fiennes has told us much about the 'folly, faction and wickedness' of contemporary politicians, and how their behaviour is not just to their own personal discredit. It undermines the foundations of England's hard-won constitution which she so admires. At the end of the seventeenth century, most rational, honest thinkers – including those of a Whiggish mind and even many of a Tory bent – would have agreed with her.

8

Worcester to Exeter

TRADE, FREIGHT AND SLAVERY

Packhorses come and take it in sacks,
and so carry it to the places all about.
The roads were full of these carriers.

However much Celia Fiennes is angered by the idea of corrupt MPs and proud of the country's long history of constitutional law, she never loses sight of the fact that these are practical matters important for the economic health of the nation. When outsiders have bribed their way into Parliament, then they'll know little about the place they're supposed to represent, and they'll be unable 'to promote designs for its advantage and trade.' And she rightly identifies the foundation stone of the independence of towns and cities: 'Magna Carta, from which is derived all the charters, full of privileges, for each corporation in the kingdom.' Clause 13 of the original Magna Carta of 1215 had guaranteed that London and 'all other cities, boroughs, towns and ports shall enjoy all their liberties and free customs'. Towns were the beating heart of commerce and manufacturing.

It's a subject which of course fits with her own restless nature. Whenever she comes across people hard at work, she stops and investigates. Whether they're making things – weaving stockings, spinning glass, producing bricks and tiles – or extracting from the earth what it has to offer for human benefit – iron, copper, coal, salt. Whether they're producing or buying and selling in the markets of Carlisle, Nottingham, Ripon or a score of other towns, she always wants to know more.

As well as production, manufacture and marketing, there's a fourth vital ingredient in any vibrant trading economy. We saw it at Hull and at Newcastle where she told us about the ships loading and unloading. And it springs to my mind as I drive south from Worcester along the M5 to pick up her route towards Bristol.

The motorway this morning is droning with herds of high-sided lorries, carrying everything from 10,000 gallons of petrol, a glinting pile of steel sheeting, ten cars rakishly angled on a transporter, several mansions-worth of furniture, food, food and more food, to countless speeding loads of nameless products for Amazon and a hundred less famous online suppliers of household goods. Freight trade – since before humans invented the wheel, unless they were just going to sell a pig to a neighbour (you get the idea), they've had to transport their goods, sometimes long distances. It's why the Industrial Revolution only really shot the country's economic growth sky high with the arrival of the railways. So, how was freight transported back in 1698?

One problem – among many – was that, in the age of the cart and horse, there was no equivalent of the huge single load carried by the diesel-powered eighteen-wheeler of the twenty-first century. Or was there? The speed of today's carriers was of course out of the question. But what about the bulk? Listen to what Celia Fiennes says as she moves on south.

> *From Worcester we passed a large stone bridge over the Severn, on which were many barges that were towed by strength of men, 6 or 8 at a time.*

The men who worked at this arduous job were known as 'bow haulers'. Using horses to pull a barge wasn't always possible because riverside footpaths were often blocked by stiles and fences before tow paths were cleared. Bow haulers have been seen as early trades unionists. In 1786 – forty-eight years before the Tolpuddle Martyrs – they opposed improvements to the navigability of the river which would have put them out of a job. And even by 1832, the bow haulers of Worcester were still resisting the introduction of horses.

Since before the Romans occupied Britain 2,000 years ago, the most efficient method of transporting heavy goods had been by water. Most inland towns and cities all over the world – if they have a long history – grew up next to a river, or sometimes two, and that includes ones on the coast, often sited alongside a river estuary. Think of towns and cities we've visited with Celia Fiennes: Cambridge (the Cam), Ely (the Great Ouse), Nottingham (the Trent), Hull (the Humber and the Hull), Newcastle (the Tyne), Leeds (the Aire) and London (the Thames). The list is endless.

The Severn, which she crosses on the stone bridge near Worcester, is the longest river in Britain at 220 miles. It rises in west Wales, flows north-east to Shrewsbury then bends south through Worcester and Gloucester before widening out to its estuary. She identifies what makes it so navigable, even though it's not always broad.

> ***It's very deep and is esteemed the finest river in England to carry such a depth of water for 80 or more miles together ere it runs into the sea which is at Bristol.***

In the late seventeenth century, the Severn played a crucial role in England's economy, and carried more freight traffic than any other waterway in Europe. Much of the cargo was taken upstream from Bristol for the populations of the Midlands and the North. Among the small goods carried were tobacco from the West Indies and wine from France, as well as home-produced groceries, drapery and hats.

It's a mark of the importance of rivers to the economy that in the century following Celia Fiennes' great journeys, the Industrial Revolution's first impact on transport came – not from the railways – but with the construction of canals. Many of them, like the Worcester and Birmingham Canal, were designed to take goods from the new manufacturing centres to rivers like the Severn.

There's ever a reminder in her diary of why the alternative to the water – land transport – was such a poor option for long-distance deliveries. It's a problem here in the dozen or so miles south of Worcester, summer or winter.

> *Rains, which just before we began our journey had fallen, made the roads – full of stones and up hills and down, so steep that the waters stood or else ran down the hills – exceeding bad for travelling. This is the worst way I ever went in Worcestershire or Herefordshire. It's always a deep sand and so in the winter with muck is a bad way. But this being in August, it was strange, and being so stony made it more difficult to travel.*

But the existence of navigable rivers like the Severn still didn't always make freight transport a straightforward process and would not begin to do so for another century or more. Even eighty years after Celia Fiennes observed traffic on the Severn, transporting produce from factory to market could involve an extraordinarily slow and lengthy journey. In 1775, a company near Coalbrookdale in Shropshire needed to deliver a consignment of pig-iron to Chester, which was 40 miles north by road. However, that was judged too difficult. Instead, the iron was loaded into carts and taken the short distance to the Severn, where it was transferred onto riverboats for a trip in the opposite direction from Chester south to Bristol. There, it was transhipped to seagoing vessels which then sailed right around the length of the Welsh coast, into the mouth of the River Dee, where it was offloaded and stacked onto wagons for the last leg to Chester. A trip of over 400 miles, with the cargo having to be heaved on or off carts and boats eight times! But it was still quicker, cheaper and more reliable than the 40-mile road trip.

Our next stop as we head south alongside the Severn is Gloucester. Her first impression of the place highlights its reliance on the river in the seventeenth century.

> *Gloucester town lies all along on the banks of the Severn and so looks like a very huge place, being stretched out in length.*

And it's clearly prone to flooding.

> *It's a low moist place. Therefore, one must travel on causeways, which are here in good repair. I passed over a bridge where two arms of the river meet.*

From Gloucester's cathedral – 'Large, lofty and very neat' – she has a fine view.

> *You have a prospect of the whole town, gardens and buildings and grounds beyond, and the River Severn in its twistings and windings.*

Today, from the corner of the open square alongside the cathedral nave, all I can see is a line of elegant Georgian houses – high rectangular windows, doorways adorned with stone columns topped by triangular mouldings – which must have been built after the time of her visit.

She heads down to the riverside.

> *Here is a very large, good quay on the river. They are supplied with coals by the ships and barges which make it plentiful. They carry it on sledges through the town – it's the great Warwickshire coal I saw unloading.*

This is another form of transport, what she calls a 'sledge'. It was nothing like the image the word conjures up for us today – laughing kids sliding down a snowy bank, or something bigger with a few reindeer. Instead, think of a horse dragging two long wooden shafts

'The streets are well pitched, and preserved by their using sledges to carry all things about.' (Public Domain)

along the ground. These shafts have crossbars fixed to them where the load is carried. This 'sledge', or 'slide-car' as it was sometimes called, was a primitive way to carry loads going back to before the invention of the wheel.

My first thought is that sledges would be slower and more cumbersome than a conventional cart. But, as she explains later when she visits Southampton, they did less damage to the road surface than wheels.

> *Southampton is a very neat, clean town and the streets well pitched, and kept so by their carrying all their loads on sledges as they do in Holland, and permit no cart to go about in the town.*

Presumably it was the iron rim on the cartwheels that were the problem. Out in the countryside, sledges were most often used for carrying lighter loads such as hay. But her observation that in Gloucester, sledges were transporting coal seems unusual, and perhaps that was only for short distances over well-paved roads in towns.

I go next in search of the quayside where she observed the 'ships and barges' bringing in the coal. Today, there's a modern apartment block here with balconies overlooking the water in an architectural style with a nod towards the old warehouses opposite and alongside it. These buildings are six or more storeys high and have that dark, slightly gothic appearance that makes it clear they're later than Celia Fiennes' time, from the mid to late nineteenth century. And there's no sign of cargo being loaded on or off any barges. There are boats, but they're the sort that people live on or sail in for pleasure.

There is a crane. It's a steam-powered one – not thumping or hissing any more. It's outside a building with NATIONAL WATERWAYS MUSEUM, LLANTHONY WAREHOUSE in red letters across the front. This is encouraging. And I'm soon inside searching for exhibits and information about transport on the Severn in the late seventeenth century. It's not overcrowded today, so I can have a relaxed look around. It's a fine museum. There are lots of steam engines which once powered cargo ships, their cogwheels greasy and turning. There's a narrowboat, and mannequins dressed up as a canal boat family alongside plenty of those black tin pots – painted with brightly coloured flowers – that we associate with canals. And there are information boards to tell us all about the role of the canals, the River Severn and Gloucester in the trading history of England. Gloucester, it turns out, was further from the coast than any other port in the country.

But after half an hour, I'm still searching for something – anything – about the waterways in the period immediately before the canal age. I ask one of the attendants once she's finished explaining the purpose of some lengths of chain to a family of four. She shrugs, apologises, and says that unfortunately it's not what the museum is about. On the way out, I come across a board summarising the importance of Gloucester as a port. It says:

> In 1581 Gloucester was given the status of a port by Queen Elizabeth I. This allowed ships to trade directly between Gloucester and foreign ports without having to pay dues to Bristol.
>
> The opening of the Sharpness and Gloucester Canal in 1827 allowed seagoing ships to bypass a dangerous stretch of the River Severn. This led to a boom period for Gloucester Docks in the 1860s.

I'm sure the museum's curators didn't intend it, but the sign does imply that nothing much worth recounting happened at the docks between 1581 and 1827. We're used to Celia Fiennes being forgotten. Perhaps the era that she wrote about at the end of the seventeenth century can sometimes be overlooked as well – at least when it comes to transport history.

From Gloucester, she moves on to Bath.

> *A pretty place full of good houses all for the accommodation of the company that resort thither to drink or bathe in the summer.*

Then it's westward. At Kingswood – today a suburb of Bristol, back then a small country town – she again takes note of how they transport the area's most important product, neither sledges nor carts this time.

> *I passed through Kingswood and was met with a great many horses passing and returning loaded with coals dug just thereabout. They give 12 pence a horseload which carries two bushels* [a volume equivalent to 16 gallons]. *It makes very good fires, this is the coking coal.*

In the twenty-first century, it's easy to forget that South Gloucestershire played a long and distinguished role in the history of the mining industry. Coal was first dug out in any quantity around Kingswood about the time Fiennes was here. Again it would have been from bell pits. Within thirty years of her visit, deep mines would start to take over with the invention of the first steam-powered engine to pump flood water up from the pit bottom. Mines were still being worked around Kingswood until 1963, with opencast mining continuing for several years after that.

Coal may be dead and buried in Kingswood nowadays, but the unmined mineral still struggles in its grave. Locals can suddenly find mysterious sinkholes appearing in their gardens – caused by subsidence from the old shafts and galleries shifting 1,000ft beneath. The problem is so serious that the local MP has called for full surveys of the mines under the town.

In Bristol itself, there's an innocent passing reference in Celia Fiennes' diary that reminds us of the most shameful and brutal side to trade in the late seventeenth century. It's all the more of jolt because it occurs in her account of an upmarket residential home for the elderly.

> *There is a noble alms-house more like a gentleman's house, that is all of stonework, a handsome court with gates and palisades before four grass plots divided by paved walks. The one side is for women, the other for men. The middle building is 2 kitchens for either, and a middle room in common for washing and brewing. Over all is a chapel. They have gardens behind it with all things convenient. They have their coals and 3 shillings per week allowed to each to maintain them. It is for decayed* [impoverished] *tradesmen and wives that have lived well.*
>
> *It was set up and is allowed to* [funded] *by Mr Colston, a merchant in London.*

This is Edward Colston, the slave-trader whose name, denounced by the Black Lives Matter movement, has become notorious across the globe. It's in Bristol that protesters in 2020 pulled down his statue. I make my way up the steep pavement of Saint Michael's Hill climbing above the docks, and there on the right is the almshouse, much as she saw it. Its design might be described as restrained neoclassical – white stucco wings on each flank, the walls set out with regular lines of tall rectangular windows, and on the far side, beyond a square lawn, a façade of understated design, symmetrical and gleaming. Today it's run by the Society of Merchant Venturers as a home for over-60s who are receiving state benefits.

Colston founded this almshouse in 1691, and by the time Fiennes came here seven years later, he'd already transported some 100,000 enslaved Africans to the Americas, branding their chests with his company's initials. In order to maximise profits, as many slaves as possible were crammed below the decks of his ships for months on the transatlantic crossing. The bodies of those who died as a result were thrown overboard.

Whether Celia Fiennes was aware of how the founder of the almshouses made his vast wealth, beyond that he was 'a merchant in London', we don't know. So, what did she, and her contemporaries in England, think about the slave trade?

In the late seventeenth and early eighteenth centuries, there were a few who outwardly disapproved of black slavery. Quakers and some evangelicals condemned it as un-Christian. It's not likely that Celia Fiennes would have lined up with them. The Quaker ways of prayer and life were not to her liking, as she points out on her visit to Scarborough. Incidentally, it's an example of how – for her – being displeased with something doesn't mean avoid it. In fact, the reverse, it sparks her curiosity.

> *I was at a Quakers' meeting in the town where 4 men and 2 women spoke one after another had done. But it seemed such a confusion and so incoherent that it very much moved my compassion and pity to see their delusion and ignorance, and no less excited my thankfulness for the grace of God that upheld others from such errors.*

This is clearly a general opinion about the Quakers' faith – and as with Catholics, she pities rather than condemns. Her words carry no opinion of the Quakers' attitude towards slavery. She, of course, counted herself a Presbyterian Dissenter, those who wished to practise their religion outside the hierarchy of the Anglican Church. Did Dissenters have a view about the morality of slavery? She does tell us about a book she's read on Dissenter beliefs. It's written by someone she almost met in Durham.

> *They have two very eminent men, one of their name was Dr Gilpin whose book I have read, but – he not being at home – could not have the advantage of hearing him.*

It's a pity Dr Richard Gilpin wasn't around for a discussion with her. He was a noted Nonconformist minister and physician. The book of his that she'd read and liked was almost certainly *Daemonologia Sacra, or A Treatise of Satan's Temptations.* It's an account of all the ways that the Devil manipulates and hurts humans, with tips on how to resist. Some of Satan's tricks involve him luring people into doing his job for him and harming others. Though Gilpin doesn't deal directly with the rights and wrongs of slavery, he does so in passing when he comments on the Old Testament's mention of the tortures inflicted by one human being on another, 'These cruelties were acted not only upon slaves, and captives,' he wrote, 'but upon children whose age and innocency might have commanded the compassions of their parents.' He does appear to be saying that brutality against any human being – slave or free – is wrong, though there may be a hint that such ill-treatment of slaves or prisoners was more acceptable. The question of whether slavery is – as we would believe – a form of institutionalised cruelty, Gilpin leaves open.

Opinion was divided among Nonconformists. Many Puritans – whose beliefs were a strong element in the Fiennes family – deemed race-based slavery was in accordance with the way that God had ordered the world, and some of them fully participated in the trade. However, there were some Dissenters, closer to Celia Fiennes' own faith, who – like the Quakers – preached that slavery was against God's will.

There were also a few secular thinkers who increasingly during the Age of Enlightenment criticised slavery for violating the rights of man. In 1700, Lord Chief Justice Sir John Holt ruled that 'as soon as a man sets foot on English ground, he is free', which again leaves open the question of enslaving Africans. Celia Fiennes' one comment on the subject occurs in her discussion of justice and punishment.

> *Here are no wracks or tortures, nor slaves made, only such as are banished sometimes into our foreign plantations there to work,*

She seems to be saying that while slavery does not exist at this time in England itself (a contention that could be disputed), the practice is permissible in 'our foreign plantations'. She must surely have been aware that there were African slaves in such places as well as the convicted English criminals she refers to.

What's certain is that in 1698 a majority of the population in the country either had no opinion on the rights and wrongs of slavery or would not have objected to Colston's profiteering from the slave trade. We can well imagine that those elderly people who'd fallen on hard times and now found themselves enjoying the splendour of Colston's almshouses in Bristol must have praised the man and all his work. But in the wider community, slavery was not an issue that was widely debated. Abolitionists were in a small minority, and the first laws that would start to curb the practice would not be passed for another 135 years.

Celia Fiennes recognises the importance of Bristol to the nation's economy.

> *This town is a very great trading city, as much as any in England, and is esteemed the largest next to London.*

Her assessment is borne out in a study by Dr Richard Stone from the University of Bristol. 'The seventeenth century,' he writes, 'was a pivotal period in Bristol's commercial history.' And Dr Stone adds something that parallels what we saw at the Gloucester Waterways Museum, 'It has, however, received relatively little attention from modern historians.' He also questions the idea that Bristol's commercial success in the Americas depended wholly on the slave trade. More important, he suggests, was the growing demand by the American colonists for English manufactured goods such as cloth, shoes, saddles, nails and even candles. Coming back through Bristol the other way were those indulgences which the English now increasingly craved: tobacco and sugar.

However, it seems to be more the domestic trade that Celia Fiennes observes.

> *The River Avon, which flows by the sea into the Severn and so to the town, bears ships and barges up to the quay, where I saw the harbour was full of ships carrying coals and all sorts of commodities to other parts. They have little boats which are called wherries such as we use on the Thames. They use them here to convey persons from place to place.*

In the town itself, as in Gloucester, there's a no-wheeled-carts rule.

> *The streets are well pitched, and preserved by their using sledges to carry all things about.*

I drive west out of Bristol. As anyone who's visited Clifton will know, it can come as a delightful contrast to leave the city and come on the spectacular landscape where the suspension bridge crosses the River Avon between the sides of a high narrow gorge. Today, I pull into a layby to admire the craggy cliffs reflecting the sunlight off hard grey-white stone mottled with the green of struggling plants. Celia Fiennes stops here to sample a special mineral found in Clifton Gorge.

> *They dig the Bristol Diamonds, which look very bright and sparkling, and in their native rudeness have a great lustre and are pointed. I had a piece just as it came out of the rock, and it appeared to me as a cluster of diamonds polished and irregularly cut. Some of these are hard and will endure the cutting and polishing by art, and so they make rings and earrings of them.*

It's quartz. She was probably not the sort to go for earrings, but she can recognise the artistry in their production.

From Clifton, she rides south to Glastonbury – 'now a ragged poor place' – and on into Somerset. At Taunton, she passes several times over the River Tone.

> *Here, at this little place where the boats unloaded the coal, the pack-horses come and take it in sacks, and so carry it to the places all about. The roads were full of these carriers going and returning.*

Just outside Exeter, at Topsham, she sees a dramatic example of the effort – and heavy investment – being devoted to speeding up the movement of freight.

> *The River Exe runs to Topsham where the ships come up to the bar. This is 7 miles by water which they are attempting to make navigable to the town. This will be of mighty advantage to have ships come up close to take their serges* [locally produced textiles, of which more shortly], *which now they are forced to send to Topsham on horses by land, which is about 4 miles. They had just agreed with a man that was to accomplish this work, for which they were to give £5,000 or £6,000, who had made a beginning on it.*

That sum would be the equivalent of between £3.5–4 million today.

Her account of freight trade in the late seventeenth century is a tribute to human ingenuity and hard work. As we've seen many times, rural roads had seen little improvement since Britain was part of the Roman Empire. It would be decades before the first canals would be excavated, and 150 years till railways would bring the first fast mass transport across the country, and centuries would pass before the invention of the diesel engine and a myriad of other mechanical devices which would allow thousands of giant trucks to speed along a network of motorways.

There was nothing new about the problem of long-distance freight transport – it had existed for centuries. What had changed was that the country was now manufacturing and mining more than ever before, so it was selling more. Add to that the produce and needs of a burgeoning overseas empire, and the result was a requirement for more and more resources to serve a fast-growing demand. What strikes us most about Celia Fiennes' account of freight movements is not just the variety of modes of transport – carts, sledges, packhorses, barges, boats and ships of all kinds – but the sheer numbers involved. She's forever telling us that 'the harbour was full of ships' and about 'a great many horses passing and returning loaded'. Transporting freight was labour intensive and expensive. But the traders of the late seventeenth century coped, and the economy of the country began to thrive in a way that set this period apart from the earlier years of the century which had been dominated by religious and political conflict. The England Fiennes describes makes the England of Tudor times a century earlier seem like a foreign, primitive land.

The picture she paints for us of a country often heaving with goods on their way to market, meets her approval. And not only that, she wants the economy to grow. That's clear from her insistence that each MP needs to understand the strengths and weaknesses of his constituency 'so as to promote and improve manufacture and trade'.

Although she could not have guessed at the many changes that would soon come to the economy, she's nevertheless forward-looking. It's in her nature to admire industriousness, but she also wants to see improvement, better ways of doing things – progress. The Victorians often regarded the age before the Industrial Revolution as 'unprogressive'. Celia Fiennes shows us they were wrong.

9

Devon

WEAVING WEALTH AND PERIL ON THE SEA

I went to Cremyll Ferry,
which is a very hazardous passage
by reason of 3 tides meeting.

It's fairly rare for Celia Fiennes to comment on the way people dress, unless it's to complain of women showing too much flesh, as she did in Scotland, or to marvel at the lifelike garments on a marble effigy in a church. However, in Devon she notices an unusual local fashion.

> *You meet all sorts of country women wrapped up in the mantles called West Country rochets* [the loose garment falling off the shoulder as worn by bishops], *a large mantle doubled together of a sort of serge, some are linsey-woolsey* [linen or cotton woven with wool] *and a deep fringe or fag* [knot] *at the lower end. These hang down, some to their feet, some only just below the waist. In the summer, they are all in white garments of this sort, in the winter they are in red ones. I call them garments because they never go out without them, and this is the universal fashion in Somerset and Devonshire and Cornwall.*

Her opinion of the women themselves is puzzling.

> *I must say they are as comely sort of women as I have seen anywhere though in ordinary dress – good black eyes and crafty enough and very neat.*

By 'crafty', she probably means clever or skilful rather than devious or cunning, though what she intends by 'good black eyes' is more of a mystery.

Her observations on what these women wore, however, serves as a prelude to a subject much closer to her heart. She now takes us on a guided tour to explain how their clothing is made and the contribution Devon's textile manufacture makes to England's economy.

The whole town and country is employed for at least 20 miles around in spinning, weaving, dressing and scouring, fulling and drying of the serges.

'Serge', for those of us not familiar with the term, was made from a combination of long fibrous wool and a shorter, softer woollen yarn to produce a distinctive diagonal pattern. It was hard-wearing and in demand especially for military uniforms. It was first produced here around the year 1615.

It turns the most money in a week of anything in England. One week with another, there is £10,000 paid in ready money, sometimes £15,000.

These sums were the equivalent of tens of millions today. The trade was dominated by the wool merchants of Exeter. In order to carry on their business, they had to pay their membership dues to the Guild of the Fullers and Tuckers. 'Tucking' was another word for fulling, of which more in a moment. At the time of her visit to Exeter in 1698, the Guild of Fullers and Tuckers regulated how the wool merchants must conduct their business. Its members held a monopoly on the trade, and that made them a powerful elite in the city. Many of them extended their influence beyond the textile business into local politics by getting elected as the city's councillors.

The guild's headquarters was at the Tuckers Hall, which – according to my internet search – is still here in Exeter today on Fore Street, so I decide to go and take a look.

The map shows it to be on the left a couple of hundred yards up from Exeter's old quayside. But I soon start to think that I must have got the wrong street. There's nothing resembling the kind of grand neoclassical structure, perhaps set in well-manicured grounds leading to an intimidating entrance designed to keep the hoi-polloi at bay, which we might expect as the heart of the most powerful institution in Exeter's history. There's the Hidden Jewel Tattoo Studio and Spice Magic Indian restaurant (both with possible eighteenth-century windows on upper floors), and there's what looks like a small Nonconformist chapel (Victorian Gothic) trapped between McCoy's Arcade (circa 1930, shut) and Peachy Tipi (selling 'pre-loved' items). So I pop into Peachy and ask the assistant inside if she knows where Tuckers Hall is.

'Yes, it's next door,' she says with a helpful smile.

'You mean the chapel?'

She points to the right. 'The old place just here. I don't think it's a chapel. You can go round inside. Looks like it's open to the public this morning.'

I thank her and a minute later I'm through the front door of what I'd taken for a chapel and have made the requested donation. The inside bears no relation to the drab exterior. Its halls have high curved ceilings with curved wooden beams and stretch back several times further than the narrow little frontage outside. The guide, a middle-aged chap who welcomes me with a handshake, reveals that the place is now the home of the Incorporation of Weavers, Fullers and Shearmen.

When I express surprise that the textile trade should still be so important in Devon, he explains, 'No, we just keep up the old name. We think history is important. Members today are business leaders from a whole range of different companies.' And when I ask when it was first built, he tells me that it was founded in 1471 but, by the time the cloth industry had declined in the mid 1800s, the old hall was in a bad way, and the front wall was leaning over and about to collapse. It was restored in the 1870s and the façade remodelled. So that's why it looks so Victorian.

He directs me to the Upper Chamber. At the top of the flight of stairs, what I see could hardly be a greater contrast with the narrow little Victorian façade out in the street. A long oak dining table is surrounded by decorated oak-panelled walls, beneath a shining lion-and-unicorn coat of arms flanked by crossed pikes – all a fitting tribute to the power of Exeter's wool merchants.

The hills and moors in the south-west are perfect grazing ground for sheep, which back in the seventeenth century were reared on family-run farms. These smallholders took the fleeces to the local markets of Moretonhampstead, Crediton, and other villages and small towns in the area, and there sold the wool either direct to the weavers or to the merchants. By the year 1700, there were 1,200 weavers working across Devon. But it was Exeter's merchants who called the shots – they controlled the process of turning the raw product, the fleece, into a source of wealth. The merchants paid scores of local people to carry out the carding, spinning and weaving, the work being undertaken not in central factories but by the women, children and servants in individual households.

The cloth produced – mainly serge – was then transported to Exeter. Celia Fiennes witnesses the heavy traffic on the road.

> *The carriers I met going with it, were thick* [crowded together], *all entering into town with their loaded horses. There is an incredible quantity of serges made and sold in the town. Their market day is Friday. The large market-house set on stone pillars, which runs a great length, on which they lay their packs of serges. Just by it is another walk within pillars, which is for the yarn*

The first purpose-built wool market had been opened in Exeter in 1538 and trading took place there once a week for fleece, yarn and some woven cloth. As the trade grew, so more markets were established. The 'market house' mentioned by her was probably the one set up in 1636 in the lower hall of St John's Hospital School – long gone – the site now being occupied by a Virgin Media Store. She notes how the sellers' proceeds from the market are reinvested in the industry.

> *The weavers bring in their serges and must have their money which they employ to provide them yarn to go to work again. They bring them all just from the loom and so they are put into the fulling-mills.*

Fulling was centralised in Exeter. The wool was cleansed to get rid of oil, dirt and other impurities in a process which also thickened the fibres by matting the surface texture. She takes a close look at the whole process. As ever, her curiosity gets the better of any nose-holding distaste she might have.

> *I was an eyewitness. They lay the serges in a sack of urine, then they soap them and so put them into the fulling-mills and so work them in the mills dry till they are thick enough. Then they turn water onto them and so scour them.*

Urine contains ammonia, which was an effective cleanser. And in case you're curious (if not, look away now), it was collected each night from taverns, inns and houses in what were known as 'piss carts'. After this smelly stage, the wool was pummelled with large square wooden hammers, driven by a huge waterwheel.

> *The mill does draw out and gather in the serges. It's a pretty diversion to see it, a sort of huge, notched timber like great teeth – one would think it should injure the serges, but it does not.*

We can judge the size and power of this device by her next remark.

> *The mills draw in with such a great violence that if one stands near it and it catches a bit of your garments, it would be ready to draw in the person even in a trice.*

The next step is to dry the serges outside in the fresh air. Again, we see the vast scale of Exeter's textile industry.

> *When they are thus scoured, they dry them in racks strained out* [stretched tight] *which are as thick set one by another as will permit the dressers to pass between, and huge, large fields are occupied this way almost all round the town.*

Incidentally, the phrase 'being on tenterhooks' – meaning a tense period of waiting – has its origin in this process. The lengths of cloth – like your nerves – were stretched, on frames called tenters, using tenterhooks.

Next, the cloth is pressed flat at contrasting temperatures.

> *Then when dry, they pick out all knots, then fold them with a paper between every fold, and so set them on an iron plate, and screw down the press on them which has another iron plate on the top. Under this is a furnace of fire of coal. This is the hot press. Then they fold them exceeding exact, and press them in a cold press.*

After that, colour is added, though not to serge bound for London, presumably because the buyers there didn't trust Devonians to do the job.

> *Some they dye, but most are sent up for London white. I saw the several vats they were dyeing in of black, yellow, blue and green. They hang the serges on a great beam or pole on the top of the vat, and so keep turning it from one to another. So they do it backwards and forwards till it's*

Serge dyeing in Devon. 'Indeed, I think they make as fine a colour as the dyes at Bow in London.' The serge was soaked in dye in a brass or copper cauldron. (*The Young Tradesman; or Book of English Trades (A new and enlarged edition)*, 1839)

> *tinged deep enough. Indeed, I think they make as fine a colour as the dyes at Bow* [in the East End] *in London. Two men do continually roll on and off the pieces of serge till dipped enough. The length of these pieces is, or should be, 26 yards.*

What's striking about the process Fiennes describes is its complexity and the number of stages in manufacture. Remember, this is before the days of factories that would come with the Industrial Revolution.

As well as serving the home market, Devon's woollen products were also shipped overseas. By the early seventeenth century, the export trade, mainly to France and Spain, had become a monopoly – or rather duopoly – in the hands of the Merchant Adventurer Company in London and the local Exeter French Company which controlled trade with France. All woollen exports had to be conducted through them. But following the Civil War, individual merchants started to sell their own cloth overseas in defiance of the two regulating bodies. And when in 1667, the French imposed high tariffs on imported wool, the merchants turned to Holland, and that became the main market for their goods. When Celia Fiennes witnessed the production process in 1698, the wool business was on the verge of its heyday, and during the eighteenth century, Exeter's wool merchants earned the title the 'Golden Tuckers' because of the riches they accumulated.

From Exeter, she rides south-west towards Plymouth. Her route is via Chudleigh and Ashburton, along the southern boundary of Dartmoor.

> *Mostly lanes and a continual going uphill and down, some of them pretty steep hills.*

Anyone who's driven the narrow country lanes in this area will recognise her description.

The roads are not to be seen, being all along in lanes covered over with the shelter of the hedges and trees.

The effect of being so enclosed on the way here in south Devon must have been especially striking. She remarks on it again a few miles further on.

Here the roads contract and the lanes are exceeding narrow and so covered up you can see little about. An army might be marching undiscovered by anybody, for when you are on those heights that shew a vast country about, you cannot see one road.

And so to Plymouth. Her description of the town as being in two different parts could hold good today 320 years later, though for very different reasons.

Plymouth is 2 parishes called the old town and the new. The sea here runs into several creeks, one place it runs up to the dock and Millbrook, another arm of the sea goes up to Saltash and Port Elliot.

Plymouth in the twenty-first century is also split into the new and the old. The new is a product of the Second World War. Its huge naval base was the target of devastating enemy bombing raids. Nearly 1,200 civilians were killed as well as an unknown number of Royal Navy personnel – their casualty figures were kept secret for security reasons. For a city of its size, Plymouth suffered more than any other in the country. Over 72,000 homes were damaged or destroyed and almost every civic building went the same way. Unstoppable fires raged, and reports at the time described the city centre as a 'brick-filled desert'. After the war, the planners pulled down much of what the Nazi bombs had missed. Hence the 'new' part.

The old sector of Plymouth on the south and west side is marked out by rows of Georgian mansions and small waterside cottages as well as two huge iconic ancient structures. Facing west on the quayside by the Tamar Estuary is the Royal William Yard, a massive, elegant, solid-looking neoclassical building. It was completed in the 1830s as the navy's main victualling base, to supply the ships and their crews with everything from beer to bread. The second great structure is the Royal Citadel, which, unlike the Royal William, was already established here in Celia Fiennes' time. She makes a beeline for it.

> *There are no great houses in the town, the streets are good and clean. The fine and only thing in Plymouth town is the Citadel or Castle which stands very high above the town.*

The Citadel dominates Plymouth, from wherever she looks.

> *Walking round I had the view of all the town and also part of the main ocean in which are some islands. The walls and battlements round it with all their works* [fortifications] *and platforms are in very good repair.*

I decide to do the same walk myself around the circuit of its dark, solid walls with my FitBit distance calculator on. I've clocked up three-quarters of a mile by the time I reach the entrance again. The gateway itself looks more like a pinnacled mausoleum memorialising the dead rather than the threshold of a military barracks. But I couldn't disagree with Celia Fiennes' judgement.

> *The entrance being by an ascent up a hill, looks very noble over 2 draw-bridges and gates, which are marble, well-carved, the gate with armoury and statues all gilt and on the top 7 gold balls.*

The Citadel lies between the Hoe and Sutton Harbour. The Hoe, to the west, is Plymouth's spreading green park which overlooks the Channel, and is where Sir Francis Drake was – allegedly – playing bowls when news came through of the approaching Spanish

Armada in 1588. To the east lies Sutton Harbour, the main docks area at the end of the seventeenth century. For sheer size, the Royal Citadel remains today the inescapable feature of the south-eastern waterside area, and this despite the many modern buildings around here now – along much of the quayside I can see several new blocks of luxury flats, their balconies overlooking the water.

The Citadel's history goes back to 1590, when Drake was appointed to strengthen Plymouth's defences and oversaw construction of the first castle here. But most of the structure that Celia Fiennes saw and which remains today was designed and built during the 1660s. Its Baroque style wasn't to everyone's liking, and when Samuel Pepys visited in 1683, he wrote that the architect 'hath built sillily'. Pepys' view counted – he was Chief Secretary to the Admiralty at the time. Fiennes, sixteen years later, was more impressed than he'd been by the defensive measures in place.

> *There is a long building which is the arsenal for the arms and ammunition, and just by it a round building well secured which is for the powder. Around the works* [fortifications] *is the platform for the guns, which are well mounted and very well kept.*

Over the next 100 years and longer, Plymouth's Royal Citadel was a vital element in the nation's defences. It was designed to be the impregnable headquarters for troops and armaments to protect the naval base here in case of enemy attack. Its walls and barracks have been regularly maintained and strengthened over the centuries. Today it's still occupied by the military, as the base for 29 Commando Regiment of the Royal Artillery.

The reasons for Plymouth's importance as a haven for shipping – both military and civilian – are obvious. Not only is it located by the entry to the English Channel from the Atlantic, but it has several large natural harbours, including the estuary of the River Tamar and two large inlets at Millbay and Sutton Harbour.

> *The mouth of the river just at the town is a very good harbour for ships. The dockyards are about 2 miles from the town by boat – it's one of the best in England. A great many good ships built are there. The water runs for 2 miles between the land, which also shelters the ships. There are a great deal of buildings on the dock,*

However, despite the town's natural advantages for shipping, in the days when larger vessels relied on the wind for their power and had only the crew's navigational skills to avoid the pull of currents, tides and gales, the sea here could be treacherous, as she notes.

> *Here up to the town there is a depth of water for ships of the first rate to ride. It's a great sea and dangerous by reason of the several points of land between which the sea runs up a great way. And there are several little islands also, all which bear the tides hard one against the other.*

From the walls of the Citadel, she observes something else.

> *There you can just discover a lighthouse which is built on a mere rock in the middle of the sea. This is 7 leagues off. It will be of great advantage for the guide of the ships that pass that way. From this, you have a good reflection on the great care and provision the wise God makes for all persons and things in his creation, that there should be in some places, where there is any difficulty, rocks even in the midst of the deep, which can be made use of for a constant guide and mark for the passengers on their voyages.*

This was the Eddystone Light, the first lighthouse to be built on a rock in the open sea. It had only just been completed earlier in the year that Celia Fiennes saw it. Eddystone was the brainchild of an eccentric engineer named Henry Winstanley, who'd begun its construction in 1696. England was at war with France, and such was the importance of the project that the Admiralty provided Winstanley with a warship to patrol around the rock for protection. One morning at the end of June 1697, the naval vessel failed to turn up on time. A French ship arrived, took Winstanley prisoner and delivered him to the French authorities. At that point, the French king, Louis XIV, stepped in and – recognising that a lighthouse was a benefit to all – ordered that Winstanley be released, saying, 'France is at war with England, not with humanity.' But that wasn't the end of the story. The beneficent God that Fiennes praised – or at least the forces of nature – would soon look less beneficent.

On 24 November 1703, what became known as 'The Great Storm' hit Britain. It's reckoned to have been the most severe gale ever recorded in the country and lasted several days. Before the era of weather forecasts, no one was prepared for what happened. It claimed 8,000 lives and wrecked countless commercial vessels as well as fifteen Royal Navy ships. In towns across the country, buildings were smashed to pieces and the streets were filled with fallen masonry. In London, 700 boats were heaped together on the Thames, Westminster Abbey had its lead roof ripped off, and Queen Anne took shelter in the cellars of her palace. The Bishop of Bath and Wells was killed by a falling chimney while he slept.

On the fourth day of the storm, the Eddystone Lighthouse caught the full force of the hurricane winds and was lashed by gigantic waves. Winstanley was there, supervising additions to the structure. He must have regretted his earlier boast that his lighthouse was so well built that he'd like to see it hit by 'the greatest storm that ever blew under the face of heaven'. Not a stone of the Eddystone Lighthouse was left standing, and Winstanley's body, and those of his crew, were never recovered. The storm was considered at the time to be God's retribution for 'the crying sins of this nation'.

The Eddystone was rebuilt six years later but burned down in 1755. The third lighthouse on the rock there had to be demolished when its walls started to wobble. The fourth structure, erected in 1882, has lasted – with many repairs – to this day.

Winstanley's experiences at the Eddystone are relevant to Fiennes' story. As we'll see shortly, the varied dangers that he faced can help us understand what makes her so fearful when she reaches Land's End.

Celia Fiennes gets a first-hand experience of the waters off Plymouth when it's time to leave and head west into Cornwall. She chooses to take the Cremyll ferry across the Tamar Estuary. The sea that day was nothing like as fierce of course as it would be in November 1703, but even on the calmest days, as she explains, it could be a frightening experience on a small boat.

> *From Plymouth I went 1 mile to Cremyll Ferry, which is a very hazardous passage by reason of 3 tides meeting. Had I known the danger before, I should not have been very willing to have gone it.*

The Cremyll ferry has been in operation, in one form or another, for at least 1,000 years. In Celia Fiennes' day, it departed Plymouth from Devil's Point near the Royal William Yard, several hundred yards south-east from where you embark today. When I take the ferry, crammed on the deck alongside hikers and families of holidaymakers, the little motorboat takes eight minutes to reach the Cornish side, and there's barely a bump on the waves big enough to make me miss a lick of my ice cream. Her story is very different.

> *I was at least an hour going over. It was about a mile, but indeed in some places notwithstanding there were 5 men rowed – and I set my own men to row also – I do believe we made not a step of way for almost a quarter of an hour.*

Nowadays, it's foot passengers and bikes only on board. In 1698, Celia Fiennes' horses have to balance on the decks. In the end, she reaches Cornwall suffering nothing worse than a sniffle.

> *But blessed be God, I came safely over. But those ferryboats are so wet and then the sea and wind is always cold to be upon, that I never fail to catch cold, as I did this day.*

And so into Cornwall and the last stage of her Great Journey. But there's no end yet to the dangers and discomfort she encounters.

10

Cornwall then to London

TIN, PIRATES AND A WET DASH HOME

My horse … his feet failed
and he could no way recover himself.
And so I was shot off his neck.

She's now on the final stage of her second Great Journey. Over the two summers of 1697 and 1698, we've come to admire her energy, determination, optimism, stolid religious faith, and especially her constant urge to investigate the world around her. We're about to witness their persistence in the face of more adversity. And at the same time, her actions and words will show us that she's not some predictable cardboard cut-out. As with anyone we think we know well, her behaviour can be puzzling at times. We'll see that too. And with Celia Fiennes, mysteries about her character are compounded because she comes from a land which at times can appear familiar and at others can seem an alien planet.

Once she's in Cornwall, she sticks close to the coast for the first 35 miles or so, and as anyone who's walked this section of the South West Path knows, it provides plenty of variety for the leg muscles, or in her case for her riding skills.

> *Here I had some 2 or 3 miles of exceeding good way on the downs, and then I came to the steep precipices – great rocky hills. Ever and anon I came down to the sea and rode by its side on the sand, then mounted up again on the hills which carried me along mostly in sight of the south sea.*

She passes through Looe, where she crosses 'a little arm of the sea on a bridge of 14 arches'. Note here the precision of her observation. There's been a storm, making it hard to judge the depth of the rain-filled craters in the road.

> *A deeper clay road, by the rain the night before, had made it very dirty and full of water in many places. In the road there are many holes and sloughs wherever there is clay ground, and when they are filled with water it's difficult to shun danger. Here my horse was quite down in one of these holes full of water. But – by the good hand of God's Providence, which has always been with me, ever a present help in time of need – by giving the horse a good strap, he flounced up again, though he had gotten quite down his head and all, yet did retrieve his feet and got clear of the place with me on his back,*

What she doesn't know is that it's an omen of worse to come.

Beyond St Austell, there are signs of an industry which many of us today will associate with Cornwall.

> *I went a mile farther on the hills and so came where they were digging in the tin mines. There were at least 20 mines all in sight.*

Today, we've probably got to know something about tin mining in Cornwall from one of two sources. Either from a holiday visit to one of the mines which has been turned into a museum with underground tours, or from TV drama images of waist-high water at the bottom of a tin mine with a bare-chested Ross Poldark wading through. What claims to be Britain's only complete tin mine that's open to the public, the Wheal Roots, is now known as the Poldark Mine, which no doubt encourages more of us to visit.

To get a taste of its underground experience, I follow the A39 then branch off on the 394. Poldark Mine is situated 25 miles beyond St Austell. Like most historic attractions these days, it aims to combine education with entertainment. I wander through its

The Carclaze tin mine near St Austell. (Public Domain)

museum and learn of the many variations of the steam-powered pump engine in use over the centuries, and stop before the images of the miners, with illustrations and information boards explaining that many were children working twelve-hour days.

Then I join twenty-odd other visitors in donning yellow hard hats before following our guide, a giant of a bearded Cornishman, along an ill-lit narrow passageway into the hillside then down a narrow ladder. The guide – John is his name – stops at intervals to expand on the 'wet, miserable, cold' endured by the workers. And he's got a taste for the kind of anecdote that brings home to us what working life must have been like here 200 years ago. He explains that the only light on the treacherous ledges deep underground came from candles stuck into small clumps of clay. The candles were made from beef tallow, and sometimes the workers got so hungry that they ate them. The mine-owners begrudged the expense of replacing the candles, and so added a poison to the tallow which made those who devoured it sick.

This morning, there's the constant noise of dripping and running water. And our guide tells us that the price for keeping this mine dry enough for public access today is an enormous bill for running the now-electric pumps and maintaining the pipes to suck out the water night and day 24-7.

Now, I have a problem with the Poldark Mine experience. Don't get me wrong. If you've not been, I recommend it. It's fun for the family, and helps you understand the trials and hazards of underground working. But it's a problem we followers of Fiennes are all too familiar with now. The Poldark Mine tells us all about the heyday of its historic activities, which came with the Industrial Revolution. In other words, decades after Celia Fiennes witnessed mining in Cornwall. Again, the late seventeenth century is all but overlooked.

But of course for us, this is not a loss. It shows that what she has to tell us about tin mining, just as what she told us about freight traffic on the River Severn, is a rare source of first-hand information about the times she lived in, and for that reason is significant.

In her own account of tin mining pre-Industrial Revolution, what strikes her first off is the size of the labour force needed. There are:

> *a great many people at work almost night and day, but constantly all and every day including the Lord's Day, which they are forced to do to prevent their mines being overflowed with water. More than 1000 men are taken up at them. There were few mines without at least 20 men and boys attending them, either down in the mines digging and carrying the ore to the little bucket which conveys it up, or else others are draining the water and looking to the engines that are draining it.*

By 'engines' she doesn't mean, as we would, fuel-powered machinery, but is referring to a simpler contraption with wheels and pulleys, as she's about to describe. What she's seeing are not deep mines with shafts going 200ft down like the Poldark Mine of the nineteenth century. But they're deep enough to be facing a problem with flooding.

> *They had a great labour and great expense to drain the mines of the water with mills that horses turn. And so now they have the mills or engines that are turned by the water, which is conveyed on frames of timber and trunks to hold the water, which falls down on the wheels as an overshot mill* [like a traditional water millwheel].

Though it's not entirely clear, she seems to be describing an ingenious system whereby at least part of the power required to turn the pumping engine comes from the very same water that the pump has brough up from the mine bottom. This water, channelled in such a way that it falls on the millwheel, helps to power the pump itself. Presumably additional water was supplied from a local stream diverted from its natural course for the purpose.

> *They do five times more good than the mills they used to turn with horses, but then they are much more chargeable* [costly]. *Those mines do require a great deal of timber to support them and to make all those engines and mills.*

We've talked a great deal on our travels with Celia Fiennes about the approaching birth of the Industrial Revolution. And it's here, in the tin mines of Cornwall, where that revolution first threatened the old ways. On 2 July 1698, only a few weeks before her description of the tin mine's water-powered pump, a man named Thomas Savery from Devon patented 'A new invention for raising of water and occasioning motion to all sorts of mill work by the impellent force of fire, which will be of great use and advantage for draining mines'. Just four years later, in 1702, Savery's invention was in operation at several Cornish tin mines. Alas, designed without mechanical moving parts, it didn't work too well. It sucked up the water directly by the vacuum created as the steam condensed. But it inspired others. In 1712, Thomas Newcomen – like Savery, a Devonian – devised his beam engine in which the condensing steam drove pistons which then turned the wheels to pump the water from the mine bottom.

Newcomen's engine had its problems too. It required huge amounts of coal so was of more use where plenty of fuel was at hand, at coal pits rather than tin mines. During the eighteenth century, pumping efficiency was gradually improved. But it was not until 100 years after Celia Fiennes was here that Cornish mines got the complete solution to their flooding problems. That was the brainchild of Richard Trevithick, the son of a Cornish tin worker, who developed the high-pressure steam engine.

In Fiennes' day, there were four kinds of power source available, and all were primitive in their effectiveness: wind, water, trudging horses or human muscles. The last of these was the weakest, though – provided the labour force was compliant – was the easiest and probably the cheapest to organise, and that's what was used to haul the tin ore itself to the surface at the mine she's describing.

> *Those above are attending the drawing up of the ore in a sort of windlass, as is to a well. Two men keep turning, bringing up one and letting down another – they are much like the leather buckets they use in London to put out fire. The ore, as it's just dug, looks like the thunderstones, a greenish hue full of pin-dust. The shining part is white.*

Strictly speaking, 'pin-dust' meant the fine dust or metal filings produced in the manufacture of pins. However, in the seventeenth century it also denoted the fine chalky powder known as 'pounce' used to blot ink. 'Thunderstones' were fossils or flint tools that turned up in fields and were mistakenly believed to have been hurled down from the sky by lightning strikes, a myth that persisted into the nineteenth century.

> *In the tin-mines there is stone dug out, a sort of spar something like what I have seen in the lead-mines at Derbyshire, but it seemed more solid and hard. It shines and looks like mother of pearl. They also dig out stones as clear as crystal which are called Cornish Diamonds. I saw*

> *one as big as my two fists, very clear and like some pieces of crystal my father brought from the Alps in Italy which I have by me.*

The main source of tin ore is the mineral cassiterite, which is often brown or black from iron impurities in it. It can also have translucent crystals embedded in it, which seem from what Celia Fiennes says to be as hard as real diamonds. These crystals were a valuable by-product of tin mining and could be used to make items of jewellery

> *I got one of those pieces of their Cornish Diamonds as long as half my finger which had three or four flat sides with edges, the top was sharp and so hard it would cut a letter on glass.*

Demand for the tin itself was growing all around the country at the time of her Cornwall trip. It's one of the main components of pewter, which was then the popular material for tableware. The process of extracting it from the ore took place close to where it was mined.

> *Half a mile hence* [from St Austell], *they blow their tin, which I went to see. They take the ore and pound it in a stamping-mill which resembles the paper mills, until it's fine as the finest sand – some of which I saw and took,*

Again, they use water power, this time to smash the chunks of raw ore.

> *The mills are all turned with a little stream or channel of water you may step over. Indeed, they have no other mills but such in all the country* [this region]. *I saw not a windmill all over Cornwall or Devonshire though they have wind and hills enough – it may be it's too bleak for them.*

Then comes the smelting process. The ore that's been pounded into a sand is then heated.

Cassiterite. (Public Domain, Robert Lavinsky)

> *This they fling into a furnace and with it coal to make the fire. So they burn together and make a violent heat and fierce flame, the metal by the fire being separated from the coal and from its own dross, which, being heavy, falls down to a trench made to receive it at the furnace hole below.*

Today we know that the temperature required to extract pure tin from the ore has to be as high as 1,400 degrees centigrade. The tin then forms a molten mass.

> *This liquid metal I saw them shovel up with an iron shovel and so pour it into moulds in which it cools, and so they take it thence in sort*

> *of wedges, or 'pigs' I think they call them. It's a fine metal in its first melting – looks like silver. I had a piece poured out and made cold for to take with me.*

And judge for yourself from her next remark how the tin industry dominated this part of the West Country, and how vulnerable it was to flooding.

> *Thence I went to Tregony – 6 miles good way, and passed by 100 mines, some on which they were at work, others that were lost by the waters overwhelming them.*

We've spoken throughout here as though Cornish tin mining exists now only in museums, period TV series and of course in Celia Fiennes' diaries, and that there's none still working. But that may soon no longer be true. The market for tin collapsed during the last century as plastics began to replace it as the favourite material for food containers. But the arrival of the age of electronic technology has reversed that decline. The world's billions of devices, from smartphones to nuclear powerplant control centres, require trillions of little bits of tin to carry computerised messages within them. Chinese and Indonesian tin miners have cashed in. Now Cornish entrepreneurs plan to reopen some of the county's old mines to do the same, with – it's argued – far less damage to the environment than their Asian competitors.

From Tregony, she rides on to Falmouth – 'the best harbour for ships'– then 6 miles further to Truro. Although she doesn't tell us what month it is now, we can assume it's getting into autumn and a wet one. So much so that she almost abandons her plan to go to the far south-west.

> *From thence I turned back, intending not to go to the Land's End, which was 30 miles farther, for fear of the rains that fell in the night, which made me doubt what travelling I should have. The next day, finding it fair weather on the change of the moon, I altered my resolution and so went for the Land's End by Redruth 18 miles, mostly over heath and downs, which was very bleak and full of mines.*

There were many legends about the influence of the moon on the weather. Seventeenth-century farmers identified what they called a 'dripping moon'. They saw a crescent moon as a dish holding water. If the dish was tilted down, then the water spilled out. If it was on its back, like a dish on a table, then they believed it wouldn't rain. Silly as this may sound to us, recent research has shown that there may be some truth in it. Observations do seem to show that rain sometimes follows the full and new phases of the moon, i.e. when there's a crescent moon. No one is quite sure, however, why this should be. One theory is that, as the moon's orbit takes it closer to the earth, its gravitational pull is stronger. That might affect atmospheric pressure which in turn could influence rain patterns. Meteorologists can't be sure though, and, of course. there are many other, more powerful, causes of storms or fine weather.

As she gets closer to Land's End, she discovers that the source of Cornwall's mineral wealth isn't only tin.

> *Here I came by the copper mines, which have the same order in the digging and draining, though here it seems drier and I believe not quite so annoyed with water.*

During the late seventeenth and the eighteenth centuries, the area to the south of Carn Brea, where she is now, was rich with copper deposits which were closer to the surface than the ore in the tin mines she'd visited, so the shafts were shallower and hence drier. Over the next 150 years, Cornish copper would become a source of great wealth. By the late eighteenth and early nineteenth centuries, the copper mines around Gwennap near Redruth earned that little parish the title 'the richest square mile on the Old World'.

She notes the packhorses they use, peculiar to this area.

> *Of a market day, which was Friday, you see a great number of horses little of size which they call Cornish Canelles* [also known as 'Goonhillies', from the nearby Goonhilly Down]. *They are well made and strong and will trip along as light on the stony road without injury to themselves, whereas my horses went so heavy that they wore their shoes immediately thin and off. But here I met with a very good smith that shoed the horses as well as they do in London.*

From Redruth she proceeds to Penzance, a distance of 15 miles. The weather is getting very cold. But she's optimistic.

> *So I went up pretty high hills and over some heath or common, on which a great storm of hail and rain met me and drove fiercely on me. But the wind soon dried my dust-coat.*

In all her diaries this is the only mention she makes of what she wears, whether to dine with a lordly relation or to struggle over marsh and moor. A dust-coat was a full-length overcoat with a cape, or capes, protecting the shoulders. It was commonly worn by coachmen, but also by both men and women when out riding.

She now approaches the only place on all her thousands of miles of travel where she appears to become fearful. Land's End itself.

At first, it seems she's reluctant to explore too far here because of the difficult terrain.

> *The Land's End terminates in a point or peak of great rocks which run a good way into the sea. I clambered over them as far as safety*

> *permitted me. There are abundance of rocks and shoals of stones that stand up in the sea a mile off. These many rocks and stones make it hazardous for ships to double the point especially in stormy weather.*

To today's visitor, it's not immediately obvious how remote Land's End must have felt at the end of the seventeenth century. The approach to it can seem just another tourist magnet – even this afternoon, when a continuous misty rain and chill wind make the most hardened hikers pull their woolly caps down and zip up their padded waterproof jackets. I have to take my turn in a queue of cars waiting for two coaches to swing around and exit the road by the West Country Shopping Village and the Land's End Hotel. Once past them, I manage to find a place to stop amid several score Minis, SUVs and campervans. But once all that's at my back, I clamber – as Celia Fiennes must have done somewhere very near here – just a few yards over the dark and jagged rocks. Before me, 100ft down, the lashing white waves are being thrown in and back. It provides some impression of how hostile this place must have looked to her.

However, rough, steep, rocky hills don't usually phase her. There's something she finds more threatening to this place.

> *Here at the Land's End, they are but a little way off of France, 2 days' sail at farthest convey them to Havre de Grace* [now Le Havre] *in France. But the peace being but newly entered into with the French, I was not willing to venture at least by myself into a foreign kingdom. And being then at the End of the Land, my horse's legs could not carry me through the deep, and so I returned again to Penzance*

It's such a strange remark: 'I was not willing to venture at least by myself into a foreign kingdom.' If we didn't now know better, we might think she was joking. But she doesn't do humour, at least not in her diaries. Does she think she might fall into enemy hands, that she might be snatched from Land's End's cliff top by a hostile invader and end up a prisoner across the Channel? She's mistaken about Le Havre, too far east to be the threat, which was more likely to have come from the much closer French port of Brest. But was that really a danger?

The Nine Years' War between Louis XIV's France and an alliance that included England, the Netherlands and Spain, had ended in October 1697 with the Peace of Ryswick. Fiennes, with her comment about 'peace being but newly entered into with the French', seems to be saying that the new treaty couldn't be relied on to guarantee peace. In a broader sense than the safety of Land's End, history proved her right. The Nine Years' War was only one of a series of conflicts between France and its neighbours between 1666 to 1714. Ryswick itself was regarded at the time as little more than a temporary truce, and three years after Celia Fiennes came to Land's End, France was again at war with the so-called Grand Alliance, which included England.

Another comment in the same section might suggest what she believes to be the real threat here. English cargo ships avoid the area:

> *because since the war, they could not double the point at the Land's End, being so near France – pirates or privateers meet them.*

Privateers were commonly used by all Europe's nations to outsource part of their maritime warfare. Governments would commission a privately owned ship and its crew to attack the enemy's merchant vessels, thus weakening its economy. It was legalised piracy. The spoils – enemy ships and their cargo – were then auctioned off, with the proceeds being split between the privateer's owner, crew and the government.

The French called their own privateers 'corsaires'. Between 1668 and 1717, they caused significant damage to the English economy. Technically, French corsaires shouldn't have been operating in 1698 after the Peace of Ryswick. A privateer who continued raiding after a peace treaty was regarded as a criminal vessel, a pirate ship.

However, given their swashbuckling tradition, it's doubtful whether their captains all obeyed the letter of the law and quit their raids when they were supposed to.

However, these activities were ship-against-ship, and ought not to have worried Celia Fiennes on land. Nevertheless, real pirates – as opposed to state-sponsored privateers – had been a threat to on-shore communities on the Devon and Cornwall coasts throughout much of the seventeenth century. Barbary pirates sailed all the way up here from North Africa. In 1625 they landed at Mount's Bay, near Marazion in Cornwall, captured sixty men, women and children, then sold them into slavery. In 1645, Barbary pirates kidnapped 240 Cornish folk. During the 1650s Oliver Cromwell tried to deter further raids by decreeing that any pirates who were captured be taken to Bristol and slowly drowned. But that had little effect. And not till 1676, when the English gave the pirates a taste of their own medicine by attacking their base in North Africa, was there an end to the threat of raids by Barbary pirates on south-west England.

The French threat, however, continued. And as we saw earlier at Plymouth, the French vessel that captured Henry Winstanley, the engineer working on the Eddystone Lighthouse in the year before Celia Fiennes came to Land's End, was one such privateer. That did at least show that if the opportunity arose when there was no armed resistance to hand, French privateers felt no need to stick to attacking English ships at sea. If there was an easy target, they went for it, be it on land or sea. So perhaps Celia Fiennes' wariness about straying too near the 'peak of great rocks' on the most remote point in the kingdom, may be more understandable than we first thought.

The English too, like other nations, made widespread use of the system. There was a fine line between legal privateering and criminal piracy, as the career of Captain William Kidd illustrates. Kidd – financed by London merchants – began as a legitimate hunter of pirates. But by 1697, he'd realised there was more profit to be had from attacking and robbing innocent vessels. When his investors

Sir John Knaresborough's attack on the Barbary pirate base at Tripoli in 1676. (Wikimedia Commons)

back in England heard that he'd switched to the wrong side of the law, they panicked and dropped any connection with him. Kidd was brought to trial for piracy in 1701. He was hanged and his body put in an iron cage and hung by the Thames. One of those merchants who'd backed Kidd with cash was Celia Fiennes' own brother-in-law, Edmund Harrison. However, Harrison's doubtful connection with this notorious pirate did little to damage his reputation – he was knighted in 1698.

The weather now is turning against her. And she starts to head back to the east, first to Penzance.

> *Just by here lay some ships, and I perceived as I went, there being a storm, it seemed very tempestuous and is a hazardous place in the high tides.*

By the time she gets to Truro, her thoughts are turning to home.

> *The season of the year inclined to rain and, the days declining, I was afraid to delay my return.*

It's a reminder of how unreliable the roads were, of how impossible it would have been to undertake any of her travels during winter months. She reaches north Cornwall.

> *Here I met with some showers which by fits or storms held me at Launceston.*

When she does resume her journey, the weather's no better.

> *This day was the wettest day I had in all my summers' travels, hitherto having had no more than a shower in a day and that not above 3 times in all, so that by that time I came through lanes and some commons to Okehampton, which was 15 miles, I was very wet.*

But it's not all bad news, and as ever she looks on the bright side.

> *This was a little market town. And I met with a very good inn and accommodation, very good chamber and bed, and I came in by 5 of the clock, so had good time to take off my wet clothes and be well dried and warm to eat my supper, and rested very well without sustaining the least damage by the wet.*

And Celia Fiennes being Celia Fiennes, she has an opinion as to how the roads could be made more floodproof. She's seen the solution elsewhere.

> *These rains fully convinced me of the need of great stone bridges with arches so high that the waters seemed shallow streams, though they were so swelled by one night's and a day's rains that they came up*

pretty near the arches and ran in most places with such rapidity and looked so thick and troubled as if they would clear all before them. This causes great floods, and the lower grounds are overwhelmed for a season after such rains.

A few days later, it happens. The accident she's managed so far to escape on all the thousands of miles she's travelled on horseback.

She calls in at Newton Toney Manor, which she twice refers to as 'home'. It's of course the house where she spent her childhood, now occupied by her half-brother William and his wife Katherine. It's likely we're into October. Two months later, on 10 December, William died. He was 59 years old.

Then she rides on to Winchester and the village of Alresford, whose name means 'the ford over the river by the alder trees'. A glance at the OS map shows that even today when many rivers have been straightened and flood plains drained, Alresford is still surrounded by a tangle of ponds and streams formed by the River Itchen and its tiny tributaries.

After crossing a bridge on the B3047, I turn left onto the old Drove Lane. This may well follow the track that she rode. The land hereabouts is flat, and I can see the stream to my right bending in an oxbow, then around a corner it widens out into an expanse of water lapping its grassy banks. It looks marshy. Celia Fiennes takes up her story.

The little rains I had in the morning before I left Newton Toney made the ways very slippery, and it being mostly on chalk a little before I came to Alresford, forcing my horse out of the hollow way, his feet failed and he could no way recover himself. And so I was shot off his neck upon the bank. But no harm – I bless God – and as soon as he could roll himself up, stood stock still by me, which I looked on as a great mercy – indeed mercy and truth always have attended me.

When we consider that she was – as ever – riding side-saddle, and take into account the many steep and stony tracks she's negotiated on much of her travels, not to mention the number of times she's had to ford a river or pass over flooded ground, it's remarkable that this is the only time she was thrown from her horse. God's mercy she blesses. We could add praise her own skill as a horsewoman.

There's no let-up in the weather the next day.

> *After an hour's riding in the morning, it never ceased more or less to rain, which made me put in at Farnham and stay all the day after I came in at noon. But then it began to rain much faster and so continued.*

She takes a ferry over the Thames, and who can blame her for taking a short cut:

> *which is a private road made for the king's coaches. Thence to Hounslow Heath and so to London 12 miles more.*

She's home again. The second of her Great Journeys is over. Often along unmapped and unsigned roads, from the Scottish borders through the ports and cities of England to its remotest coastal point, she's endured flood, precipitous hills, filthy infested lodgings, an attempted armed robbery, and been thrown from her horse. Back in London, we can imagine Celia now being embraced by her younger sister, Mary, and being greeted by an enthusiastic brother-in-law, Edmund. We could guess at the tears and laughter and questions as she's reunited with her family. 'Imagine' and 'guess' I'm afraid is all we can do. They're not the kind of matters Celia Fiennes would think suitable for her diary.

We've got more to tell about her. Before we say goodbye, we're going to review the rest of her long life. But for now, we'll leave the closing words from 1698 to Celia Fiennes herself, with her optimism, her faith, a hint of pride and, by my calculation, an underestimate both of the bad weather and of the miles she's covered.

> *Here ends my long journey this summer, in which I had but 3 days of wet, except some refreshing showers sometimes, and I think that it was not above 4 in all the way. And it was in all above 1,551 miles, and many of them long miles, in all which way and time I desire with thankfulness to own the good providence of God, protecting me from all hazard or dangerous accident.*

Epilogue

A MOST CURIOUS WOMAN

To remind him time passes.

One of the frustrations for students of Celia Fiennes is that we know so little about her life other than what her journals tell us, and most of those pages are devoted to her two great journeys of 1697 and 1698. When she reaches her London home in the autumn after her second trip around the country, she's 36 years old. According to life expectancy in the late seventeenth century, that makes her middle-aged – she might have hoped to survive another twenty years or so, perhaps till she was 60. It would have been beyond her dreams to live, as she indeed did, into her 80th year.

Her diaries continue, for a while at least, beyond her second great journey. It's difficult to judge how long, because she doesn't provide us with dates. Sometimes we can work them out for ourselves. When she tells us about attending the coronation of Queen Anne at Westminster Abbey, we know that's April 1702. She recounts in page after page the exact sequence of lords, ladies and prelates escorting the new monarch. She also notes the Queen's difficulty walking.

> *She, because of lameness of the gout, had an elbow-chair of crimson velvet with a low back,*

The gout was brought on by Anne's love of brandy. Celia Fiennes also however makes it clear that the Queen was not as disabled as is sometimes supposed.

> *The chair she left at the Abbey door.*

And again after the ceremony:

> *The Queen walked to the door of the Abbey with obliging looks and bows to all that saluted her … To Westminster Hall, where the Queen again quitted her chair which was carried by four men.*

And during these later years, Celia Fiennes continues with some of her old habits. Her love of spas is undiminished, and she tells us about the wells at Epsom in Surrey where it seems she's as picky as ever about the entertainment on offer.

> *There is a house built where people have caraways* [probably tea made from caraway seeds, which was believed to be a cure for indigestion], *sweetmeats and tea etc. But the place looked so dark and unpleasant, more like a dungeon, that I would not choose to drink there.*

And there's a clue as to when this was. From Epsom, she travels to Leatherhead and Box Hill. Near there she talks of 'Mr Moore's fine house'. This was Fetcham Park, home of Arthur Moore, a self-made tycoon and MP. He bought it for £8,250 in 1705, and then proceeded to spend much of his fortune on rebuilding it. It seems from her description that this work was complete.

> *The house is built with brick and quoined stone. The top is in a peak painted fresco.*

We know that Fetcham House's remodelling was finished by 1710, so her visit here must have been after this date. In other words she's at least 48 years old now.

And her travelling days are not over. She records half a dozen more trips. Her preference now is to avoid wayside inns with all their uncertainties of food quality and bed cleanliness. Instead she sticks to the grand homes of her relatives – eight weeks with her favourite folk, the Wolseley family in Staffordshire, a visit to her childhood home at Newton Toney, a week at Broughton Castle with her nephew, Lord Saye and Sele.

But the echoes of her great journeys can still sometimes be heard. In Bedfordshire, she complains about the way being 'narrow, and lanes rooty and long'. Near Lutterworth in Leicestershire, she spots 'a hand pointing 4 ways to Coventry, Leicester, London and Lichfield'. The fact that she bothers mentioning it shows such signposts were still a rarity, despite the 1697 law requiring local authorities to erect them at all crossroads. And she still offers some gems that can make us wonder and smile – this back at Epsom:

> *Monday morning is the day the company meet, and then they have some little diversion, as racing for boys, or rabbits, or pigs.*

And so her diary, which has told us so much about her and about life in the late seventeenth century fades away, and with it almost all we know about the rest of her life.

Apart from the 1705 House of Lords record we've already mentioned, which indicates she has a mortgage on a salt-works in Cheshire, there's one other document which sheds a little light on her later years. That's her will, made in 1738, when she's 76 years old. In it, she says she's 'in perfect health, praised be my good God, but … increasing in infirmities of body and sudden seizures'. We don't know what caused these seizures. The most likely explanation is early signs of heart failure.

It's revealed in her will that she's moved from her home in London, and is living in Hackney, now in the East End of the capital. In the mid-eighteenth century it looked like one of those East Anglian villages she'd described on her Great Journey. It was bounded by impassable marshes to the east, cows grazed to the north, and much of the land was owned by the squire of Hackney Wick Manor. Not till the nineteenth century was the area swallowed up by London's houses and factories. Her address is given as Well Street. Today it's a 200yds length of square-windowed, brick-built, half-empty offices over the Cocktail Nail Bar and Nicky's Café. But she's not forgotten here. Just around the corner is a sign announcing, 'CELIA FIENNES HOUSE 8–20 Well Street London E9 7PX'. And nearby, high on the wall – rather too high to be read easily – next to Mumtaz Dry Cleaners is a blue plaque.

It was 6 November 1738 that she made her will. Mary, her sister and we believe her closest confidante, had died a few months earlier. That's almost certainly what prompted her to move to Hackney, where she could be close to the home of her niece, Jane – Mary's daughter. And it may well have been the death of her sister that prompted Celia to plan for the end of her own life. In January 1741, she added a final codicil to the will, adjusting some of the details of who is to get what.

Three months later, on 10 April 1741, in her eightieth year, Celia Fiennes died.

The will had specified how and where she was to be buried. The funeral was to be in the village where she was born, at Newton Toney.

> *Without ostentation only put into a leaden coffin ... be as private as can be a hearse and one coach.*

The will also revealed that, though far from poor, her 'temporal estate' apparently was not what it had been.

> *By depredations on my lands, little but annuities remain which conclude at death.*

But she was not resentful, and as ever had put her trust in her Maker.

> *My good God gives and has the power to take away ... and He still affords me sufficiency.*

She left the income from a £40 investment to 'purchase bread for to be distributed to the prisoners at Ludgate and White Chapel.' Another £50 went to her manservant, William Butcher, who'd been with her for fifteen years. There was a long list of small items and who was to receive them.

> *Let my washerwoman have my cotton nightgown and one pair of my ordinary couch sheets and ordinary apron.*

She apologised to her nieces for the small value of what she was leaving them, though she specified some splendid presents which they'd receive on their wedding days, among them, 'a diamond necklace of 48 diamonds … a large silver salver … my ring set with diamonds and rubies.' To her nephew – with a hint not to waste his life – she bequeathed 'my repeating clock for his closet, to remind him time passes.' The rest of her estate – and its greatest portion – was to benefit the Nonconformist faith to which she'd been devoted throughout her life. It was to go to 'the fund for country ministers of the Dissenting denomination'.

The most intriguing discovery in her will is the name of one of the witnesses – Daniel Defoe. It's not the Daniel Defoe who wrote *Robinson Crusoe* and who over the centuries has overshadowed Celia Fiennes with his *A Tour thro' the Whole Island of Great Britain*, written twenty-five years *after* her own Great Journeys. He had died in 1731. The will's witness of the same name was almost certainly his son, or just possibly his nephew. However, this connection with the Defoe family might well suggest that she'd been acquainted with the more famous Defoe before he died. If that's the case, they must surely have compared notes with each other about their similar long trips around the country.

Would she, we might wonder, ever have felt that it was unfair that this man's travel journal had been printed, published and admired by so many, while a woman's great journeys, made twenty-five years before his, lay unrecognised by all but a few close relatives in a handwritten manuscript?

We today can certainly find plenty of grounds for her to be resentful, if she'd chosen to be so. Her description of the country she explored at the end of the seventeenth century was exceptional by all standards. It was the first comprehensive survey of England undertaken by anyone, man or woman, since Elizabethan times. In fact, she was probably the first woman to make such journeys, and certainly the first woman to leave such a detailed record of her travels. And unlike Defoe's account a quarter of a century after her, Fiennes' journal was authentic. She wrote only of what she'd witnessed at first hand.

Why, then, isn't she up there and remembered alongside other diarists such as Samuel Pepys, Daniel Defoe and William Cobbett? There are several reasons. Unlike the other three, her journals were not published for almost 200 years, and even then in 1888, when they were privately printed by her descendant Emily Griffiths, they would have reached only a very limited readership. Celia Fiennes may not have been surprised. She'd spelled out in her Introduction that she felt the diary was 'not likely to fall into the hands of any but my near relations'.

To what extent is her lack of recognition because she was a woman? There's no evidence she ever approached a publisher herself, and even if she had, it's probable her journal would have been rejected on the grounds that the wider public wouldn't be interested in what a woman had to say about such things.

But this doesn't explain why her groundbreaking journeys and what she tells us about life in England at the end of the seventeenth century, have been so neglected in more recent decades. She's been relegated to a few references in academic papers by social historians and the occasional passing mention in books or guides to country houses she visited, and – as far as I can see – once in a TV travel programme. There's one exception: a 1982 publication of her diaries by the historian Professor Christopher Morris with many valuable footnotes. However, mention the name of Celia Fiennes to most amateur lovers of history, and you'll get a blank look.

And if there's been scant mention of what she had to say about life in the late seventeenth century, there's been nothing written or said or explored in any way about the character of this highly unusual woman, and nothing about her role in the developing history of gender equality. Consider this – on International Women's day in 2016, that bastion of liberal opinion, the *Guardian* newspaper published an historical survey of 'the top ten incredible women who defied convention to undertake inspiring journeys'. And, you guessed it, Celia Fiennes is nowhere on the list.

I believe that one reason why she's been ignored – and it's somehow become embedded over the centuries – is that her writing, in its original, unedited form, isn't always easy to read. I've added an example extract in the Appendix. The problem is more than the lack of standardisation of spelling, capital letters and abbreviations which were usual in this period. Celia Fiennes shared those peculiarities with all other writers of her time, so that should have put her on an equal footing with her male counterparts. But there's something else that makes her diaries less accessible. And the underlying cause is significant. As she herself showed us – without comment – in Manchester, girls and young women in the late seventeenth century did not receive the same education as boys and young men. And that disadvantage to some extent applied to a minor aristocrat like Celia Fiennes just as it did to women of lower social standing. The result is that her grammar, punctuation and sentence construction can at times be confusing. It's for this reason that in the hundreds of quotes I've used, I've ironed out these discrepancies. I've wanted to be sure that we can appreciate the true value of what she says without the unfair handicap her work has suffered because, as a woman, she was denied the education given to her male contemporaries.

Celia Fiennes was not an intellectual. She was not a polished writer, she was not a profound philosopher and she was not a campaigner. Above all, she was a doer. Without hesitation, she broke free from what in the late seventeenth century might be considered women's interests. Coalmining, shipping, political shenanigans, brutal punishments all may have been male preserves, but to her they were what people did regardless of their sex. If it grabbed her attention, she would go for it. She could so easily have sat back like other women of her rank and enjoyed a relaxed, stress-free life among friends and family at home. She didn't have to go and stay in filthy, overcrowded, noisy lodgings choking with smoke. Nor did she have to spend her days negotiating flooded, narrow lanes pitted with deep craters. She didn't have to ride up and down the stony precipices of the Derbyshire Peak District. No one and nothing forced her to ford the tides of the Dee Estuary or risk getting drowned on the Ely causeway as her horse stumbled and fell. And when armed thugs harassed her on a remote Cheshire track, she held her nerve. She must surely have enjoyed the perils and the uncertainties of life on the road, or at the very least, have relished her daily triumphs over the latest tribulations.

She never married, and that was highly unusual for a woman of her class. We don't know why she stayed single. Did no man ever propose to her? Did she reject suitors? Or is it not more likely that in an age when marriage gave a woman security but denied her any independence, she had no desire to become subservient to a man? It would have been contrary to everything she was.

Celia Fiennes was a child of her time in many ways: in her moderate Puritanical outlook, her pity for Catholics and Quakers, her nationalism and prejudice against the Welsh and the Scots, her loyalty to her own social class, and her disdain for wild landscape. These all plant her firmly in the late seventeenth century. All the more astonishing then that she chose to lead a life so different from her female peers.

When, on that day in May 1697, she mounted her horse, made sure her servants and packhorses were all ready, and set off on her travels from her London home, it was 180 years before married women in Britain acquired even basic legal rights to own property. It was 220 years before they got the vote. And it was 260 years ahead of the modern feminist movement's campaign for gender equality in all legal, economic, social and cultural matters.

The journeys she made, her tenacity, skill, bravery and especially her undiluted curiosity about the world out there beyond her comfort zone, place her ahead of her time. She showed that a woman at the end of the seventeenth century, as much as any man, could lead an independent life, with all the dangers and inconveniences that involved. She's a unique figure and deserves our admiration.

The final words go to her. From the heyday of her first great journey, here she is, excited, doing what she does best, without the least regard for late seventeenth-century assumptions about what was suitable behaviour for a high-ranking lady.

> *They dig down their mines like a well for one man to be let down with a rope and pulley. When they find ore, they keep digging underground. In the mine that I saw, there were 3 or 4 miners at work. They dig sometimes a great way before they come to ore. They wall round the wells to secure them from mouldering in upon them … And sometimes they are forced to use gunpowder to break the stones, and it is sometimes hazardous to the people and destroys them at the work.*

And while it's her actions and observations that we've enjoyed as we've travelled with her around England in the summers of 1697 and 1698, there's something else we should not forget. When a little later in life she writes the Introduction to her journals, she becomes more than a woman of action. She begins to recognise a fundamental handicap suffered by women in her day – their lack of education. The answer is in true Celia Fiennes spirit. Take control yourself.

> *I shall conclude with a hearty wish and recommendation to all, but especially my own sex, the study of those things which tend to improve the mind and make our lives pleasant and comfortable as well as profitable in all the stages and stations of our lives, and render suffering and age supportable, and death less formidable, and a future state more happy.*

Appendix

An extract from Celia Fiennes' manuscript, unedited. Here, when she arrives in Colchester.

Out of these great streetes runs many Little streetes, but not very narrow – mostly old buildings Except a few houses builded by some Quakers, y^t are brick and of the London mode. The town did Extend itself to the sea but now its ruines sets it 3 mile off. Y^e low Grounds all about ye town are used for ye whitening their Bayes for wch this town is remarkable, and also for Exceeding good oysters, but it's a dear place and to Grattifye my Curiosity to Eate them on ye place I paid dear. It's a town full of Dessenters, 2 meeteings very full besides anabaptists and quakers. Formerly the famous Mr Stockton was minister there till he Dyed. From Colchester to jpswitch is 10 miles, and thence to Dedom 9 miles, the way pretty good Except 4 or 5 miles they Call ye severalls, a sort of deep moore Ground and woody. At this place I passed over a wooden bridge, pretty Large, wth timber railes of wch make they build their bridges in these parts; and now I go into Suffolk wch is not so rich Land as ye part of Essex I passed through, wch was meadows and grounds wth great burdens of grass and Corn. So I went to jpswitch 9 mile more; this is a very Clean town and much bigger than Colchester is now. Ipswitch has 12 Churches, their streetes of a good size well pitch'd wth small stones – a good market Cross railed in. I was there on Satturday wch is their market day and saw they sold their Butter by ye pinte 20 ounces for 6 pence and often for 5d or 4d they make it up in a Mold just in the shape of a pinte pot and so sell it. Their Market Cross has good Carving, ye ffigure of justice Carv'd and Gilt. There is but 3 or 4 good houses in ye town – ye rest is much Like ye Colchester buildings, but it seems more shatter'd, and Indeed *the town Looks a Little disregarded, and by Enquiry found it to be thro' pride and sloth, for tho' the sea would bear a ship of 300 tun up quite to ye Key, and ye ships of ye first Rate Can Ride wth in two mile of the town, yet they make no advantage thereof by any sort of manufacture, wch they might do as well as Colchester and Norwitch, so that ye shipps that brings their Coales goes Light away, neither do they address themselves to victual or provide for shipps. They have a Little dock where formerly they built ships of 2 or 3 tun, but now Little or Nothing is minded save a Little ffishing for ye supply of ye town.*

The reader will find a reproduction of the 1888 publication of her original manuscript on Kindle.

Acknowledgements

My special thanks to Martin Fiennes for inviting me to examine the original manuscripts of his ancestor's diaries, and for his enthusiastic support for this book. And I'm also most grateful to the many friends and professional contacts who've provided me with detailed insights into particular aspects of her story. Special mention goes to John Culverhouse, Curator at Burghley House; Alan Wilkinson, Sandy Fulton and Chris Fulton on health and pandemics; Dr Elaine Murphy of Plymouth University on women and naval vessels; Nigel Robbins on ornithology; and Lindsay and Trevor Stanberry-Flynn on the history of Plymouth's Cremyll Ferry.

Though I've consulted many books and academic papers in researching the background to Celia Fiennes' great journeys, I've found only one source that discusses the woman herself: Professor Christopher Morris's 1982 *The Illustrated Journeys of Celia Fiennes, 1685–1712* and his numerous footnotes to the text. I pay tribute to him.

My thanks too to my agents, Diane Banks and Martin Redfern of Northbank Talent, who have, as ever, been encouraging throughout, as well as to Mark Beynon, Jezz Palmer and Alex Boulton at The History Press. It's been a pleasure working with them.

Most of all, I'm delighted to thank Maggie Cox for her unerring judgement, guidance and editorial oversight. The book could not have been written without her.

Index

About the Author

Derek J. Taylor is a best-selling history writer and former international TV news correspondent. He studied law and history at Oxford before joining Independent Television News of London. As an on-screen correspondent, he reported from Northern Ireland, Rome, South Africa and the United States, and reported on five wars in the Middle East. He is the author of *Magna Carta: The Places that Shaped the Great Charter* (The History Press, 2015), *Who Do the English Think They Are? From the Anglo-Saxons to Brexit* (The History Press, 2017) and *Fayke Newes: The Media vs the Mighty, From Henry VIII to Donald Trump* (The History Press, 2018).

www.derekjtaylorbooks.com

By the same author ...

978 0 7509 8915 2

978 0 7509 9475 0

978 0 7509 8778 3